*Psychology Revivals*

# Experimental Psychology: its scope and method
## VII Intelligence

First published in English in 1969, the book opens with a chapter by Pierre Oléron on intellectual activities. These fall into three groups: inductive activities (the apprehension of laws, relations and concepts), reasoning and problem solving. It describes typical methods and essential results obtained by relevant experiments.

There are two chapters by Jean Piaget and his collaborator Bärbel Inhelder. The first, on mental images, breaks new ground: it describes original experiments carried out by Piaget and associates with children of various ages. Piaget examines the relations between images and motor activity, imitation, drawing and operations. He also classifies images according to their degree of complexity and show why children have inadequate images of some processes. The second chapter is on intellectual operations and Piaget gives a summary of the main findings of a number of his earlier books, on the child's notions of conservation, classification, seriation, number, measurement, time, speed and chance.

In the last chapter, Pierre Gréco discusses learning and intellectual structures. He describes the work of psychologists with rats in mazes and formulating theories of animal learning. Gestalt psychology and various other interpretations are examined and Gréco also pays attention to Piaget's view of 'structural learning' based on experience.

# Experimental Psychology: its scope and method
## VII Intelligence

Pierre Oléron, Jean Piaget,
Bärbel Inhelder and Pierre Gréco

LONDON AND NEW YORK

Originally published in French as
*Traité de Psychologie Expérimentale: VII L'Intelligence*
By Presses Universitaires de France, Paris 1963

Copyright © 1963 Presses Universitaires de France

First published 1969 by Routledge & Kegan Paul
This edition first published in 2014 by Psychology Press

Published 2022 by Routledge
2 Park Square, Milton Park, Abingdon, Oxon OX14 4RN
605 Third Avenue, New York, NY 10017

*Routledge is an imprint of the Taylor & Francis Group, an informa business*

English translation © 1969 Taylor & Francis

All rights reserved. No part of this book may be reprinted or reproduced or utilised in any form or by any electronic, mechanical, or other means, now known or hereafter invented, including photocopying and recording, or in any information storage or retrieval system, without permission in writing from the publishers.

Notice:
Product or corporate names may be trademarks or registered trademarks, and are used only for identification and explanation without intent to infringe.

Publisher's Note

The publisher has gone to great lengths to ensure the quality of this reprint but points out that some imperfections in the original copies may be apparent.

**Disclaimer**
The publisher has made every effort to trace copyright holders and welcomes correspondence from those they have been unable to contact.

ISBN: 978-1-84872-467-9 (hbk)
ISBN: 978-1-848-72464-8 (pbk)
ISBN: 978-1-315-75654-7 (ebk)

# Experimental Psychology
## its scope and method
edited by Paul Fraisse and Jean Piaget

## VII Intelligence
by Pierre Oléron, Jean Piaget,
Bärbel Inhelder and Pierre Gréco

Translated by Thérèse Surridge

Routledge & Kegan Paul     London

*Translated from the French*
TRAITÉ DE PSYCHOLOGIE EXPÉRIMENTALE
*VII L'Intelligence*

© *1963 Presses Universitaires de France*
*First published in Great Britain 1969*
*by Routledge & Kegan Paul Limited*
*Broadway House, 68–74 Carter Lane*
*London, E.C.4*
*Printed in Great Britain by*
*Western Printing Services Limited*
*Bristol*
*English translation*
© *Routledge & Kegan Paul 1969*
*No part of this book may be reproduced*
*in any form without permission from*
*the publisher, except for the quotation*
*of brief passages in criticism*
SBN 7100 6544 2

# Contents

**CHAPTER 22** *Pierre Oléron*     page
INTELLECTUAL ACTIVITIES

1 *Introduction*
  1 The psychologist and the question of intellectual activities    1
  2 Three key-concepts    3
  3 Main types of intellectual activities    5

2 *Inductive activities*
  1 Experimental study of various forms of induction    7
  2 Conditions affecting induction    20
  3 The bases of abstraction and of generality    26
  4 Information gained by the use of complex tests    31

3 *Reasoning*
  1 The various aspects of reasoning    36
  2 Conditions affecting reasoning    40

4 *Problem solving*
  1 Several types of classical problems    49
  2 Conditions on which problem solving depends    50

*Bibliography*    74

**CHAPTER 23** *Jean Piaget and Bärbel Inhelder*
MENTAL IMAGES

1 *Statement of Problems*
  1 Figurative and operative aspects of cognitive functions    87
  2 Meaning and symbolic function    88
  3 Classification of problems    90

2 *Psychophysiological data and the problem of whether images are sensory or motor*
  1 Quasi-sensory character of images    93
  2 The role of motor activity    94
  3 Eye movements    96
  4 Auditory images    98

## Contents

**3** *Genetic data concerning the stage at which and the manner in which images are formed: images and imitation*
   1 Level at which images appear    99
   2 Symbolic function and imitation    101

**4** *Experiments on elementary reproductive images*
   1 Reproductive image of a rod    103
   2 Graphic and digital estimations    105

**5** *Classification of images as a function of their development*
   1 Kinetic reproductive images    109
   2 Anticipation of the rotation of a rod    110
   3 Interpretation and control experiment    112

**6** *Mechanism of the evolution of images*
   1 Introduction    114
   2 Transformation of an arc into a straight line    115
   3 Interpretation    118
   4 Images of a somersault    119
   5 Reversal of the ends    121
   6 The displacement of a square    122
   7 Kinetic anticipatory images    124
   8 The evolution of images    128

**7** *Images and thought: the role of images in the preparation and functioning of operations*
   1 Introduction    129
   2 Anticipation of the seriation of lengths    130
   3 Interpretation    132
   4 Anticipation of conservation    133

**8** *Spatial images and 'geometrical intuition'*
   1 Distinctive character of spatial images    136
   2 Images of development    137

**9** *Conclusion*    139
   *Bibliography*    142

*Contents*

CHAPTER 24 *Jean Piaget and Barbel Inhelder*
INTELLECTUAL OPERATIONS AND THEIR DEVELOPMENT

1 *Historico-critical survey*
   1 From associationism to 'strategies' — 147
   2 Claparède's 'implication' — 148
   3 Spearman's 'noegenesis' — 149
   4 *Gestalt* structures — 150
   5 'Thought psychology' — 152
   6 Method to be followed — 153

2 *Notions of conservation*
   1 Introduction — 155
   2 The ball of clay — 157
   3 Qualitative and quantitative results — 158
   4 American and English controls — 160
   5 Transfer of liquids or beads — 161
   6 The problem of integrated structures — 164

3 *'Groupings' of classes and of relations and the construction of number*
   1 Classifications — 165
   2 'All' and 'some' — 167
   3 Quantification of inclusion — 168
   4 Seriation — 170
   5 'Grouping' structures — 172
   6 Multiplicative 'groupings' — 173
   7 Construction of the whole number — 175
   8 So-called intuition of number and numerical correspondences — 176
   9 Operational nature of number — 178

4 *Spatio-temporal operations and chance*
   1 Spontaneous measurement — 180
   2 Other spatial operations — 182
   3 Temporal operations — 183
   4 Speed — 185

## Contents

 5 Chance   187
 6 Chance (continued) and the game of heads or tails   188

5 *Propositional or formal operations*
 1 The combinatorial system   190
 2 Propositional logic   191
 3 The group of the two reversibilities   194
 4 Action and reaction; proportions   195

6 *General Interpretation*
 1 Maturation   197
 2 Acquired experience   197
 3 Language and social transmission   200
 4 Equilibration   201

*Bibliography*   203

## CHAPTER 25   Pierre Gréco
### LEARNING AND INTELLECTUAL STRUCTURES

1 *Introduction*   206

2 *'Intuition' and groping*
 1 Learning through 'trial and error' and learning through 'ideas'   209
 2 The notion of insight and Gestalt views   210
 3 Cognitive structures in animal learning   213
 4 'Inferential expectation': the experiment of Tolman and Honzik   215
 5 Control experiments and discussion   217
 6 'Cognitive' and behaviourist formulations   219
 7 Transposition and generalization of learning: Spence's models   222
 8 Criticisms and discussion   225

3 *Thinking and learning*
 1 Method and concepts   227
 2 Problem-solving tests   229
 3 'Mental mazes' and pre-experimental artifact   231

|   |   |
|---|---:|
| 4 'Concept formation': discussion of a classic example | 232 |
| 5 Specificity of intellectual structures: *Gestaltheorie* and *Denkpsychologie* | 234 |
| 6 Reductionism or unification: two recent models | 236 |

4 *Logical structures, learning and development*
1 Notions of conservation, transitivity and learning        242
2 Empirical observation and operational practice           251
3 Learning and structurization                              257
4 Tentative conclusion                                      265

*Bibliography*                                              269

*Index*                                                     275

# Chapter 22

# Intellectual Activities[1]

## Pierre Oléron

## 1 Introduction

### 1 The psychologist and the question of intellectual activities

The standpoint adopted in this chapter is that of the psychology of behaviour. That is why the term 'activités intellectuelles' (intellectual activities) has been used in preference to 'pensée' (thought),—although contemporary authors writing in English commonly refer to *thinking* and *thought* (cf. Humphrey, 1951; Vinacke, 1952; Osgood, 1953; Johnson, 1955; Bruner, Goodnow, Austin, 1956; Bartlett, 1958; Harms, 1960). It is presumably possible to employ these terms without reference to a subjective standpoint—and that is indeed what most of the above authors have done—but in dealing with a subject of this kind it is desirable to avoid as far as possible all risk of ambiguity and misunderstanding.

Experimental research is concerned directly with behaviour, at least nowadays when there is no longer any attempt to base experiments on introspection, as Binet and the Würzburg school had done. This is a point in its favour and it deserves recognition. On the other hand, the work that has been published failed, on

---

[1] It was neither possible nor desirable to turn the present chapter into an exhaustive summary of the research devoted to the questions with which it deals. Nor did we feel that we could select particular pieces of research and define them as objectively the most important (we must admit that there are no grounds for objectivity). We have therefore included only those which illustrate the points that we feel to be significant. The bibliography likewise does not claim to be exhaustive but is more open, thus compensating for the limitations of the summary presented in the chapter itself.

the whole, to organize itself around a general view of the facts under consideration. A frame was supplied by the *Gestalttheorie* and has been used to good purpose in research on problem solving (Köhler, 1917; Maier, 1930, 1931, 1933; Duncker, 1935; Wertheimer, 1945). Learning theories appear to find a natural extension in the study of intellectual processes, some of which are a form of learning (concept formation) or present characteristics with which the theories are concerned (generalization, discrimination), or depend on factors of which the role is widely studied in elementary learning (reinforcement, motivation). Information theory (or, more precisely, the concept of information which goes considerably beyond it) is mentioned in connection with research on concept formation or problem solving. Even theories about decision have contributed a terminology of which some authors have availed themselves ('strategies' in operations of classification (Bruner, Goodnow and Austin, 1956; cf. Piaget, 1957, vol. II, ch. 2), or else have supplied the material for the mathematical analysis of various problems (Kochen and Galanter, 1958),—not to mention the recent (and possibly fundamental) perspectives opened up by the performance of 'electronic brains', capable of reasoning logically and of proving theorems (Newell, Shaw and Simon, 1958, 1960; Gelernter and Rochester, 1958; Gelernter, 1960 . . .).

The experiments themselves do not present any great degree of coherence, and are not conspicuously better in this respect than everyday language in which expressions such as reasoning, judging, understanding, explaining, inventing, inducing, deducing, evaluating, abstracting and solving a problem . . . all refer to real acts which are not, however, assigned a position in relation to one another. Indeed, it is hard to believe that all these different words correspond to separate realities.

As any summary must refer to psychology in its present state and not to an ideal state of affairs, we have to accept this situation. We have, however, felt that it was possible to reduce the lack of coherence by devoting only a little space to theoretical notions. What matters, in the present state of things, is surely the psychologist's ability to establish a correspondence between notions and objectively observable behaviour and to determine what are the conditions upon which he can show this behaviour to depend. This is the aspect upon which we have concentrated.

At the same time, it is not entirely impossible, without sacrificing any essential, to reach a standpoint from which a tentative organization begins to emerge.

## 2 Three key-concepts

This tentative organization could be as follows:

(A) TWO ESSENTIAL FEATURES OF INTELLIGENCE

Intellectual activities can, we feel, be characterized by two essential features (cf. Oléron, 1961 *b*).

In the first place, they are activities which operate by means of *long circuits*. This can be clearly seen by comparison with reflex actions. In the latter, a response is immediately evoked by a stimulus according to a mechanism which is at once ready for action. This is not so with the *détour*, a familiar notion to all who have studied intelligence. The *détour* is the long-circuit type of behaviour. Using a tool, *a fortiori* making one, both typical manifestations of intelligence, also belong to this type, by comparison with responses which involve only the organism itself (direct grasping, etc.).

In the second place, intellectual activities involve constructing and using *schemata or models* relating to the objects which the subject perceives and upon which he acts. The most elaborate of these models are the symbolic systems with which civilized man is constantly concerned. These include language, specialized languages such as mathematics, and various figurative plans and schemata. Nevertheless there are others, less socialized and less completely objectified (and therefore less accessible to the psychologist) upon which the subject may also rely in approaching a task or solving a problem.

There are close links between these two features of intelligence and it would be a misconception to try to make them correspond respectively to the two 'forms of intelligence' which are classically set against each other: 'practical intelligence' and 'abstract (or symbolic) intelligence'. In actual fact, every response which brings into play any properties of objects which go beyond their immediate appearance can be considered to imply a model that is at least implicit, not necessarily conscious or expressible by the subject but liable, without fundamental change, to become so.

*Pierre Oléron*

As for models which can be completely objectified, they play a part only in so far as they are integrated to response schemata actually made use of by the subject and so do not remain external objects which may be contemplated but no more (it is only on this condition that language is effective, otherwise one has the classical case of the subject who can describe a situation but not respond to it adequately).

(B) THE NOTION OF SCHEMA

The two concepts referred to above are no more than the elements of an, as yet, external description and it is possible to go beyond this.

In the psychology of behaviour, only stimuli (or situations) and responses are considered admissible as factual data. However, what matters in psychological activities in general, and in intellectual activities in particular, are the connections which are established between given stimuli and given responses, so it is normal to use concepts which seek to express these by providing a convenient expression or, possibly, by suggesting a hypothesis concerning the underlying mechanisms. It is in this way that the concept of schema can profitably be used, as has already been done by several authors, from Kant to Burloud and to Piaget (in contexts which, however, are far from being identical).

The connections between stimuli and responses are flexible and multiform. This is particularly marked in the case of intellectual activities but it is also a general characteristic of psychical processes. A relatively wide range of stimuli can arouse an identical response (generality or generalization). An identical stimulus may evoke perfectly distinct responses according to the existing constellation of the stimuli—or to their sequence (abstraction, invention). (This characteristic can easily be linked to the existence of long circuits, which are naturally multiple, and to that of models, which introduce new and varied elements into the stimulus-response cycle.) This diversity does not mean anarchy; on the contrary, it presents regularities, for example we find that stimuli of a particular category all provoke the same response (stimuli of a given colour or shape) and the responses concerned belong to well defined categories (actions centred on a particular element of an experimental set-up, such as a bolt in the

## Intellectual Activities

case of a practical problem, etc.). The notion of schema makes it possible to express this regularity, as a connection between a class of stimuli and a class of responses.

At the same time, in so far as a schema can be assimilated to a habit, it allows the intervention, not only of the plasticity just mentioned, but also of energizing (or dynamic) aspects by which it is possible to express the availability (or greater facility) of a particular response, the interactions (substitution, conflict, dominance) and the transformations which are determined at once by stimuli and responses and by other schemata belonging for instance to other systems (language as distinct from action proper). From this angle, the notion of schema leads us back to certain notions put forward by authors such as Hull (habit strength, habit-family hierarchy, convergent or divergent mechanisms), which are almost certainly valuable (cf. Maltzman, 1955).

### 3 Main types of intellectual activities

As mentioned above, intellectual activities are diverse, as suggested by the number of words used to designate them. One can try to find a guiding thread to present them—and first to represent them to oneself—by using the concepts mentioned above.

If we take first the basic situation in which the subject finds himself confronted by stimuli to which he must respond, not in a reflex or habitual manner, but in an intellectual way, several cases can arise. In one of these, the stimuli may present a regularity which is not immediately perceptible. The subject must then discover the regularity; in other words, he elaborates a response schema which is based on, and adapted to, the stimuli. It is correct to speak here of *inductive processes*. Another case, directly opposed to the first, is that in which the appropriate schema is immediately applied to the stimuli: the subject fits them into the frame which is already at his disposal. One should then speak of a process of *subsumption*, a term which has not been used by psychologists but which is logical.

It is probably somewhat academic to draw a radical distinction between these two types of process, since a schema is not constructed *ex nihilo* and the subject always approaches stimuli with an equipment of responses already constituted (especially when the experiments are carried out on adults, as is usually the case).

*Pierre Oléron*

It is none the less true, that, from the point of view of what might be called the 'dosage' of accommodation and assimilation, to use the terms aptly used by Piaget, the distinction is justified when applied to tasks which can be submitted to experimental enquiry.

It should be added that subsumptive processes have been relatively neglected. This is understandable as subsumption is typically an immediate and automatic process, which hardly seems to present a problem and indeed scarcely appears distinguishable from a habitual or reflex action. Classifying is a subsumptive process but it interests psychologists in so far as it has an inductive aspect, consisting in the discovery or adaptation of classes appropriate to the stimuli. That is why we shall not devote a special section to subsumptive processes.

The nature of *reasoning* (or inference or deduction) is quite different. Here the subject does no more than combine schemata without reference, in extreme cases, to stimuli which would control or modify them. These combinations normally refer to symbolic material and in the ideal case they obey formal laws of a logical or mathematical nature.

*Problem solving* is a combination of the processes of induction and of subsumption. For in solving a problem one approaches a situation armed with a number of response schemata which one tries to apply to it but which prove ineffective and so must be modified or replaced by others, which one has to invent. A problem can be said to exist when the subject finds himself really disarmed in the face of the stimuli, hence the importance attached to invention (which, nevertheless, it must be remembered, never arises *ex nihilo*).

## 2  Inductive activities

Induction is the process in which the subject extracts, from data presented to him, regularities or constancies which are not immediately apparent. The term 'education', invented by Spearman (1932–1936), is also apt in this connection since it means 'to draw out from' and it is possible to present inductive processes as calling for an operation of this kind.

*Intellectual Activities*

*1   Experimental study of various forms of induction*

The regularities which the subject may be led to discover take various forms. We have found it convenient to divide them into three groups: laws, relations and concepts. Admittedly, on the theoretical plane, this division is hard to justify (a law is in a sense a relation—while a concept may be considered as a system of relations or laws). However, on the practical plane—and that is all we ask of it—it enables us to distinguish and classify various experimental situations which have been used by psychologists.

(A) THE INDUCTION OF LAWS

The law which has to be discovered may be a physical one and the subject may find himself in the same situation as the scientist who tries to formulate a law about a given phenomenon. This is the situation which Inhelder and Piaget (1958) adopted in their study of adolescents.

Usually authors, concerned with less mature subjects and having more analytical ends in view, have had recourse to simpler situations.

A number of classical experiments draw on temporal or spatio-temporal laws. Let us recall the main ones. Révesz had the idea of using serial laws, with monkeys and children as his subjects. The subject is confronted with the task of choosing the 'right one' from a series of boxes. The 'right one' (which contains a reward) varies from one trial to the next, being in turn the first, the second, the third, etc., or the first, the last, the second, etc. (Révesz, 1923 *a*, 1923 *b*. For an adaptation of this set-up, see Oléron, 1957).

Jenkins' three-plate apparatus is based on a similar principle (cf. Fig. 1).

In the double alternation temporal maze (Hunter, 1920; Gellermann, 1931 *a*), the subject must learn to go twice to the right, then twice to the left, before he can get out (the apparatus is worked by a system of doors which the experimenter bolts and unbolts, without the subject's knowledge, as he proceeds through the apparatus). From this was derived the double alternation box-apparatus, in which the subject has to discover that, out of two stimuli, first the right-hand one and then the left

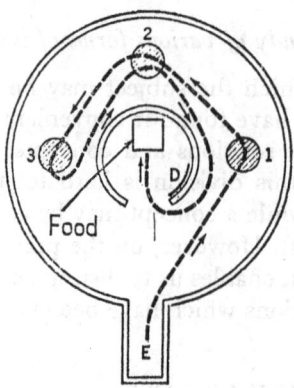

Fig. 1 JENKINS' THREE-PLATE APPARATUS

A door, D, opens when the animal steps on the plates in the correct order. In the above example, he must step on plates 1, 2, and 3, then come back to 2 to open the door and obtain a reward. (After Fjeld, *Genet. Psychol. Monogr.*, 1934, **15**, 403)

are positive twice consecutively, etc. (Gellermann, 1931 *b*, Hunter and Bartlett, 1948 (Figs. 2 and 3).

These types of apparatus can be adapted for work on more complicated laws (*inter alia* triple alternation, which has been used to assess the capacity for generalization of subjects who had already solved double alternation, Oléron, 1957). However,

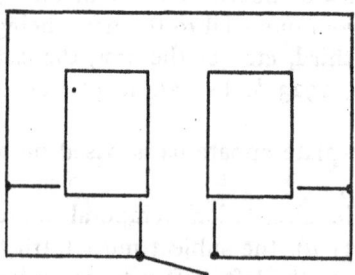

Fig. 2 TEMPORAL MAZE USED WITH HUMAN SUBJECTS BY GELLERMANN (1931)

Owing to the bolting and unbolting of the various doors, the subject cannot escape from the maze until he has been twice round the right-hand block and twice round the left-hand block (or vice versa). (After *J. Genet. Psychol.*, 1931, **39**, 52)

## Intellectual Activities

double alternation and especially the temporal maze have proved quite difficult enough for the subjects tested (animals, young children). (For details of other experimental set-ups, see de Montpellier, 1949, 157.)

Many other laws can be imagined besides those just mentioned, but in experimental research psychologists have not made undue efforts to invent any (as an example of an original type of law we can mention that formulated by Gréco who watched children and adults discovering it (in Piaget *et alia*, 1959 vol. X) and as an example of a set-up which lends itself to a great variety of combinations we have the P S I devised by John and Miller, 1957).

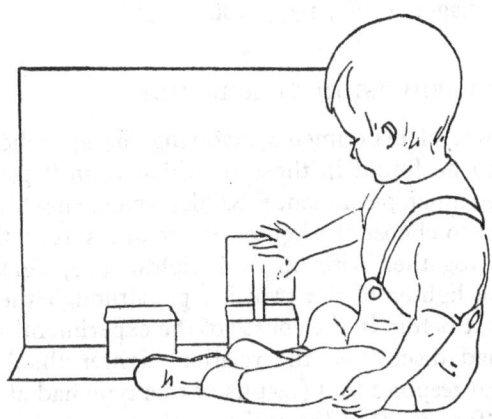

Fig. 3 APPARATUS USED BY HUNTER AND BARTLETT (1948) TO STUDY DOUBLE ALTERNATION

A system of bolts behind the panel makes it possible to open the left-hand box once and then a second time, then to open the right-hand box twice, and so on. (After *J. exp. Psychol.*, 1948, 38, 559.)

On the other hand, the authors of tests show a great variety of invention. Symbolic material lends itself to the most varied combinations and it is possible to devise problems with a high degree of complexity. A basic form of these tests is to be found in mathematical progressions where reason supplies the law, which has to be discovered from given elements; another basic form consists in classifications, where the subject must find the characteristics common to several figures, etc.

*Pierre Oléron*

One form of law which has relatively recently been studied is that of probabilistic laws. A typical experiment consists in presenting to the subject a succession of alternating events, each appearing with a well defined (and complementary) probability. For example, there are two lights, a white and a red; one or the other appears and, in the course of a series, one flash in two may be red, or one in three, one in four, etc. The subject must state in advance which light is going to appear. Naturally, exact prediction is impossible since the event occurs at random, but the interesting fact is that the subject succeeds in making predictions which come very close to the probability of the event. (References will be found in Hake, edited by Quastler, 1955, 257, and in Matalon in Piaget *et alia*, 1959, vol. X, 90.)

(B) THE APPREHENSION OF RELATIONS

The prototype of experiments involving the apprehension of a relation is to be found in those to which *Gestalt* psychologists have given so much prominence. Köhler's chicken (cf. Ellis, 1938, 217), trained to choose the lighter of two greys, ($g\bar{r}$), then put in front of $g\bar{r}$ together with an even lighter grey ($g\mathring{r}$), went on choosing the lighter of the two, i.e. $g\mathring{r}$, although they had not come across it before in the course of the experiment. It was as if the birds had discovered the relation 'lighter than' and were continuing to respond to it (results of this type had already been observed before Köhler; for a historical account, see Gulliksen, 1932).

Psychologists have used a fairly wide range of relations; besides lightness, they have introduced size, weight, speed (Oléron, 1957) and multiplicity (for references, see de Montpellier, 1949, 142).

Experimentation has been extended to more complicated situations involving three terms or even more. For instance, there is the relation of 'middleness', where the subject is trained to respond to a stimulus that is intermediate between two others. There is also 'oddity' and here the subject must respond to the 'odd' item, the only one of its kind. Thus, given three objects of which two are identical and the third is different, he must learn to choose the last (Fig. 4) (for descriptions and references, see de Montpellier, 1949, 148). The identity-dissimilarity relation has also been studied; subjects must discriminate in their response

*Intellectual Activities*

Fig. 4  CHOOSING THE OBJECT WHICH IS THE ONLY ONE OF ITS KIND (ODDITY PROBLEM)
The subject's response is independent of the form of the stimulus since all that counts is that it should be the only one of its kind. (After Harlow in Stone, *Comparative Psychology*, 3rd ed., New York, Prentice Hall, 1951, 189.)

to pairs of stimuli, some made up of identical stimuli, others of different stimuli (Fig. 5) (Oléron, 1962 *a*).

It can be disputed whether the term 'induction' is appropriate in the case of an experiment such as Köhler's, which involves a spontaneous reaction of the organism (one can also dispute the use of the word 'relation' in place of 'structure'). Nevertheless, in the other experiments, it is through learning that the subject succeeds in isolating the element to which he must respond while neglecting those that are not reinforced.

(C) APPREHENSION OR FORMATION OF CONCEPTS

*a) The meaning of 'concept' in experimentation.* From the standpoint of the psychology of behaviour, a concept is not an object. When a subject apprehends a concept, he is not undergoing a specific cognitive experience: he is manifesting regular kinds of behaviour which can be observed by psychologists.

It is true, of course, that in the case of a child, for example, forming concepts is indeed acquiring knowledge, but this acquisition of knowledge is nothing more than an increase in his 'know-how'. The child who learns what a dog is learns to react to

Fig. 5  STIMULI AND MODELS USED IN THE STUDY OF RESPONSES TO THE IDENTITY-DISSIMILARITY RELATION WITHOUT RECOURSE TO LANGUAGE

The set-up comprises two models (identical human figures: 2 men and different human figures: a man and a woman) in front of which the stimuli must be placed according to whether the pairs that they form are identical or different. From top to bottom one finds specimens of stimuli for speed (rotating discs surmounted by human figures), shape, colour, size and resistance (small bars which are more or less rigid under pressure). (Oléron, *Psychol. franç.*, 1962, **7**, 6.)

real dogs and to words relating to dogs in a way which conforms more and more to the habits of those around him, both in his conduct and in his remarks. The study of this evolution remains on the plane of observation.

The study of children can teach us facts that are of great interest by showing us how the ideas which they form on a given subject evolve, but it comes up against a number of difficulties. In particular, some investigators have been too inclined to limit their investigations to the verbal field, seeking to find the meaning which the child attaches to particular words, that is to say, the systems of translations which he can establish between the words in question and other words. From this standpoint, difficulties of communication arise between the subject and the psychologist who is questioning him, as the latter sometimes forgets that the words used by the child do not necessarily mean what he himself takes them to mean. Besides, descriptive study, though interesting, is limited, as it does not reveal much about the conditions on which the evolution of concepts depends nor about the mechanisms involved.

Experimental research, on the contrary, is relatively indifferent to language; behaviour which is attributed to concepts is essentially considered from a formal point of view and although the form it takes can be expressed with words, it is usually envisaged in terms of actual behaviour.

The formal properties of concepts, in the eyes of psychologists, lie in the fact that concepts can be considered as *classes*: behaviour is attributed to a concept when the subject makes an identical response to stimuli belonging to the same class, whatever differences there may otherwise be. Hence, typical experimental situations consist in putting before the subject various instances of the concept that is being considered and observing his reactions to see whether he responds in a coherent manner.

*b) Fundamental methods.* The concepts that are used may be 'natural' in that they form part of the subject's actual experience (size, shape colour, . . . ) or 'artificial' (often they are made up of an arbitrary combination of real concepts). The former, excluding complex cases of 'masking', are easier to apprehend, in principle, than the latter, with the result that they are used mainly in experiments with animals and children.

1. In experiments using the first type of concept, there is a

## Pierre Oléron

method accessible to subjects of the lowest level and similar to the one described in connection with relations. The subject is trained to choose a positive stimulus while neglecting another (negative stimulus). When this has been learned, the positive stimulus undergoes a number of variations. These are intended to test whether the subject is in fact responding to the general aspect common to the various stimuli or, failing this, to widen his learning and see whether it is possible in this way to assist him to develop a response to the general aspect.

Experiments of this type include those carried out by Fields (Fig. 6) on rats (1932), by Gellermann (1933) and Klüver (1933)

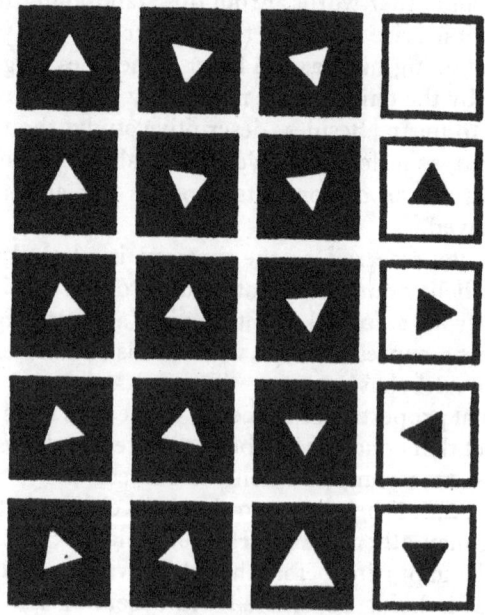

FIG. 6 SERIES OF STIMULI USED BY FIELDS (1932) TO STUDY THE RESPONSES OF THE CAT[1] TO THE 'CONCEPT' OF TRIANGULARITY. (After *Comp. Psychol. Monogr.*, 1932, 9, 8.)

on monkeys, and by Gellermann again (same reference) and Long (1940) on young children. (For a summary analysis of this kind of research see Munn, 1955, 134–135 and 318.)

With subjects of a higher level Hull's method is often used, as described below, but with figures referring to real concepts. Thus,

[1] Translator's Note: Rats, not cats, were used in Fields' experiment.

*Intellectual Activities*

Heidbreder (1946) used drawings of concrete objects (faces, buildings, trees), numbers (2, 5, 6) and geometrical figures (which apart from the circle do not, however, correspond to anything that is part of everyday reality) (Fig. 7).

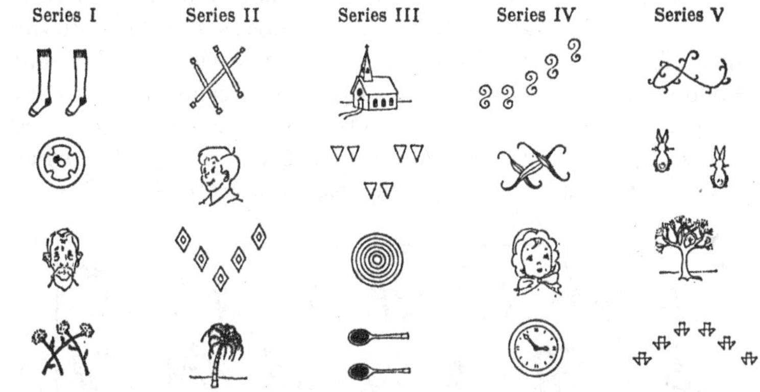

Fig. 7   MATERIALS USED BY HEIDBREDER (1946 a) IN ONE OF HER EXPERIMENTS

The above shows only some of the series presented, each of which contains a specimen of each concept: face, building, tree, the numbers 2, 5 and 6, and three geometrical figures, among them a circle. (*J. gen. Psychol.*, 1946, **35**, 182.)

Instead of figures, one can use words on the same principle (cf. Reed, 1946; Underwood and Richardson, 1956 a, 1956 b; Underwood, 1957).

*Pierre Oléron*

2. Experiments with the second type of concept are inspired by those devised by Hull (1920). Figures—in this case Chinese characters—are associated with nonsense syllables (*oo, yer, ii, ta,* ... ). The subjects must learn to produce the syllable corresponding to the character presented to them. The same syllable corresponds to several characters, but all those associated with the syllable have a *common element* (a root) interwoven with different elements. After a number of trials, subjects called upon to say the syllable associated with the type of character succeeded more and more and managed to give the right syllable when shown characters *which they had never seen before* (Fig. 8).

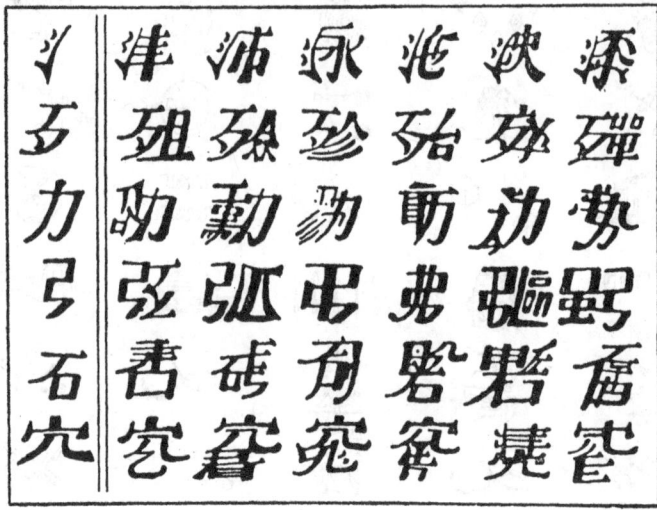

Fig. 8 SPECIMENS OF HULL'S MATERIAL (1920)
Each stimulus of a series contains one of the roots shown on the left, which is the common element, characterizing the 'concept'. (After *Psychol. Monogr.*, 1920, **123**, 10.)

Subsequent experiments, beginning with Smoke (1932) eliminated recourse to a common element as stemming from a naïvely empirical conception whereby a concept is characterized by the presence of a common *material* element.

Smoke used geometrical figures in which the elements present definite relations and these relations form the essence of the concept (Fig. 9). Many authors use concepts made up of the combination of several 'natural' characteristics (this is the principle underlying the Hanfmann-Kasanin test) (Oseas and Underwood, 1952: size and shade; Kurtz and Hovland, 1956: shape and position, etc.). As the nature and number of these combinations are almost infinite, the degree of complexity of

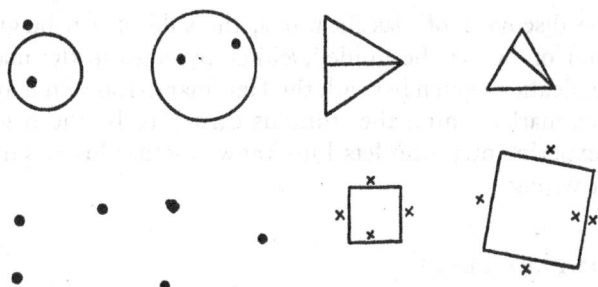

FIG. 9  SPECIMENS OF 'CONCEPTS' USED BY SMOKE (1932)
On the left, a specimen of the concept, on the right a related figure which does not, however, conform to the definition. *Dax*: a circle with a dot inside and a dot outside. *Vec*: an equilateral triangle with a perpendicular. *Zif*: three dots, the distance between the two furthest being twice that between the two nearest. *Tov*: a square with four crosses, each side of the square having a cross that is nearer to it than to any other side. (After *Psychol. Monogr.*, 1932, **191**, 12.)

the material and, consequently, the difficulty of the test can vary widely. As a result, it is sometimes difficult to compare experimental situations and results. Hovland (1952) greatly helped to facilitate analysis by distinguishing between *dimensions* and *values*. A dimension can, for instance, be shape and its values are triangles, squares, circles, etc., just as yellow, green and red are values on the dimension of colour. He showed that the complexity of material increases as a function of the increase in the number of dimensions and values, according to the formula: $V^d$, where V = the number of values and $d$ the number of dimensions.

3. The reader may have noticed that with these procedures the 'class' aspect of the concept plays no specific part. However, an affirmation that a given stimulus is a 'Vec' while another is not is indeed a way of classifying the stimuli. The classification technique makes the matter more explicit. It is clear that grouping all the objects which are 'Vecs' amounts to the same thing as

stating the 'name' each time. The advantage, however, lies in the elimination of a superimposed symbolic element which makes the task harder for some subjects and of a factor of association and memorization, which is in no way implied in intellectual activity as such (cf. Richardson and Bergum, 1954).

In the discovery of classifications, the subject can be given a free hand or he can be guided, either by clues in the material itself (indications given beneath the Hanfmann-Kasanin material, reference marks behind the stimulus cards), or by the reactions of the experimenter who lets him know whether his response is right or wrong.

(D) COMPLEX TESTS

The standard tests which clearly show inductive processes at work are simple, in that only one law, relation or concept is involved at a time. Many tests lack this simplicity and subjects are required to adapt to situations that include multiple regularities. They must take them all into account and combine them or consider them successively.

Where laws are concerned, let us mention Vincent's experiment (1956). Stimuli having two characteristics in common, such as form and dimension, but differing in another respect (colour) are presented. The subject must choose a third stimulus which agrees with them. The test proceeds from form-dimension combinations to form-colour and colour-dimension combinations. In the final part of the test, the three principles are present in turn. Let us also mention the test which Young and Harlow (1943) succeeded in making monkeys perform. They had to choose the 'odd' object but the colour of the tray determined whether the correct object was the one which was odd in form or the one which was odd in colour.

Where relations are concerned, it is possible to pass from responses to one type of relation to responses to another type, provided material is used which comprises several characteristics simultaneously, size-lightness for example. The most characteristic situation is reversal. The subject is for example trained to respond to the smaller of two stimuli, then suddenly the positive stimulus becomes the larger of the two (Fig. 10).

## Intellectual Activities

Lastly, where concepts are concerned, one finds that learning situations devised for adult subjects generally introduce several concepts and concrete instances of these are intermingled (cf. Hull, Heidbreder): the subject must therefore sort the various stimuli in order to group them around their respective 'nuclei'. The fundamental situation consists in what are called *multiple classifications* of which the basic example is the Weigl-Goldstein-Scheerer colour-form sorting test. The subject has a choice between two principles of classification: form or colour, but when he has adopted one of these, he is asked to change over and to adopt the other (Weigl, 1927, Goldstein, Scheerer, 1941).

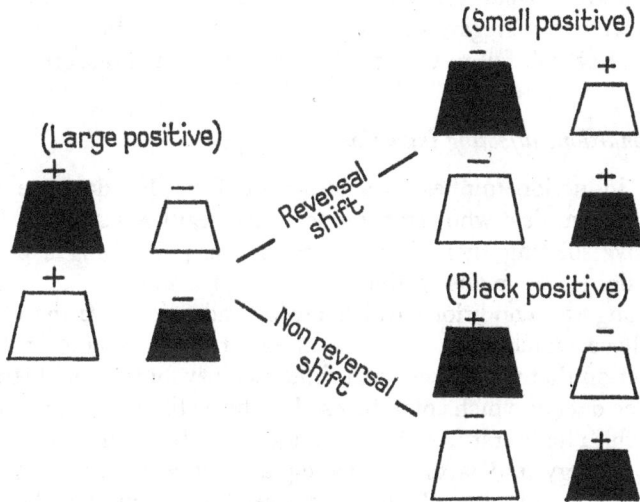

Fig. 10 EXAMPLE OF REVERSAL AND NON-REVERSAL SHIFTS IN RESPONSES TO A RELATION

In the first part of the experiment, the positive stimuli are the largest. The reversal shift consists in making the small stimuli positive. The non-reversal shift consists (in this case) in making black stimuli positive. (Kendler, in *Current Trends in Psychological Theory*, University of Pittsburgh Press, 1961, 193.)

Reversal situations all belong to one of two main types: either the subject is given verbal instructions to change his classificatory principle (Weigl-Goldstein for instance) or else the experimenter merely sets about reinforcing responses according to the new principle and the subject must adapt himself to this change

*Pierre Oléron*

(Wisconsin sorting card, for example; Berg, 1948) (cf. Fraisse, 1956, 224).

It may be useful to point out that these are very different psychological situations. In a sense, the first one makes the task easier since the subject, having been warned, is in far less danger of persevering in error. At the same time, it forces him to take the initiative in discovering the new category (or one of the new categories) while with the second method the category is chosen by the experimenter whom the subject can follow thanks to the reinforcement of his responses. That is why the same category of subjects can do badly in a test of the first type (Oléron, 1951) and achieve normal results in one of the second type (Rosenstein, 1960). If one disregards the differences between the two techniques, one will fail to understand why the results disagree.

## 2  Conditions affecting induction

Every induction implies an abstraction. Complex data are put before the subject who can respond to the regularities in the data only by isolating them from accessory or perturbing aspects. In so doing, he is abstracting.

Among the conditions which favour induction, we therefore find those which make abstraction easier. Let us note in this connection that there is no such thing as a psychology of abstraction, the data of which could be used to throw light on the present problem. The literature on abstraction dates from the early days of psychology and is totally inadequate, since it starts from a subjective standpoint. (Külpe considered abstraction to be the process of bringing certain elements into the foreground of consciousness.) Subsequently, the word has hardly found a place in books on psychology. Actually, it is through the study of specific tasks of an inductive type (mainly concept formation) that an understanding of abstraction can best be reached.

Every induction implies a certain degree of generality in the responses (we are deliberately avoiding the admittedly convenient term 'generalization' on account of the empiricist postulates which it implies). Mechanical conformity to a stimulus pattern is a matter of learning pure and simple and not an event of an intellectual order.

All laws are general, even in the context of experimental

## Intellectual Activities

situations: the proposed sequence can always be extended and it cannot be said that the subject has arrived at the law if he is not capable of this extension. The subject cannot be said to have discovered a relation unless he can apply it to different stimuli from those in which it first manifested itself. Experiments always comprise two stages: in the first stage the subject learns to respond to the positive stimulus (the one that is bigger, lighter in colour, lighter in weight, etc.). Whether he is in fact responding to this stimulus or to the relation as such can only be determined by the extent to which, when confronted with new stimuli, he continues to react in a manner that conforms with his original choices (it sometimes happens that a subject maintains his response to the original stimulus when it appears in the second situation, in which case his response is absolute and not relational). In the same way, a concept can only be general: a triangle is always a triangle whatever its position, or dimensions, and whether it be equilateral, right-angled, drawn in dotted lines, or shaded red, green or black. . . .

Thus, as in the case of abstraction, the conditions favouring the subject's apprehension of the general character of a situation must also be present among those that assist induction.

### (A) VARIATIONS IN THE STIMULUS

A general response can be obtained immediately when a stimulus is presented in one form only. A subject trained to respond to a triangle, for instance, or to the larger of two figures, will respond to triangles or to figures of different absolute sizes, which are later presented to him. Experiments have shown, however, that generality usually admits of limited extension only. Gradients of generalization have frequently been observed (cf. below) and the subject tends to cease to respond when the new stimuli are altogether too different qualitatively or quantitatively from the stimuli which aroused the original responses.

A subject who is trained to respond not to an immutable stimulus but to a range of stimuli subsequently becomes capable of reacting to varied stimuli. An example of this is found in experiments with animals. Harlow's macaque monkeys which were trained to respond positively to a triangle later showed a certain capacity for generalization. When trained to respond to

*Pierre Oléron*

various triangles, their powers of generalization improved (Andrew and Harlow, 1948).

This is also seen with human subjects. The study of failure to master certain mathematical notions shows that it is sometimes due to the fact that the subject can see no further than the particular case which was used as an illustration. This can happen with the perpendicular to the base of a triangle. The child thinks of this as an internal feature of the triangle because that is how it was introduced to him in examples given by the teacher. Thus, he is at a loss when confronted with an obtuse-angled triangle where it falls outside (Mialaret, unpublished thesis). In the same way, it often happens that with a deaf child the meaning of the word taught him in an artificial school situation remains attached to the particular example chosen by the teacher.

The fact is certainly of general significance when one wants to understand human capacity for generalization. This capacity is not due merely to a superior gift, but to a constant exercise in the course of which the child sees situations that are otherwise heterogeneous being treated in the same way. The child who is learning to form the concept of 'dog', applicable to all the various breeds which he may meet in reality or in pictures, is helped by the people around him, but it is also true that he is acquiring practice in a general exercise from which other tasks may subsequently—or simultaneously—benefit.

(B) DISSOCIATION BETWEEN THE QUALITIES OR ASPECTS OF A SITUATION

James was right in saying that the possibility of discriminating between various qualities depended on the existence of dissociations between the qualities. 'If all cold things were wet and all wet things cold, if all hard things pricked our skin, and no other things did so, is it likely that we should discriminate between coldness and wetness, and hardness and pungency respectively?' (Principles of Psychology, I, ch. XIII, p. 502.)

James's view seems so obvious that the need for an experimental verification has not made itself felt. The only experiment which, to our knowledge, is related to this passage by James was one carried out by Gengerelli (1926). However, his perspective and technique (inspired directly by Hull's first study on concept formation) make the experiment questionable. (One can, however, quote the experiment by Detambel and Stolurow (1956), who showed that synchonous variations in essential and parasitic stimuli[1] made concept learning more difficult than when the variations were 'asynchronous'.)

(c) DISTINCTIVENESS OF THE ELEMENT TO BE ABSTRACTED

We shall describe as 'essential' those elements or aspects to which the subject must react, and as 'parasitic' (or 'accessory') those which are present but do not count and so must be abstracted.

*a*) It is easy to understand that the more clearly do the essential elements or aspects appear and stand out from the total situation, the more easily can the subject be led to take them into account and respond to them.

Thus, in the apprehension of relations a determining condition is that the subject should distinguish the elements between which the relation has been established. If they are too similar, the subject finds it difficult to make a discriminative response. It has been observed that discrimination could be facilitated by practice with clearly distinct stimuli (such as black and white) before going on to stimuli that are closer to one another (greys that are more or less related) (Lashley quoted by Leeper in Stevens, 1951, 746).

A related factor is the *form of presentation, whether serial or simultaneous*. It might also seem that in the apprehension of relations, the subject's task would be made easier when the related elements are present simultaneously rather than serially. (The former is the original situation but the other, which appears far less natural, has nevertheless been widely used to test Spence's conception, opposed to the Gestalt or relational conception.) One expects the same thing to apply in the formation of concepts, when all the stimuli corresponding to a concept are given at once instead of appearing in turn, as in typical learning situations. (Examples of simultaneous presentation may be found in Bruner, Goodnow and Austin, 1956.)

[1] Translator's Note: The actual terms used by these two authors were 'relevant and irrelevant stimulus components'.

In actual fact, experiments have not given results which would warrant a definite conclusion of this kind. In the case of relations, what appears to facilitate simultaneous presentation is the presence of a perceptual structure which is of course lacking in serial presentation. However, the importance of a structure of this kind and its superiority over the interaction of responses to each element has not been clearly established. It is probably a mistake to believe in a general solution, when the fact is that the level of subjects, and particularly their ability to compare stimuli, plays an important part, indeed a decisive one (animals and man are not identifiable from this point of view). In the matter of concept formation one must take into account the complexity of data; serial presentation is, in a sense, a means of analysing this complexity by causing the data to be considered successively and not *en bloc*. But in this case the subject finds it more difficult to remember all the elements presented (cf. Reed, 1950, Cahill and Hovland, 1960).

*b*) The 'essential' element, the one to which the subject must respond, is normally mixed with parasitic or accessory elements or aspects. It is easy to understand that the greater the number of these elements, the more difficult it becomes to abstract the essential (Archer, Bourne and Brown, 1955).

As mentioned above, a number of concept learning situations are so arranged that instances of several concepts are put before the subject simultaneously. In that case, obviously, the elements corresponding to each concept are disturbing elements in relation to other concepts. The greater the number of concepts involved, the more is it to be expected that the task will be difficult. Similarly, the more the concepts to be induced are kept separate, the easier the task (Kurtz and Hovland, 1956).

(D) CONDITIONS OF LEARNING

An element of learning enters into every induction. The subject learns what is important in the situation which confronts him. The factors which condition all learning are present here.

The most essential of these is obviously reinforcement. It plays an indispensable part in most experiments, since it serves to indicate what is important among the multiple aspects presented by the situation. The subject chooses at random or according to a hypothesis and it is the experimenter's sanction which reveals to him whether or not his choice is correct. Where the response is left free (e.g. in the Goldstein type of classification), habits formed by previous reinforcements undeniably play a part.

Some authors have tried to show how the factors operating in classical learning tasks also play a part in the formation of concepts and in the apprehension and transposition of relations: distributed practice (Oseas and Underwood, 1952; Richardson and Bergum, 1954; Underwood, 1957); fixed-ratio schedules of reinforcement (Buss, 1950; Green, 1955); nature of reinforcement (Juzak, 1953; Terrell and Kennedy, 1957), etc. Research of this kind is not the most relevant where intellectual activity is concerned.

(E) QUANTITY AND NATURE OF INFORMATION

In every inductive task—at least in the tasks which are set in laboratory experiments—the subject is at the beginning in a state of uncertainty: he is given multiple data and cannot know in advance which will correspond to positive stimuli. The choices he makes and the approval they meet with lessen his uncertainty by supplying him with some information. Hovland (1952) analysed in this light some 'concept learning' situations, reduced to the problem of discovering which combinations, among the various characteristics or aspects of the stimuli, the experimenter had at the outset chosen as positive.

An interesting feature of an analysis of this kind is that it can be used to determine a subject's ability to utilize information, since it is possible to define the information supplied by each stimulus. In theory, the subject, given a particular combination and succession of stimuli, should discover the relevant principle at the end of a given number of trials; if he succeeds, he has used the information perfectly, if not he has failed to use some of it.

Already, Whitfield (1951), using a problem that is admittedly different (since the subject has to allocate objects to a number of cells and is told each time by the experimenter how many objects he has correctly placed), had found (not surprisingly) that a human subject's performance is inferior to that of a machine capable of using all the information supplied. This is in part due to the intervention of a factor of forgetfulness; as experiments extend over a period of time, the subject forgets part of the information received.

Hovland and Weiss (1953) showed that subjects do not use information supplied by positive and negative stimuli with equal effectiveness. When the subject learns that some stimuli *are not* instances of the concept in question, he has more difficulty in discovering the concept than when offered stimuli that do represent it. This had already been discovered by Smoke (1933), in a less detailed analysis.

Nevertheless, negative stimuli also supply information and assist in eliminating incorrect hypotheses. In general, a greater number of negative than positive stimuli is required to convey the same amount of information. A further difference is due to the fact that 'concepts' are not abstract entities but are derived from figures that are perceptually presented. As a result, the characteristic 'big' or 'black' is obviously suggested more directly when the subject sees big or black stimuli than when he sees small or white stimuli.

This observation goes beyond the narrow and artificial frame of the experiments which led up to it. Educationalists have noticed that there are drawbacks in presenting to the pupil what the notion they wish to teach him *is not*, even if at the same time they present what it is. The pupil becomes confused and makes poor use of the information conveyed by the negative stimulus.

Since the subject cannot exploit to the best advantage the information supplied to him, a certain amount of redundancy appears necessary, as in verbal communications. This was shown by Bourne and Haygood (1959) still within the framework of 'concept formation'.

## 3  The bases of abstraction and generality

Since induction is characterized by the abstraction and generality of responses, one is naturally led to ask what makes both these possible. It is true that, in so doing, one is led beyond a simple statement of factual conditions to embark upon considerations that are more general but can only be said to be probable.

It is difficult to dispense with these, however, since we are concerned with fundamental processes.

It must be remembered that these processes, while conditioning induction, extend well beyond it. Generalization, for instance, enters into learning, even in its most elementary forms, and into conditioning (not only the stimulus which sets off the conditioned reaction is effective, but also similar stimuli), even in its most complex forms (transfer of a skill, whether manual or intellectual). This already suggests that a fundamental process is involved and this must be taken into account even if there is no question of considering it in all its aspects.

(A) INTERPRETATIONS BASED ON THE PROPERTIES OF THE STIMULI

The first explanation which can be put forward considers the properties of stimuli.

*a) Empiricist conception of the common element.* From an empiricist standpoint—which the psychologist willingly adopts, probably because he manipulates his stimuli like objects that are mutually independent—the objects to which the subjects react each have at the outset a distinct entity and are perceived in their individuality. Abstracting or forming a general concept consists in isolating what these objects may have in common.

Associationalists have had recourse to singularly acrobatic reasoning in their attempt to show that the common element was literally an *identical* element present in the various objects concerned. Hull, in his fundamental experiment on concept formation (cf. above), still adhered to this view.

The classical objection to this conception is well known: in nearly all cases, there is no element which is identical in all the various instances of a concept. What element is there that is common to a basset hound, a greyhound and a spaniel . . . and yet, they are all specimens of the dog species.

*b) The role of relations.* One might hope to resolve the difficulty by invoking, instead of an identical element, a common relation present in the various stimuli. This was suggested by Smoke (1932). In actual fact, it has taken us no further, since either the relation in question is given in the stimulus, that is, perceived within it, in which case we come back to the notion of an identical element, or else the relation is introduced by the subject, in which case we move beyond the empiricist standpoint towards a type of explanation that will be considered later.

The *Gestalttheorie* has, it is true, shown that the alternative is not so simple and that the relation could at once be given perceptually and apprehended in a general way, as shown by the transposition experiments of the type mentioned above, the relation—or, more precisely in this case, the structure—being grasped like a melody which is still there when transposed into another register. Experiments, however, have shown that there are limits to the transposition of a relation and that transposition ceases to take place if the new stimuli are too far removed from the original stimuli. Relations—or structures—are like elementary stimuli in this and a gradient of generalization[1] can be shown to apply to them, as to the stimuli, calling for the same kind of explanation. At the same time, we are indeed dealing with relations and the 'explanation' valid in their case does not appear to extend to concepts.

## (B) INTERPRETATIONS BASED ON THE SUBJECT'S REACTIONS

Another line of approach consists in considering the subject's response rather than the properties of the stimuli.

Two standpoints have to be considered here, corresponding in fact to two models of 'generalization' and of abstraction.

*a) Ignorance of differences.* A subject's response may be general simply because he is unaware of differences between stimuli.

First of all, it must be noted that what we might call a 'physicalist' attitude towards stimuli can lead to the setting of pseudo-problems of generalization. It is possible in effect, in considering the physical nature of stimuli, to pulverize them into a large number of separate elements (for example, when one takes into account wavelengths or vibratory frequencies). The fact remains that the subject's response cannot be said to be general when he fails to discriminate between stimuli.

---

[1] The existence of this gradient has caused the Gestalt thesis to be brought into question. Spence (1937) tried to account for transposition phenomena by considering the relations between elements and not their structure. The hypothesis has led to numerous experiments but these cannot be considered here. Besides, the results obtained have often failed to agree.

A subject is often unaware of differences which he is in fact capable of perceiving (this can be verified by discrimination tests which make it possible, for instance, to determine differential thresholds). This is something which goes back to the fundamental nature of perception, which in the first place is utilitarian and not a contemplation of objects in their individuality, as could be said of the vision of an artist who paints the portrait of a particular person. It is a response to objects and it appears from the start to admit more or less broad variations in their appearance. Even the physical and geometrical laws of the universe are responsible for variations in the manner in which objects present themselves to the subject. As objects recede, they change in apparent size; as they revolve, they change shape; and as lighting alters, so they change colour. One is familiar with the way in which the organism reacts to maintain its constancy of perception. Similarly, the work of Piaget has shown that the child constructs the unity of an object by integrating the diversity and multiplicity of impressions to which the object gives rise. Objects lead to concepts in so far as they too comprise a number of characteristics and extend to a number of specimens.

Experiments on instinctive behaviour have shown that animals can respond to lures (models) which are no more than a crude imitation of natural stimuli: the fighting fish takes up an aggressive pose when confronted with models which give but a distant imitation of a male of its species (cf. Piéron, 1941, 93), the robin will attack a stuffed model of its species and even a mere bundle of feathers (Scott, 1958, 140).

*b) Active assimilation.* A response may be general because it entails common treatment of different stimuli.

It must not be forgotten that an organism's reaction does not depend on what objects are in themselves but on the interest which they hold for it. Stimuli that are perceptually, and even objectively, different produce the same response because they have the same meaning for the organism. Dissimilar liquids and even fruits and roots can all quench thirst just as certain mushrooms albeit different in colour, shape and size, can all poison or upset the organism. Classes are thus set up by the organism's own reactions. It was for this reason that Rignano (1927) laid stress on affective classifications, to which he attributed an important role in concept formation.

Similarly, he insisted on the part played by 'use', as a result of which objects with different intrinsic properties are none the less treated in the same way. This is true but calls for further generalization, since the subject is constantly led, and in fact compelled, to bring stimuli together in order to give them a common treatment. The influence of environment is more pressing here than nature alone can be since it introduces a large number of obligations and points of view. Is it not through this influence that a child learns to group in categories, to which he responds in an appropriate manner, the members of his family (as opposed to 'strangers'), the objects with which he may play (as opposed to those which he must not touch), the clothes he puts on to go out, those which he wears at home, etc.? All these everyday categories are not based purely or simply on a likeness, for likeness alone could lead to the establishing of quite different categories. Even live categories such as an animal species, dogs for instance, are established as a result of social pressure. This applies *a fortiori* to notions, such as those in geography, the natural sciences or grammar, which are actually taught in school.

The subject is not passive in all this. He does not accept external constraints but meets them half-way or else offers resistance. The way in which a child gropes in his use of words, his 'abusive' extensions or restrictions of meaning are classical evidence of this.

This activity increases considerably in the case of more markedly intellectual tasks, free from the narrow restrictions imposed by a context. It is thus greater when the subject is dealing with the realities of scientific laws or, quite simply, is placed in various situations used in experimental psychology. These are strictly speaking problems and the subject plays a part by evolving hypotheses which can be tested in the course of the experiment.

It would be a mistake, however, to overestimate the conscious and voluntary aspect of this activity. In many cases—if we exclude the case where the subject has to invent a completely new law— or even quite simply those occasions where the choice of subjects is not limited to psychology students, who have a ready tendency to look for principles that are infinitely more complicated than those thought of by the psychologist—we find that the subject is guided by the situation itself towards the regularity to which he

## Intellectual Activities

is to respond. This is so in the classical experiments on concept formation, in which similarity emerges and forces itself on the subject even before he has become conscious of it. Active intervention on his part is not thereby excluded but it operates on a particular level by making available responses which are formed during the course of the experiment or which, having been formed previously, are released and mobilized in accordance with the suggestions contained in the situation.

### 4 Information gained by the use of complex tests

It must be remembered that one of the uses of these tests, particularly the multiple classification tests, is to make it possible to determine the capacity for abstract thought and the plasticity of a subject or category of subjects. It is quite clear that 'abstract thought', considered as a level or a possibility of functioning, is much better assessed by tests which require the subject to manipulate simultaneously, and to arrange in time sequence several principles of response than it is when he is merely required to follow indications more or less directly suggested by the stimuli perceived. (cf. Oléron, 1951.) This explains the use that Goldstein made of these tests on women patients with brain injuries, and other (more or less convincing) applications in psychiatry.

#### (A) LEARNING SETS

One of the first general facts to emerge from situations in which the subject must pass from one principle to another is that there is a phenomenon of facilitation, which causes him to adapt himself to changes better and better. This applies to the reversal of relations so that after the first reversal he takes quite a long time to respond correctly and makes many errors but, after subsequent reversals, he makes fewer errors and succeeds more and more quickly in giving the right response.

Harlow (1949, 1950) suggested using the expression *learning set* to express this fact and he emphasized its bearing upon the conception of learning which, in such cases, cannot be reduced to mere stimulus-response connections.

It is clear that its significance extends beyond the field of

*Pierre Oléron*

learning (as he also pointed out) and concerns intellectual activities. If subjects can be trained to make plastic inductions in an experimental situation, there is little doubt that everyday life itself offers opportunities for this kind of exercise, at least to adults. The child is trained to consider things from many aspects, if only because the words that designate them or the verbal expressions that relate to them imply multiplicity. It is certainly not easy to make a detailed genetic study of this training, but there is little doubt that it creates abilities which the normal man can use to deal with the natural or artificial tasks set before him. It is not easy to interpret cultural differences to which little study has been devoted in this connection. Nevertheless, it is not surprising to find a greater rigidity among subjects who are not used to the variations made possible by a highly developed culture and language.

(B) REVERSAL SHIFTS AND NON-REVERSAL SHIFTS

The most ingenious applications of reversal experiments were made by Kendler with various collaborators (see Kendler, 1961, for a general account and references). Kendler distinguishes two categories: reversal shifts in which the subject must respond to the characteristic which is the opposite of the previously positive characteristic and non-reversal shifts in which he must respond to a characteristic which is merely different (previously 'parasitic') (cf. Fig. 10).

It has been found, at least with human subjects, that the first type of shift is easier than the second. This may appear a paradoxical result since it seems harder to acquire a response to a stimulus entirely opposed to the original stimulus than to a stimulus which is merely different

The interpretation proposed by Kendler (1961) makes reference to a process of mediation illustrated by the diagram on the next page.

The mediator here corresponds to size, which evidently establishes a community between the big and the small stimuli by virtue of being a more general category to which they both belong.

Thus it appears that the response is not simply the result of the subject's discovery of the characteristic which is immediately present (and reinforced). The response schema which is brought into play in fact goes beyond the direct stimulus-response connection which alone is apt to receive attention at first. It is rich in generality and ambivalence.

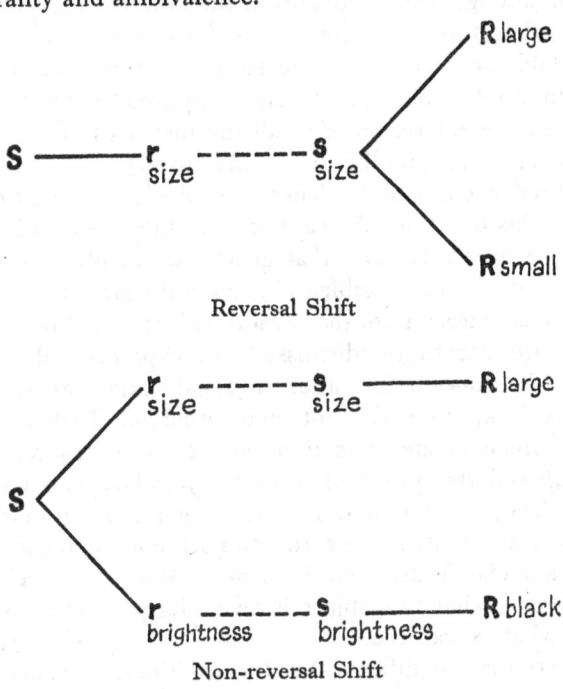

(C) ORDER OF DOMINANCE OF CONCEPTS

Another category of facts concerns what, following Heidbreder, has been termed the order of dominance of concepts. Originally, the phenomenon was found to occur in situations where, according to a technique derived from Hull's, the subject had to discover the 'concepts' corresponding to various figurative examples (cf. Heidbreder, 1946 a, 1946 b, 1947). It was observed that some of these concepts were on the whole discovered before the others.

An order, parallel to the one just mentioned, was also found when using a completely different technique, that of multiple classifications.[1] If subjects are left free to choose several principles of classification suggested by the material presented to

[1] Translator's Note: Heidbreder's term is *free classification*.

them, it is generally found that most of them will adopt the same order of preference and, broadly speaking, their choice of first, second and third principles will be the same (Heidbreder, 1948).

Thus, among natural categories, the object comes first, number comes last, form and colour occupying intermediate positions.[1] (In the table on page 35, the measure of performance is given by the mean number of series attempts required to obtain from the subject a coherent response to all the instances of the concept, Heidbreder, 1947; Heidbreder *et alia*, 1948.)

Heidbreder engaged in lengthy analyses in an attempt to elucidate this question. We cannot enter into the details of them here. It seems to us—and that is why we mention her experiments—that it is not possible to interpret the facts by considering only the characteristics of the stimuli. It is true that these characteristics are not to be dismissed. In experimental situations dealing with concept formation or classification, as in real life, one must take into account perceptual similarities between stimuli, which create attractions and thus contribute to form groupings (on this point, cf. Grant, 1951; Dattman and Israel, 1951; Oléron, 1961). One must not exaggerate the importance of perceptual similarities since the subject does not base his induction and classification on them alone. What he perceives is an indication of what the object is, with its properties which go beyond what he can see.

It is extremely significant that the order of dominance is again similar when using figures or words corresponding to them (Oléron, 1953). Words do not act through their perceptual value but through their meanings, which refer to what they designate. Cf. also Sigel (1954) who found that stimuli presented in three different forms of symbolization i.e. toy objects (concrete form), photographs and word-names of the objects, were treated in a comparable way throughout repeated classifications. The experiment is, however, disputable from a methodological point of view as the various forms of stimuli were presented to the same subjects.

---

[1] Naturally an order can be observed only with subjects who are capable of distinguishing clearly between various standpoints. This is a matter of genetic evolution. Ascoli (1950) observed that the ability to combine several principles of similarity increases with age. Subjects dominated by a concrete attitude also fail to establish a clear order of classification, since for them all qualities are as it were given at once and adhere to one another (Oléron, 1951).

| Experiment A | | | Experiment B | | | Experiment E | | | Experiment F | | |
|---|---|---|---|---|---|---|---|---|---|---|---|
| Face | 3 | 35 | Bird | 3 | 85 | Form E1 | 6 | 76 | Shoe | 6 | 44 |
| Building | 3 | 48 | Hat | 4 | 70 | Form E2 | 9 | 20 | Bird | 6 | 60 |
| Tree | 3 | 94 | Face | 4 | 90 | Form E3 | 9 | 72 | Book | 6 | 92 |
| Form A1 | 4 | 46 | Form B1 | 4 | 70 | Red | 11 | 04 | Red | 9 | 32 |
| Form A2 | 5 | 05 | Form B2 | 7 | 00 | Yellow | 11 | 16 | Yellow | 9 | 92 |
| Form A3 | 5 | 19 | Form B3 | 8 | 65 | Blue | 12 | 12 | Blue | 11 | 24 |
| Number 2 | 6 | 14 | Number 6 | 9 | 35 | Number 2 | 14 | 80 | Number 2 | 14 | 28 |
| Number 6 | 8 | 76 | Number 3 | 9 | 40 | Number 4 | 16 | 12 | Number 4 | 15 | 40 |
| Number 5 | 10 | 22 | Number 4 | 9 | 60 | Number 5 | 16 | 32 | Number 5 | 15 | 56 |

(Forms A1 and B1 are circles.)

*Pierre Oléron*

It is easier to understand what takes place if one envisages the subject as actualizing certain reactive tendencies when presented with the stimuli. Is it not true that the earliest, most firmly anchored, but at the same time most readily available tendencies are those which concern objects? An object is something that one touches, manipulates and moves, and to which one adapts oneself most frequently and most immediately.

Heidbreder emphasized the 'thinglike' character of stimuli, which could well govern the hierarchy of responses. It would appear that this character is not an attribute of the stimuli themselves but that it lies in the implicit relations existing between them and the subject's activities, and thus in the reactive tendencies present within the subject himself.

## 3 Reasoning

Ambiguities of terminology are even more pronounced in the area of intellectual activity which we are now about to consider than in the others. The words 'inference', 'reasoning' and 'deduction' could equally well (or ill) be used as headings for this section.

The intellectual activities to which we refer are operations—concatenation, combination—by which it is possible to arrive at affirmations and decisions from a given starting point without reference to additional data.

### 1 *The various aspects of reasoning*

(A) ITS THREE MAIN FORMS

It is possible to distinguish three forms which to a certain extent correspond to three levels.

*a) Actually experienced inferences.* The subject simply puts into operation response schemata which have already been constituted and which establish a connection between a given category of stimuli and gestures or actions which the stimuli could not spontaneously have produced.

*b) 'Material' reasonings.* These draw on a symbolism which is usually verbal but which may be made up of representations of an even more concrete nature. The way in which they unfold is determined by content, that is, by the objects to which the symbols refer and by the connections between them, as revealed by experience. Almost every inference which man uses is of this type, whether it be the deductions of a detective, those of a scientist or of a human relations expert.... The forms of reasoning found in pre-scientific thought, or in the early stages of a science are particularly instructive because they often reveal faulty chains of reasoning, the inaccuracy of which (now apparent to us) serves to bring out the mechanism involved.

*c) Formal reasonings.* These also have a symbolic basis, which may be verbal or specialized (symbols used by mathematicians and logicians). Chains and combinations of propositions proceed *vi formae*, i.e. they are not a mere reproduction of empirical connections. They obey rules defined within the system concerned. For example, syllogistic reasonings proceed by combining propositions in a way which takes into account the relations of comprehension and extension between the terms (hence they can be symbolized by means of Euler's circles).[1] This type of reasoning provides a framework into which any content can be inserted, even if it is devoid of sense (or if the combinations are devoid of sense). In logic, $a \supset b$. $b \supset c$. $\therefore a \supset c$ is valid whatever is designated by $a$, $b$, and $c$. The rules of logical sequence are determined as rules governing the use of the sign $\supset$ ('implies'). These rules are themselves formally defined on the basis of the relations between the various terms which may be introduced and their 'truth' or 'affirmation'.

---

[1] We do not propose to give here the theory of syllogisms, but in order to make it easier to understand experiments which will be described later, it may be useful to point out that syllogistic reasoning involves three terms (known in classical terminology as the major, middle and minor terms). These enter into three propositions, which are the two premises and the conclusion. Propositions may vary in quality (affirmative or negative) and in quantity (universal or particular). They are indicated as follows according to traditional notation: A = universal affirmative, I = particular affirmative, E = universal negative, O = particular negative. The only valid syllogisms are those in which the propositions respect the mutual inclusions or exclusions of the concepts corresponding to the three terms, thus it is not possible to conclude anything from two I premises, nor from two O premises, etc.

*Pierre Oléron*

(B) ACTUALLY EXPERIENCED INFERENCE

Reasonings of type *a*), as described above, have not been specifically studied. They enter, however, into most of the steps involved in solving a problem. By virtue of this, experiments concerned with problem solving bring in this type of reasoning but do not examine it in any systematic fashion.

Let us not forget, however, that Maier (1929, 1936) drew on the notion of *combination* to characterize reasoning. His classical experiments on rats and on young children bring into play the idea that reasoning exists when the subject can use elements

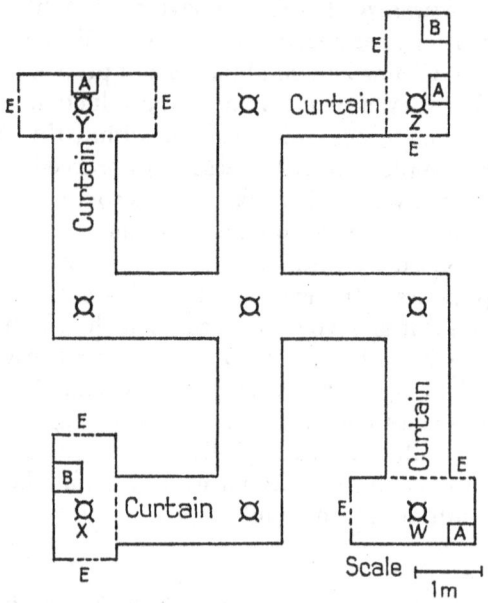

Fig. 11  APPARATUS USED BY MAIER (1936) TO TEST REASONING IN CHILDREN

It consists of pathways and four little booths to which they lead. The child explores the apparatus then is led into Y (first experiment). He is taken round the outside of the apparatus from Y to W, where there is a toy which he can set in motion with a coin (2nd experiment). He goes out to get another coin and the experimenter makes him enter X, whence he must go back to the place where the toy is. This can only be done by combining the first and second experience. (*J. Comp. Psychol.*, 1936, **21**, 358.)

*Intellectual Activities*

from different experiences, gone through at different times, and combine them in a single step leading to the solution of the problem (Fig. 11). The results obtained by Maier (1936) show that young children of less than five or six years of age are not capable of achieving the combination of isolated experiences called for by his experiment. Kendler and Kendler (1956), on the contrary, discovered this ability in children of three to four. Their apparatus is different from Maier's (cf. Fig. 12) and this factor must be taken into account. Maier's apparatus implies the construction of a more complex spatial model (the subject has to change his position) while Kendler's is such that he can proceed largely by associations. We feel that it is dangerous to try to assess ability to combine or to reason without reference to the objects and situations which form the context of these activities.

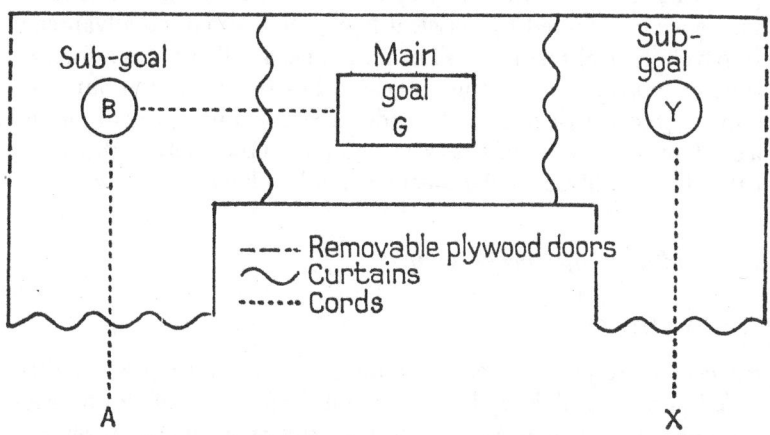

Fig. 12  APPARATUS USED BY KENDLER AND KENDLER (1956) TO STUDY REASONING IN YOUNG CHILDREN

During the first part of the experiment the subject is placed in front of the apparatus, and by pulling first cord A then X (or the other way round) he can obtain a little toy with which he is allowed to play for a few moments. During the second part, in which he is placed in front of the side opening from which the door has been removed, he can obtain a more attractive toy attached to A. During the third part, he is again placed in front of the apparatus and asked to choose the cord which will give him access to the main toy. (*J. exp. Psychol.*, 1956, **51**, 311.)

*Pierre Oléron*

(C) REASONINGS WITH A SYMBOLIC BASIS

It is mainly this type of reasoning which has been the object of experimental study. One can obviously refer to the notion of combination here as in the preceding case. It is a fact that combination is implied in reasoning but in this case the subject must not simply put together two elements in the experiment but a number of elements which refer only indirectly to the experiment.

Syllogisms have been fairly extensively used (taking into account the small number of studies which we have mentioned). This may seem a conservative attitude on the part of psychologists and suggest ignorance of modern forms of reasoning (Moore and Anderson (1954) have, it is true, indicated the use that could be made of problems dealing with the calculus of propositions). In actual fact, syllogisms, like all other forms of inference considered by classical logic, have a marked advantage in psychological research. This is because a syllogism is a formal type of reasoning the value of which lies in its pattern but it is constructed with words and words carry meanings, thus there is a content. Whence conflicts arise which lend themselves, theoretically, to an analysis of the mechanisms involved.

## 2 Conditions affecting reasoning

(A) TRAINING

Success in tests of formal reasoning is low, even among cultivated subjects. This will be apparent from some of the figures quoted below. It is partly due to the unfamiliar character of this type of task, and to the subject's lack of familiarity with the type of logical sequence involved. It is understandable that training can improve performance, whether it takes the form of a theoretical introduction or of practice with similar tests.

Morgan and Morgan (1953) observed that a test of logical reasoning was better performed following attendance at a course in logic. Probably, as they point out, some subjects who have not followed the course are capable of reaching a higher level than some of those who have. One must not, therefore, overestimate the part played by training, particularly as there are other

## Intellectual Activities

subjects with a higher university degree who do better, even though they had not had special training, than students who have followed courses in logic. Nevertheless, it appears that the influence of training can readily be understood, whether it consists in inducing familiarity with a certain type of material or in establishing rules which can then be applied to various particular cases (just as classical logic has formulated rules which determine the conditions whereby a syllogism is valid).

It is true that a test which can be dealt with simply by applying ready made laws is no longer a test of reasoning in the full sense of the word. Conversely, however, one must not be deceived into thinking that reasoning corresponds to an absolute power which is exercised *per se*. Like every intellectual activity, it brings into play a number of habits and dispositions which are in no way ready made.

### (B) THE STRUCTURE OF PROPOSITIONS

*a) Global structure: atmosphere-effect.* Woodworth and Sells (1935), Sells (1936), and Sells and Koob (1937) discovered a phenomenon which they called 'atmosphere effect'. It concerns syllogisms and it consists of the fact that subjects have a tendency to draw conclusions on the basis of the global impression of the premises. Thus, affirmative premises create an atmosphere which induces the subject to state or accept an affirmative conclusion; negative premises incline towards a negative conclusion; the same effect is produced by the universal or particular character of statements.

The test which reveals atmosphere effect in the most spectacular fashion is that of Sells and Koob. It consists in presenting two concordant premises (AA, EE, OO, II), and asking the subject to draw the conclusion of which only the terms are given, as in the example below:

All x's are y's.         No x's are y's.
And all x's are z's.     And no z's are x's.
Therefore .. y's .. z's. Therefore ... z's ... y's.

The proposed syllogisms are invalid so that no conclusion can be drawn from them. The fact remains that most subjects (students in this case) completed the conclusion that was outlined and did so in keeping with the atmosphere created by the premises.

In this form, the test is very questionable since it does all it can to induce the subjects into error. It begins by a demonstration and an example of a syllogism to be completed, both of which are correct (they are of the Barbara type, that is, the two premises are universal and affirmative and call for a conclusion of that type); the presentation of the conclusion invites the subjects to complete the syllogism but there is nothing to show that they may have to refuse. . . .

The form of experiment adopted by Sells (1936) does not incur these criticisms, since it consists in the presentation of complete syllogisms and the subject has to judge their validity by using a scale which allows rejection (giving a choice between 'absolutely true', 'probably true', 'indeterminate', 'probably false' and 'absolutely false'. One hundred and twenty-seven syllogisms put forward by Sells were invalid (out of 169). Nevertheless, a very high proportion of subjects accepted the conclusions and did so in keeping with atmosphere effect.

This effect is studied in a more precise manner than in the experiment mentioned above since combinations of premises are not confined to homogeneous propositions (of the type AA, II, etc.). It is seen that together a universal and a particular premise create an atmosphere conducive to a *particular* conclusion, while an affirmative and a negative premise incline towards a *negative* conclusion.

(In addition to atmosphere effect, Woodworth and Sells referred to a 'caution effect', which leads to preference for a 'weak' rather than a 'strong' conclusion, such as 'some are' or 'some are not' rather than 'all are' or 'none are'.)

Chapman and Chapman (1959) disputed Woodworth and Sells' conception of 'atmosphere effect'. They carried out an experiment with forty-two syllogisms, of which the premises were given and the subjects had to decide upon the conclusion by choosing between five statements. Here is an example:

Some L's are K's.
Some K's are M's.

Therefore:

1) No M's are L's.

## Intellectual Activities

2) Some M's are L's.
3) Some M's are not L's.
4) None of these.
5) All M's are L's.

Each of the forty-two syllogisms was incorrect, so that in each case the correct answer was 'None of these'. It is apparent that the subjects (222 students) were far from having reached this conclusion (approximately only twenty per cent correct answers).

Percentage of subjects choosing each type of conclusion

| Item No. | Premises | Fig. | A | E | I | O | N | Item No. | Premises | Fig. | A | E | I | O | N |
|---|---|---|---|---|---|---|---|---|---|---|---|---|---|---|---|
| 12 | AA | II | 83 | 6 | 3 | 1 | 7 | 5 | II | IV | 2 | 3 | 68 | 13 | 15 |
| 17 | AA | II | 82 | 5 | 3 | 1 | 9 | 20 | II | III | 1 | 5 | 63 | 5 | 26 |
| 39 | AA | II | 77 | 5 | 6 | 1 | 10 | 51 | II | III | 4 | 5 | 64 | 5 | 23 |
| 4 | AE | I | 3 | 81 | 3 | 5 | 8 | 7 | IO | III | 1 | 6 | 13 | 48 | 31 |
| 23 | AE | III | 1 | 85 | 0 | 5 | 8 | 34 | IO | IV | 2 | 5 | 11 | 60 | 22 |
| 41 | AE | I | 1 | 82 | 3 | 6 | 7 | 48 | IO | I | 2 | 6 | 10 | 55 | 27 |
| 8 | AI | II | 3 | 7 | 75 | 7 | 8 | 22 | OI | I | 1 | 4 | 14 | 59 | 21 |
| 15 | AI | IV | 3 | 3 | 80 | 6 | 8 | 33 | OI | III | 1 | 7 | 15 | 52 | 24 |
| 46 | AI | IV | 10 | 2 | 74 | 6 | 7 | 44 | OI | IV | 1 | 5 | 11 | 55 | 27 |
| 13 | IA | I | 5 | 5 | 78 | 8 | 5 | 29 | EE | IV | 1 | 57 | 4 | 3 | 36 |
| 19 | IA | II | 5 | 11 | 68 | 7 | 9 | 36 | EE | II | 3 | 59 | 5 | 5 | 28 |
| 42 | IA | I | 3 | 4 | 83 | 4 | 7 | 40 | EE | III | 2 | 47 | 4 | 7 | 40 |
| 11 | AO | III | 2 | 7 | 14 | 61 | 16 | 30 | EO | I | 3 | 24 | 10 | 32 | 32 |
| 24 | AO | I | 1 | 2 | 13 | 76 | 8 | 35 | EO | II | 1 | 26 | 9 | 32 | 32 |
| 52 | AO | IV | 1 | 4 | 10 | 74 | 11 | 47 | EO | III | 5 | 25 | 6 | 21 | 44 |
| 25 | OA | II | 0 | 7 | 12 | 64 | 16 | 2 | OE | IV | 2 | 28 | 12 | 24 | 34 |
| 32 | OA | IV | 3 | 4 | 11 | 70 | 12 | 27 | OE | I | 3 | 39 | 5 | 19 | 34 |
| 43 | OA | I | 1 | 6 | 7 | 78 | 8 | 50 | OE | III | 3 | 41 | 7 | 19 | 30 |
| 9 | IE | I | 1 | 62 | 6 | 13 | 18 | 3 | OO | III | 0 | 8 | 10 | 50 | 31 |
| 26 | IE | III | 2 | 59 | 5 | 16 | 19 | 14 | OO | IV | 0 | 5 | 11 | 50 | 24 |
| 49 | IE | IV | 2 | 48 | 6 | 24 | 20 | 45 | OO | II | 1 | 8 | 11 | 60 45 | 35 |

Chapman and Chapman considered that these results did not agree with the views developed by Sells and Woodworth. If these were true, the conclusions drawn from IE and OE premises should be of type O (since the premises create an atmosphere that is at once negative and particular). It was also found that particular conclusions were not more favoured than universal ones (cf. the conclusions of universal premises AA, AE, EE).

It is difficult, however, not to see a measure of agreement with the conception of atmosphere, if one takes the latter in its original sense, without entering into details that do not agree. Atmosphere effect naturally tends to bring about a conclusion of the same type as the premises; to expect it to lead to conclusions of a different type is probably unwise and Chapman and Chapman are certainly right to question the arguments advanced by Sells and Woodworth. However, their results clearly show that the choice of conclusions is closely dependent on the nature of the premises.

*b) Detailed structure.* The subject considers that propositions are to be deduced from one another and he draws a new proposition from those which are given by engaging in a number of operations by means of which the various propositions can be considered as equivalent (or not equivalent). These operations may be helped or hindered by the actual structure of the propositions, or the structure of their combination, since they may either follow from one another directly or call for manipulations in order to attain a form in which they can be confronted or combined. In the latter case, it is understandable that the process of reasoning is more difficult than in the first.

I. Hunter (1957) made a contribution to the study of this condition, which we feel should inspire further research in this direction. He studied a type of reasoning which has become a classic among psychologists, Cyril Burt having invented the prototype: Tom runs faster than Jim; Jack runs slower than Jim. Who is the slowest: Jim, Jack or Tom? (Burt, 1909).

The reasoning in a test of this kind consists in determining the serial relation of three terms, of which the positions are given two by two in each premise. Seriation has been achieved when the premises are arranged thus: $A > B$; $B > C$ ('isotropic' premises according to the terminology proposed by I. Hunter). When the presentation is different the subject must reorganize the premises to arrive at this form.

Hunter's experiment consists in comparing the relative ease with which various types of presentation lead to the solution.

*Intellectual Activities*

I. A > B; B > C.

II. A > B; C < B. (Order is re-established when the second premise is simply *converted*, that is, transformed into B > C.)

III. B < A; C < B. (This is merely a case of *reordering* the second premise, that is, putting it first.)

IV. B < A; B > C. (This can be solved in two ways: *a*) the second premise is converted, i.e. B < A, C < B, then reordered, i.e. C < B; B < A; *b*) the first premise is converted, i.e. A > B; B > C.)

Sixteen-year-olds and eleven-year-olds confronted with these various types of premises found that they presented an increasing order of difficulty, corresponding to the order above (II to IV). This implies that reordering (III) is more difficult than converting (II) and that the conversion of the premise which comes first (IV, in so far as subjects have recourse to this method) is more difficult than that of the premise which comes second, since the first premise gives, as it were, an overall orientation.

The kind of analysis used by Hunter is clearly applicable to other forms of reasoning, in particular the syllogism, which also involves the establishment of a relation between three terms on the basis of the indications given by two premises. The case of the syllogism is a little more complicated since negative propositions also occur, but it is possible to begin by considering the positive forms and then to specify the modalities of the analysis to include the other forms.

I. Hunter followed Burt and Piaget, as he himself states, in considering the effects of the global impression produced by certain premises. This impression can be likened to atmosphere effect but it, too, can be more closely defined. If, for example, the first premise is 'Jack runs slower . . .', and the question is 'Who runs slower?' the subject, remembering the first statement, may tend to reply 'Jack'. This tends to reduce the chances of correct responses. In other cases, however, the effect may be favourable. Thus, with children of eleven, I. Hunter observed that statements of type II led to a greater proportion of successes than those of type I. He attributed this to the effect just mentioned ('A is taller than B; C is smaller than B; who is the tallest?' The answer 'A', encouraged by atmosphere, is also the correct one).

An important point arises here. Analysis in terms of relation is meaningless unless subjects are capable, while considering

45

relations, of ignoring any suggestion implied by the content, and thus the level of development of the subjects is a significant factor.

(C) ATTITUDES AND HABITS

Not only do subjects who are given tasks to perform lack appropriate training but also they bring with them intellectual habits fashioned by the types of reasoning to which they are accustomed and these do not have the structure or the exactness of formal reasoning. This may account for some of their responses when confronted with the latter.

Chapman and Chapman (1959), in an attempt to account for the results reported above, advanced as their first hypothesis that subjects tend to consider that the simple conversion of propositions of type A and O is valid (conversion consists in deriving from a given proposition a new proposition in which the predicate of the first becomes the subject and the subject of the first becomes the predicate). Such a conversion is not valid. Propositions of type A are converted by 'accident', according to the terms of classical logic. That is to say that given that 'all S's are P's' one can only conclude that 'some P's are S's'. Propositions of type O cannot be converted. As Chapman and Chapman point out, training in mathematical reasoning encourages the tendency to consider that propositions of type A are simply convertible, since in mathematics, the verb 'to be' generally means 'is equal to' and not, as in classical propositions, 'is included in'. Thus it is true that if all angles of 90° are right angles, conversely all right angles are angles of 90°.

The same applies to the conversion of propositions of type O, which experience often appears to justify. For example, 'some plants are not green'—'some green things are not plants' are two equally acceptable propositions, as can be observed from reality.

Chapman and Chapman introduce a second hypothesis, which lays stress on the merely probabilistic character of most of the inferences which one is led to make in daily life or even in the course of scientific development. It appears probable that things with some properties in common are of the same type and that those which do not have common qualities are not of the same type. This can explain some reactions to IO premises as when

'Some A's are B's, some C's are not B's' is interpreted as meaning that some A's and some C's do not share the common quality B, thus seeming to justify the affirmation that some C's are not A's.

It is by no means certain that the hypotheses put forward by Chapman and Chapman prove that atmosphere effect does not exist. This effect and the factors which they adduce could well operate at different levels, atmosphere effect influencing mainly subjects who think less and who allow themselves to be overwhelmed by a distinctly abstract task while the influence of habits affects mainly those who do attempt to reason. We do not wish to belittle the role of habits, far from it, and indeed we feel that it should be studied further.

To this must be added *the interpretation put upon the meaning of words*. It is well known that the meaning of 'some' in the propositions of classical logic differs from its use in ordinary speech. To logicians it means 'at least some', while in everyday speech, it means rather 'only some' (i.e. some but not all). These are obviously different interpretations since, in the first case, 'others' may possess the characteristic which is said to belong to 'some' whereas, in the second case, they do not.

In order to assess the meaning spontaneously attributed to particular propositions, an experiment was carried out (Oléron, unpublished) in which educated but non-specialist subjects (students) were invited to choose between two interpretations of each of four statements varying in expression, but all 'particular' in form. One interpretation was 'non-exclusive' (in conformity with classical logic) while the other was 'exclusive'.

1. What, according to you, is the meaning of the statement: 'Professor Z is sometimes boring.'
   'The rest of the time he is not boring,' or
   'It is possible that the rest of the time he is also boring.'

2. What, according to you, is the meaning of the statement: 'Some oxides are conductors.'
   'Other oxides are not conductors,' or
   'It is possible that other oxides are conductors too.'

3. What, according to you, is the meaning of the statement: 'Some historians made a mistake.'
   'The other historians did not make a mistake,' or
   'It is possible that the other historians made a mistake too.'

*Pierre Oléron*

4. What, according to you, is the meaning of the statement: 'Some traders are not honest.'
'The other traders are honest,' or
'It is possible that the other traders are not honest either.'

Results were as follows (194 subjects):

Number of subjects who chose each type of interpretation

|  | *Interpretation* | | |
| --- | --- | --- | --- |
|  | *Exclusive* | *Non exclusive* | *No response* |
| 1st proposition | 168 | 21 | 5 |
| 2nd proposition | 166 | 25 | 3 |
| 3rd proposition | 121 | 67 | 6 |
| 4th proposition | 132 | 58 | 4 |

Subjects were clearly in favour of an 'exclusive' interpretation, contrary to that adopted by classical logicians. Authors who have used syllogisms warn their subjects of the meaning ascribed to particular propositions in classical logic. One is left to wonder whether warning is sufficient to counterbalance the strength of acquired habits.

## 4 Problem Solving

It may be said that in principle every situation to which a subject cannot make appropriate response by drawing on his directly available repertoire or responses is a problem.

It is well to add two qualifications to the general definition given above.

*a*) One can only speak of a problem when there exists a solution. The subject may find himself in a situation which it is completely impossible for him to overcome and which necessarily defeats him. A miner crushed by a roof fall or a condemned man confronted by the executioner who puts his head in the lunette of the guillotine cannot be said to be faced with a problem. A second degree equation or a square root are likewise not problems to a child of six or to an illiterate. . . .

*b*) The solution must be obtained by intellectual means. If a

*Intellectual Activities*

subject succeeds in dealing with a situation simply by developing an automatically acquired ability or skill, it is merely a question of adaptation or learning. One is speaking metaphorically when one says that altitude sets a problem to an organism used to the plains and likewise a subject who, after prolonged struggling, finds a way out of a difficult situation (such as a cat which has been shut in a box and keeps on jumping until finally it succeeds in jumping high enough to get out) has not properly speaking solved a problem.

## 1 Several types of classical problems

It is impossible to establish a logical classification of the problems which can be used by psychologists. In view of the very general character of a problematic situation the number of situations is practically unlimited. At the same time, there are very few which are not complex. For this reason few can be closely defined. Moreover, the absence of any clear conception of the psychological processes involved in problem solving precludes a classification on those lines.

We shall indicate here only a few types of classical problems, mainly by way of illustration and not of systematization. Others will be referred to later in connection with experiments that we shall have cause to mention.

### (A) PRACTICAL PROBLEMS

These can be characterized by saying that the subject is dealing with *concrete* set-ups, which call for some kind of action. What is interesting is that among them there are tasks that can be applied to the whole range of subjects capable of solving a problem, including animals and young children, whereas this is not the case with the other categories. The only completely practical problems are those which can be set without recourse to language (hence their applicability to the latter type of subjects) and in which the goal is clearly determined by the natural motivation of the subject (bait, freedom to be attained....).

The famous experiments by Köhler (1917) did much to popularize this type of test, even in connection with human subjects (children), although some of them had already been used

*Pierre Oléron*

before with both children and animals. Here are a few examples taken from the study by Gottschaldt (1933) who worked with children of different ages (2.8 to 9.5) and of normal and abnormal I.Q. (Fig. 13).

The problems set by Rey (1935) are also intended for children. A few specimens are reproduced below (Fig. 14).

(B) PROBLEMS RELATING TO SYMBOLIC MATERIAL

School problems in arithmetic, algebra, geometry and physics are clearly of this type. It is unusual, however, for them to be used exactly as they stand by psychologists, since they assume knowledge and abilities which are more developed in some than in others. Nevertheless an analysis of problem solving, for example with schoolchildren, has been made by some authors such as Wertheimer (1945). The most commonly used problems, however, are simple and require no specialized knowledge. This is true of Maier's excellent nine dot problem and of the problems of containers widely used by Luchins (cf. below).

The problems just mentioned imply a verbal aspect since specialized symbols can never be used alone. Language also plays a part, though in a more limited way, in many practical problems. It is possible to use problems which are stated in purely verbal terms but which refer, for example, to concrete situations (many school problems are of this type). The subject must then imagine the reality corresponding to the terms of the problem. This creates a difficulty that does not arise in concrete problems.

## 2 Conditions on which problem solving depends

(A) CONDITIONS DUE TO OBJECTS

It is clear that the relative difficulty of problems varies according to the nature of the question that is posed, but attention must also be paid to subject matter and to the way in which it is presented.

*a) Quantity of material.* Problems vary in the quantity and complexity of their terms. Thus, the whole which a subject has to take into account may be greater or smaller and more or

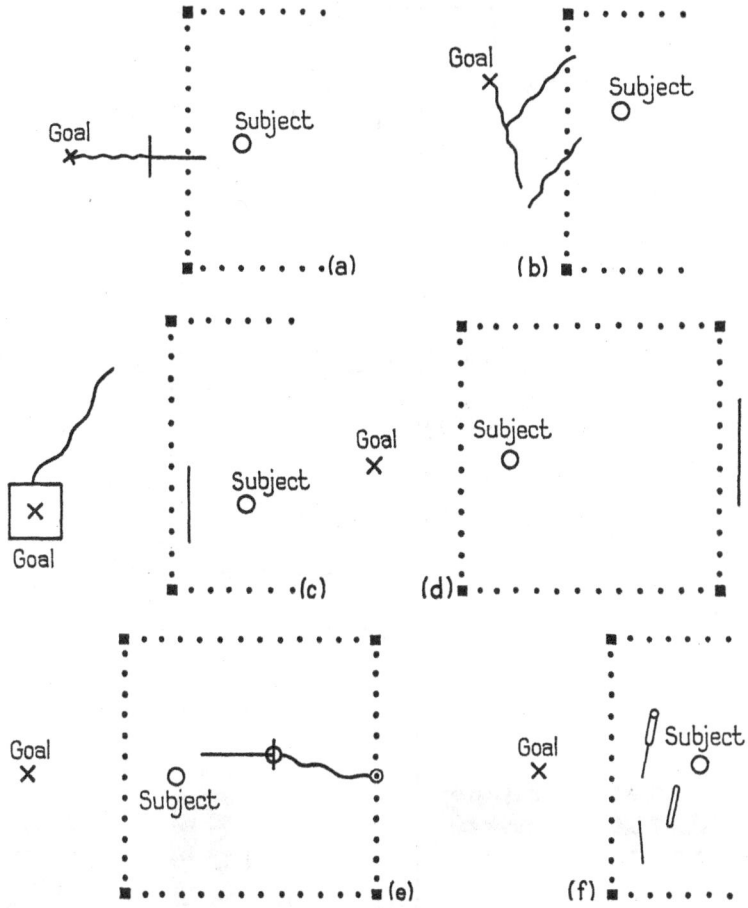

Fig. 13  Specimens of Problems used by Gottschaldt (1933) with Children

a) The goal-object is tied to a string, itself tied to a stick of which the outer end is in the shape of a T. The child must turn the stick 90° to make the bar of the T vertical so that it can pass between the bars;

b) the string which is directly tied to the goal-object does not reach the bars but a second string, tied to the middle of the first, does. The third merely has a perturbing effect;

c) the string tied to the support of the goal-object is not within hand's reach; the stick that is available in the cage does not enable the child to reach the object itself but only the end of the string.

d) the goal-object and the instrument are diametrically opposed;

e) a string tied to a bar of the cage ends in a ring through which there passes a stick with a T-shaped end; with this it is possible to reach the goal provided it has been disengaged from the ring;

f) one had to use the available elements to make an instrument long enough to reach the goal. (*Beih. Z. ang. Psychol.*, 1933, **68**, 153, 160, 164, 202, 204, 216.)

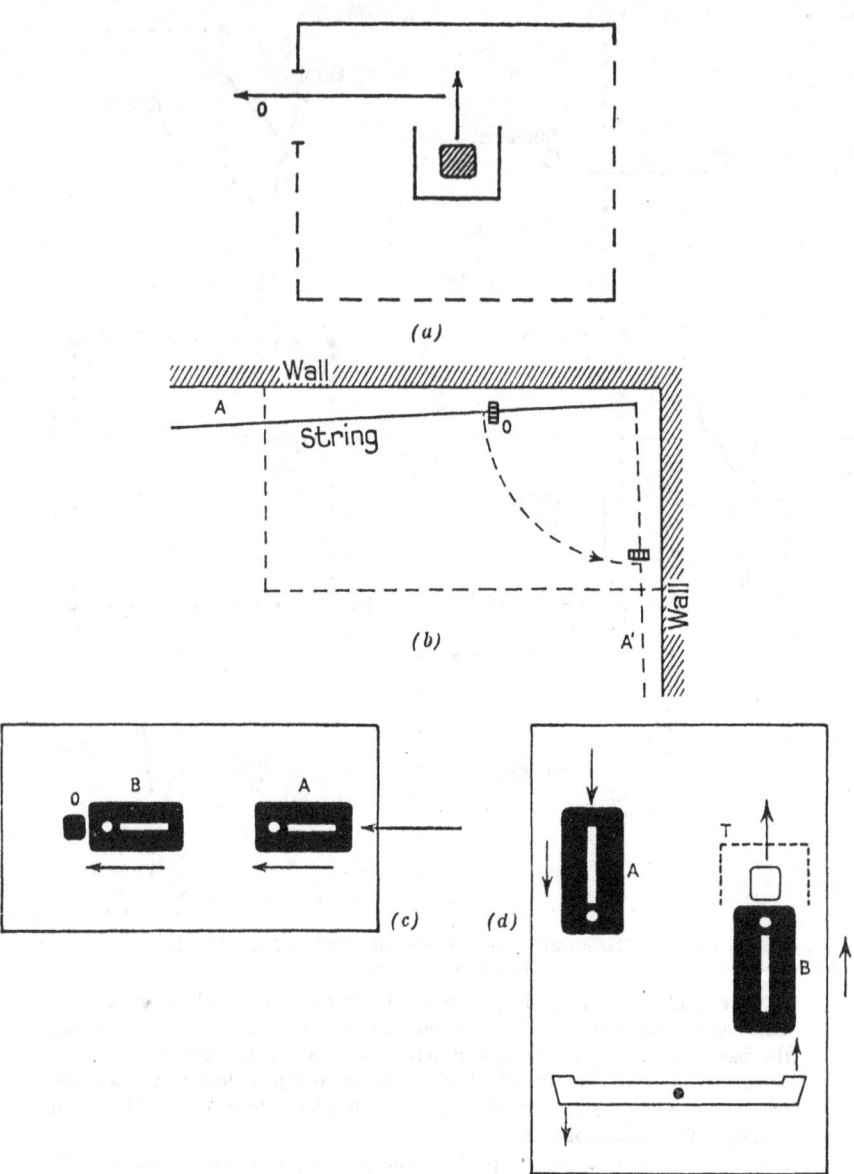

Fig. 14 EXAMPLES OF PROBLEMS USED BY REY (1935)

*a* and *b*: diagram of a box with grating, from which the bait must be removed with the aid of an instrument and by making a detour (a) or by bringing it within hand's reach using the string to which it is attached (b).

*c* and *d*: transmission of movement resolved by the interposition of blocks which fill the gaps between the pieces shown. (*L'intelligence pratique chez l'enfant*, Alcan, 1935, 46, 57, 131, 161.)

## Intellectual Activities

less difficult to embrace. The phenomenon is comparable to what one observes in all cases where the subject has to master an increasing quantity of material (perceptual field, immediate memory, memorization of elements. . . .).

Cook (1937) showed how there is an increase in the number of errors, the time taken and the number of moves when a puzzle passes from two to three and then to four elements.

Similarly, Johnson, Lincoln and Hall (1961) studied the increase in time taken by the subject in preparation and in actual solution (which an ingenious method enabled them to separate) as a function of the complexity of the problem (number of conditions which the solution must satisfy) (Fig. 15). (cf. also Solley and Snyder (1958) in a task which, admittedly, is predominantly perceptual but which brings in the concepts of information theory.)

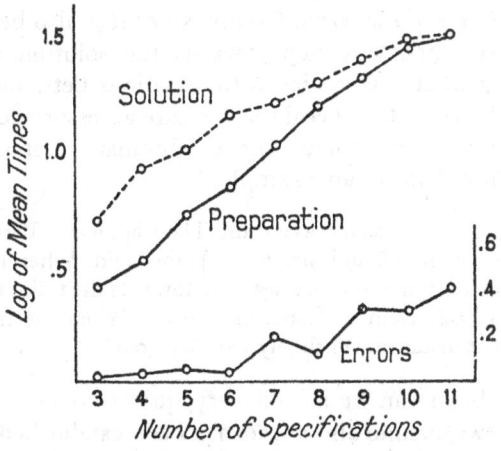

Fig. 15 INCREASE IN PREPARATION TIME AND SOLUTION TIME AND IN NUMBER OF ERRORS AS A FUNCTION OF THE NUMBER OF SPECIFICATIONS WHICH THE SUBJECT MUST TAKE INTO ACCOUNT

The use of serial-exposure apparatus makes it possible to present separately the material of the problem and a list in which the solution is to be found. In the very simple case illustrated above, the material consists of a list of digits and the problem consists in finding them among several lists. The number of specifications is the number of digits in the original list (ranging from 3 to 11). Preparation time is the time spent by the subject in examining this list. (Johnson, Lincoln and Hall, *J. Psychol.*, 1961, 51, 466.)

*b) Structure of the terms.* The Gestalt psychologists have stressed the part played by *organization* or *structure*. It is easy to understand that a problem which is close in structure to the solution is more easily solved than one in which the initial structure has to be completely recast and broken up or another in which the elements present no apparent organization. Simple examples may be found in the case of *anagrams*, which have been used by a number of psychologists. Anagrams can be presented in forms which suggest the key word more or less directly, simply by changing the order of the letters in the word more or less radically. Thus, Mayzner and Tresselt (1958) compared 'easy' orders which, in the case of the French word 'sujet', for example, would correspond to forms such as: Sujte, Ujets, Tsuje . . . . and 'difficult' orders which, for the same word, would be: Seutj, Utjse, Tuesj. . . . In the first case, reaction times are much shorter (cf. also Oléron, 1961 *a*).

*c) Complexity of the terms.* Complexity must also be taken into account. An important step towards the solution consists in determining what is essential in the relations between the terms proposed. It is easy to conceal this beneath accessory details which the subject will take some time to eliminate. Let us take the following problem as an example:

> A fly moves twice as fast as a train. The train leaves Paris for Rome. The fly leaves Rome and flies to meet the train. When it reaches it, it flies back to Rome, then comes back towards the train. On reaching it, it goes back again to Rome and so on. When the train reaches Rome, what distance will the fly have covered?

This problem can be solved very quickly once the essential relation between time and speed has been established: since the fly goes twice as fast as the train, and since it is in motion for the same length of time (this is not actually stated but is implied in the terms), it necessarily covers twice as much ground. All the rest is accessory detail, which can only lead the subject to waste time if he tries to follow all the movements or to elicit a law by analysing them.

Katz (1949) devoted a short study to what he called the 'blinding phenomenon', a term he used to express the idea that the subject can be dazzled, as it were, by some of the data. This prevents him from seeing the relevant structure and delays the discovery of the solution. Thus, taking a particular task (finding the sum of numbers from one to nine, or from one to five, according to the age of the subjects), he observed that there is an order of increasing difficulty corresponding to the following situations: 1) the numbers are presented in order; 2) they are presented out of order; 3) they are called out, then placed in a box and shaken; 4) the experimenter asks the subjects to find the smallest possible sum.

*d) 'Functional fixedness'*. The Gestalt psychologists have drawn attention to what happens when an element in the problem situation is incorporated in a structure from which it must be removed if the problem is to be solved.

Duncker (1935) gave classical instances of this factor. He spoke of 'functional fixedness', meaning that an element which has performed a function in a given context remains attached to this function and can only with difficulty be used in another function (i.e. the one required to solve the problem).

An example of this occurs in the following experiment: the subject must fix a board between the two stiles of a door (supposedly for a physics experiment). The board is too short to fit between the stiles; it has to be wedged with a suitable object. A cork would do perfectly. The subjects have a cork, among other objects, but when the cork is on a bottle, they less often have recourse to it than when it is simply placed amidst other objects.

Another example is given in the following problem: the subject must fix three little candles on a door. He needs supports to do this. Little cardboard boxes are perfectly suitable. All that need be done is to fix them to the door with drawing pins and to put the candles inside them. In one situation, the boxes are full (of candles, matches and drawing pins), in the other, they are empty. In the second case, the solution is more easily found than in the first.

Adamson (1952) resumed these experiments, using more subjects than Duncker, and obtained the same results.

Birch and Rabinowitz (1951) also confirmed them when they used Maier's two-cord problem. The subject has to bring together the free ends of two cords which are suspended from the ceiling. The distance between them is such that the subject cannot reach the end of the second while holding the end of the first (Fig. 16). The solution that is called for is the 'pendulum'; this

## Pierre Oléron

consists in making one rope swing so that it comes within reach of the subject holding the other. In the experiment by Birch and Rabinowitz, the subjects have at their disposal two objects which can be used as a weight to be attached to the cord in order to make it into a pendulum—a relay and a switch. There are two groups. In one of these, the subjects, during a preliminary experiment, are led to use the relay (to complete an electrical circuit) and in the other they use the switch (for the same purpose). It was found that the subjects in the first group did not use the relay as a weight but that they all took the switch. On the contrary, the majority of those in the second group (seven out of nine) chose the relay.

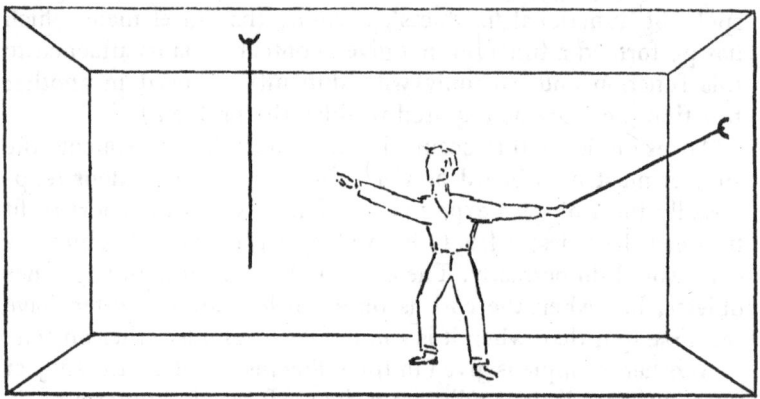

Fig. 16 DIAGRAM SHOWING MAIER'S TWO-CORD EXPERIMENT (1933)

The two cords are too far apart for the subject to be able to reach one while holding the other. (After Maier's description.)

A further confirmation, using different material, will be found in Van de Geer (1957), accompanied by a brief discussion of 'functional fixedness'.

e) *'Availability of functions'*. It is only to be expected, from the above, that problem solving should be facilitated by the availability of the object which must be used in the solution, or, more exactly, by the availability of the function which it must perform.

This question was studied by Saugstad (1955). He determined

*Intellectual Activities*

the availability of the function by asking subjects to state the uses to which the objects in question could be put, before these were submitted to them to solve the problem.

The problem used by Saugstad is an adaptation of one of those invented by Maier (1933). The subject must blow out a candle which is approximately two yards away by using several glass tubes nine and half inches long, a metal rod and putty. The solution consists in making a long tube by joining the short tubes with putty, which makes the joints air-tight, and supporting them with the metal rod. This done, the subject can extinguish the candle merely by pointing the tube towards it and blowing through it (Fig. 17).

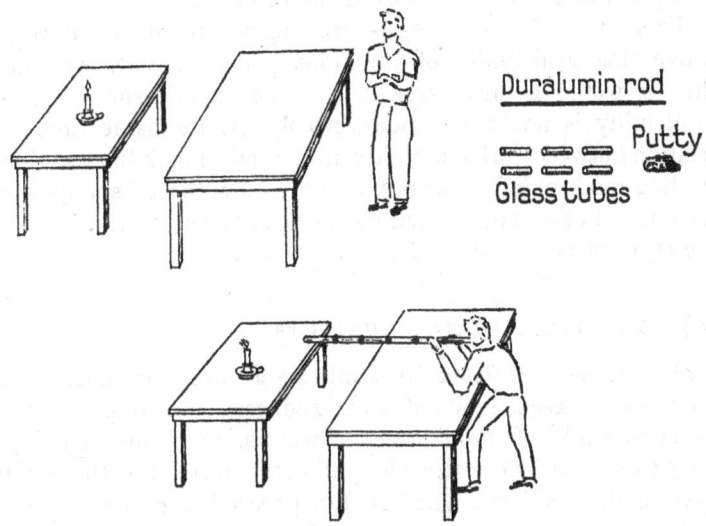

Fig. 17 ELEMENTS OF MAIER'S CANDLE PROBLEM (1933) AS ADAPTED BY SAUGSTAD (1955)

The subject must put out the candle without going up to it; he can do so by making a tube with elements held by a duralumin rod and using putty to make the joints airtight. (After Saugstad's description.)

The results obtained by Saugstad were positive in the sense that the subjects who indicated the functions of the objects used in solving the problem (sealing joints and giving support) all solved the problem while only approximately half of those who did not indicate them solved the problem.

*Pierre Oléron*

It is clear that in a study of this type 'availability of function' is tested on the verbal plane, while the problem calls for a practical and effective mobilization. Saugstad's results suggest that there is a concordance between the two types of availability. This has been questioned by Staats (1957) who also asked his subjects to state the functions of the critical object before calling on them to solve the problem. In his version of Maier's two-cord problem, using the pendulum method, the weight which must be used to make the pendulum is a screwdriver. It appears that there is no link between the mention of the 'weight' aspect of the screwdriver and its actual use as a weight in the experiment. Only seven subjects out of sixty-one gave the answer 'weight' and yet fifty-five solved the problem.

This contradicts the results previously quoted, but does not prove that availability of functions plays no part. To check this, it would be necessary to imagine experiments in which availability is not ascertained verbally. At the same time, the relation between verbal mobility and practical mobility should be studied more closely, not relying only on subjects' spontaneous responses but varying, much more than in previous experiments, the types of tasks and the types of objects.

(B) CONDITIONS DUE TO SUBJECTS

*a) Attitudes and habits.* It would be an over-simplification of the facts to present availability or fixedness of functions purely as a characteristic of the objects themselves. One must not forget the part played by the attitudes and habits formed by the subject towards these objects, whether they proceed from previous uses he has made of them in everyday life or from suggestions arising out of the existing or immediately preceding situation (as in the case of situations used to study 'functional fixedness').

Nothing is further from the truth than to consider that solving a problem is a totally new process though there is a tendency to do this because a problem is, by definition, a new situation and solving it implies invention. Observation and the study of the groping attempts made by the subject show on the contrary that he has recourse to procedures which he has already had occasion to use in previous situations. This is seen, for example, in the child who is placed before an unfamiliar apparatus (e.g. a problem box). He tries to open it by means of various procedures which are effective in the case of familiar apparatus (lifting the lid, sliding a partition, turning it over, etc.).

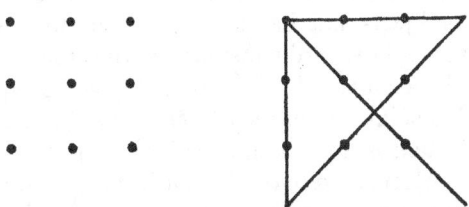

Fig. 18 MAIER'S NINE DOT PROBLEM AND ITS SOLUTION
The subject must link all the dots using only four straight lines and without raising the pencil from the paper. The problem can be solved only if the lines extend beyond the pattern of dots and do not merely assume a horizontal and vertical direction, as the position of the dots would suggest.

These factors should be taken into account when assessing the significance of the experiments carried out by Gestalt psychologists. Thus, with Maier's nine dot problem (Fig. 18), it is tempting to point to the structure of the figure, which encourages the subject to draw horizontal and vertical lines rather than oblique lines. It tends also to confine him within the limits of the square marked out by the dots, instead of going beyond them. (He must in fact break through both of these artificial limitations to solve the problem.) We have suggested (Oléron, in *Les Attitudes*, 1961, 64) that it was necessary also to take into account habits whereby, for example, a child who is learning to write, draw, draw a map, or cut out, normally expects dotted lines to indicate the directions to be traced in bold and followed exactly. Is it not a habit of this kind which determines the subject's first reaction when confronted with the nine dots?

*b) Implicit restrictions.* Some of the difficulties or failures of subjects are due to the fact that they interpret the terms of the problem in a way that involves narrower restrictions than are there. This is clearly seen when, after the solution has been given, the subject protests and claims that it violates one of the terms. The problem has to be re-read to him to convince him of his mistake (we observed this with the nine dot problem when some of our subjects claimed that the instructions forbade the lines drawn to extend beyond the limits of the figure).

*Pierre Oléron*

As an example of classical problems involving such restrictions, one can quote the problem of the four equilateral triangles to be constructed with six matches. The solution involves the construction of a tetrahedron, i.e. the use of three dimensions in space. The subjects fail because they tend to construct their triangles using only two dimensions, leaving the matches flat on the table. The problem by Bulbrook (1932) is equally typical (Fig. 19). The solution consists in *breaking* the extra bead with a hammer[1] which is among the available objects. Failures arise because the subjects tend to think that the task must be performed without destroying part of the material.

We believe that these implicit restrictions are the expression of habits: matches are normally placed on a surface where they are seen and manipulated and on which the figures they can form are constructed. Problems involving the geometrical organization of elements are not, as a rule, resolved with a hammer, particularly as the attitude of a subject to the material put before him by the experimenter is normally respectful and tends to exclude methods which would damage it!

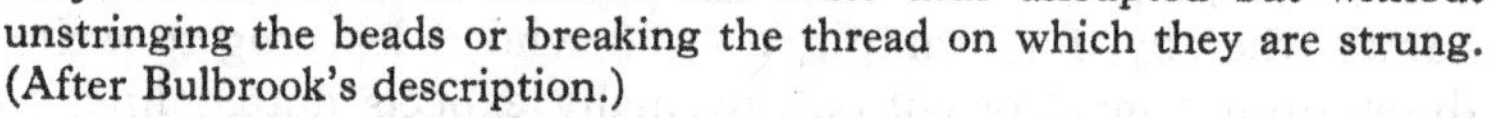

Fig. 19 BULBROOK'S PROBLEM (1932)

The material consists of a necklace in which coloured beads alternate regularly, such as two white, one yellow, two white, etc. In one place, however, the sequence is broken as there are three superfluous beads. The subject's task is to re-establish the order thus disrupted but without unstringing the beads or breaking the thread on which they are strung. (After Bulbrook's description.)

*c) Trick problems*. Psychologists have devised a number of trick problems which consist in presenting as a true problem one that contains a 'catch', in that either the solution is given in the terms or that there is no genuine problem corresponding to the question asked.

Here is an example taken from Sweeney (1953):

> A rope ladder ten feet long is hanging over the side of a ship. The rungs are a foot apart and the bottom rung is resting on the surface of the water. The tide rises at the rate of six inches an hour. When will the first three rungs be covered with water?

[1] Translator's Note: Bulbrook mentions *pliers*, not a hammer. Also, three beads have to be broken, not one.

## Intellectual Activities

The interest of these problems is that they show, once again, the importance of attitudes. These 'catches' succeed because the form of presentation and the terms imitate those of real problems and lead the subject to approach them as such, that is as serious matters calling for reflection and calculation. They therefore mobilize the problem-solving procedures to which they are accustomed, such as calculation when the terms are of an arithmetical type.

*d) Adoption of an attitude (or set).*[1] Sweeney used problems, an example of which has just been given, to study intellectual plasticity, success implying that the subject frees himself from his original attitude, which consists in treating the problems as real, and discovers the 'trap' aspect. There is, however, a drawback in presenting only this type of problem in that the attitudes adopted by the subject are not controlled and may therefore present pronounced variations which escape detection.

This risk is avoided when, for instance, these problems are introduced after genuine problems, which would determine in a more precise fashion the attitude investigated by the psychologist.

Several authors have used this kind of procedure, particularly Luchins whose problems have met with great success and have been applied in many experiments, both by Luchins himself and by others.[2]

It is possible to vary the number of problems in order to bring out the effect of certain factors. This was done by Luchins himself and by Tresselt and Leeds (1953) but in the original experiments by Luchins (1942) they fall into three groups (which naturally are not distinguishable by the subject):

1. Problems designed to establish a set. These can be solved by only one method which is either demonstrated or discovered by the subjects themselves (problems 2–6);

---

[1] In view of the many meanings of the term 'attitude' we feel that it would be advisable in the case of very specific situations, as here, where attitude amounts to a given method, to use in preference the English word 'set' (not that it is more precise in English than the word 'attitude' in French, but in transposing it into French, one can give it a more limited meaning). Luchins, in the research mentioned below, used the German word *Einstellung*, meaning the same thing, and likewise transposed it into English.

[2] Other, less successful, tests have been used for the same purpose: anagrams (Maltzman and Morrisett, 1952, 1953), mazes (Luchins and Luchins, 1954), alphabet mazes (Cowen, Wiener and Hess, 1953).

*Pierre Oléron*

2. Critical problems designed to test the application of the set. They can be solved by the preceding method and also by another method which, to make the demonstration clear, is simpler and quicker (problems 7, 8, 10, 11);

3. Extinction problems. These cannot be solved by the original method, but only by a different method which the subject must discover after abandoning the first method (problem 9).

| Problems | Available jars | | | Quantity to be obtained |
|---|---|---|---|---|
| 1 (Demonstration) | 29 | 3 | — | 20 |
| 2 E1 | 21 | 127 | 3 | 100 |
| 3 E2 | 14 | 163 | 25 | 99 |
| 4 E3 | 18 | 43 | 10 | 5 |
| 5 E4 | 9 | 42 | 6 | 21 |
| 6 E5 | 20 | 59 | 4 | 31 |
| 7 C1 | 23 | 49 | 3 | 20 |
| 8 C2 | 15 | 39 | 3 | 18 |
| 9 | 28 | 76 | 3 | 25 |
| 10 C3 | 18 | 48 | 4 | 22 |
| 11 C4 | 14 | 36 | 8 | 6 |

In each problem, the object is to succeed in obtaining a specified quantity of liquid (column 3) by using the available jars (column 2). None of these allow the subject to measure the quantity directly but the liquid can be poured from one to another so as to obtain the required result. The method which problems 2–6 aims at inducing is of the type $B-A-2C$, i.e. filling the second jar, and drawing off the amount contained by the first then twice the amount contained by the third. It can be seen that more direct methods are available for the other problems. Luchins (and his successors) do not appear to have noticed that problem 5 was ill chosen as it can be solved by other methods than $B-A-2C$, such as $A+2C$ or $(A-C)\times 7$. In a number of subsequent applications, the test was abridged, particularly by eliminating problems 10 and 11.

The results obtained with these problems were spectacular: they revealed that a large number of subjects continued to conform to the set adopted at the beginning of the experiment. Luchins spoke of blindness and mechanization of thought and

*Intellectual Activities*

these terms are very appropriate in describing the subjects' behaviour.

Here are the percentages of subjects (college students) who responded in conformity with the set in the critical problems (Luchins, 1942):

| Group | N | Type of Problem | |
|---|---|---|---|
| | | C1  C2 | C3  C4 |
| Sen. 1 | 13 | 77 | 73 |
| Sen. 2 | 14 | 82 | 64 |
| Sen. 3 | 15 | 70 | 27 |
| Jr. 1 | 12 | 100 | 84 |
| Jr. 2 | 10 | 85 | 75 |
| Fr. 1 | 15 | 77 | 63 |

*e) The subject's activity. α) Action and its consequences.* The subject succeeds in solving the problem set before him only in so far as he acts, works upon the elements given him and transforms them. Authors who have studied problem solving from the descriptive angle have devoted considerable space to the subject's activities of research and exploration and to his elaboration of hypotheses, whether stated verbally or expressed through what he does. From these studies, few precise details emerge concerning the role played by these activities, since only a more precise analysis could reveal which are useful and which are not. This kind of analysis has yet to be undertaken. Meanwhile, the fact that we are reduced, on various points, to making conjectures and noting probabilities should not be taken to mean that we fail to appreciate the importance of the points concerned.

1 *Transformations of the situation.* One of the first effects of this activity, even without precise orientation, is to bring about transformations of the situation which may lead to the solution and sometimes actually constitute it. An elementary example of this is when simple exploration leads to the discovery of the appropriate instrument or to perceiving the situation from an angle which reveals the solution by establishing, for instance, a relation between two elements in an experimental set-up where the goal is the instrument (cf. Köhler, 1917).

*Pierre Oléron*

The fact that activity plays not only a favourable but an essential role becomes fully apparent when subjects are called upon to construct or make something. Even when human subjects are given abstract problems, there should be scope for the construction of diagrams or figures or for literal 'constructions' which serve to translate in an intuitive manner problems expressed in a form that does not allow direct representation. Moreover, these constructions may enable the subject to surmount difficulties found in every problem that is at all complicated, namely difficulties in apprehending a group of elements which exceeds the normal field of apprehension. By means of concrete representation, condensation is possible and this allows what is essential to emerge.

2 *Transformations of the subject*. Activity does not only transform the situation, it also brings about changes in the subject. This is sometimes overlooked. The transformation of objects is not enough to lead to the solution. It may be quite ineffectual although in itself it contains or implies the solution. The subject may indeed not see it and it has frequently been observed that one allows to escape, temporarily if not altogether, a solution which is before one's very eyes (the story of inventions points to a number of cases of this kind).

Change is due to the fact that the failure of a given procedure leads, sooner or later, to its being inhibited, either by spontaneous exhaustion, or by a deliberate decision and this leaves room for the emergence of another response schema which may prove more effective. This is not identical with what happens in learning where the form of response remains essentially the same but is perfected. Here, there is the substitution of one type of response for another but in numerous cases the difference may be slight, if one admits that learning is not the creation of a response *ex nihilo* but the construction or adaptation of responses already formed.

β) *Groping*. The first psychologists who approached in a positive spirit the question of problem solving by animals felt that groping played a large part (Thorndike). It is easy to argue that groping is the very opposite of an intellectual process and that one cannot therefore, when seeking to explain what is essential in problem solving, admit that it plays even a subsidiary role. One should not, however, forget that groping, except in

## Intellectual Activities

the case of animals, or of a human subject who arrives at the solution by pure chance (and even then one must be capable of taking advantage of chance) is not, as a rule, an activity devoid of any psychological significance. Rey (1935, p. 215 *et seq.*) put forward an interpretation in genetic terms, to the effect that groping reproduces all or part of the scale of behaviour that can be established by chronological analysis. We feel that, more generally speaking, it expresses response schemata which have previously been used and which are more or less habitual in character. This interpretation is suggested by observing a subject faced with a practical problem where groping can be directly observed. It is the same, although observation is in this case less easy, with an abstract type of problem, such as a mathematical one. Inferences drawn from observation of animals are misleading here since the problems put before them often go beyond their repertoire of responses and it is difficult to imagine that their reactions are dictated by anything more than chance.

γ) *Analysis.* Analysis is frequently invoked as an activity which enters into problem solving. Problematic situations are often characterized, it is true, by their complexity and analysis is a procedure which enables the subject to get his bearings by picking out the essential elements.

In actual fact analysis does not correspond to a single and specific type of psychological activity and there are various procedures which go under that name. Thus breaking down a whole into its parts, a normal procedure when trying to understand a piece of mechanical apparatus, is different from a regressive search for the logical conditions on which the truth of a proposition depends.

Relatively few experimental studies have been devoted to analysis. Let us mention Marks (1951) whose problem took the form of discovering the source of an error in the computation of a square root performed with a calculating machine and a table according to a method explained at the beginning. Any of these three elements (and the subject himself) may be the cause of the error (in actual fact, it is the table which is falsified).

Duncker (1935) had pointed out the role of analysis in less contrived situations. He distinguished two aspects: *analysis of the situation* and *analysis of the goal*. The first aims at determining what elements are present and which of them create the difficulty, and then seeking what must be done to overcome the difficulty. The second aims at defining what is required to solve the problem. Duncker saw it as a decisive step in attaining the solution and he spoke of a 'functional solution', when the subject has clearly defined the conditions implied in the solution although he has not yet reached the stage where the solution is determined by the specific object which defines it completely. Reid (1951) showed the part played by the latter type of analysis, using in particular the problem of the four triangles to be constructed with six matches (cf. page 60). The experimenter offers some of the subjects a series of suggestions constituting a more and more precise analysis of the conditions which the solution must fulfil (e.g. 'twelve sides of triangles must be formed with six matches', then 'each match must form the side of two triangles'). Success is greater than in the control group, which is not offered similar suggestions.

(c) UTILIZATION OF INFORMATION

We are speaking here of information in its usual sense, that is, information about the point of a problem which is communicated by significant data. A number of authors have tried to use a more precise concept inspired by information theory. As it is mainly the information arising from the stimuli which is apt to be analysed and manipulated, the tasks to which these authors have turned are naturally of the inductive type (such as discovery of a law, or of a principle involved in the experimental set-up). That is why we mentioned them above and do not feel that there is any reason to refer to them again at this point.

It will readily be agreed that the more information a subject has about a problem, particularly about the ways of arriving at the solution, the more easily will he in fact reach it. The source of this information may lie in the problem itself (which yields more or less readily the information implied in the data) or in the subject (depending on his knowledge or training). In order to make the analysis clearer, however, we shall concentrate on information provided by external indications which are additional to the data. In an experimental study, the experimenter might try to regulate the amount of this information as precisely as possible. It should not be forgotten that, in an educational setting, the subject can be

## Intellectual Activities

guided in solving a problem by being given supplementary information. Hence the question: 'How can he be helped in the most effective way?' of which the practical significance is obvious.

*a) Teaching of principles.* The usefulness of information is clearly closely linked to the nature of problems, but one can at least distinguish between different types of information among which that bearing on principles seems to have special significance. Various studies devoted to transfer have shown that knowledge of a principle plays an important part and makes it easier to pass from one task to another of a similar type (cf. Chapter X). This knowledge may come to the subject through sudden awareness while he is performing the task, but it may also come from outside. Such is the case in the experiments by Judd (1908) and Hendrickson and Schroeder (1941) (quoted by McGeoch, 1952) in which the subjects must hit a submerged target. After a preliminary training session for a given depth of water, the subjects must adapt themselves to a new depth. Those who are taught the principle of refraction transfer easily from one situation to the other, but those who are not taught it find transfer difficult.

Katona (1940) used problems which require the subject to make new figures, from those given, by moving certain elements (Fig. 20). One group of subjects was merely shown the solution of

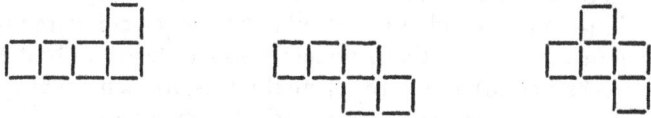

Fig. 20 PROBLEMS USED BY KATONA (1940)
The above figures are supposedly formed by matches. The task consists in finding how by moving only three of them one can obtain four squares instead of five. (Katona, *Organizing and Memorizing*, New York, Columbia University Press, 1940, 78.)

the training problem while the others were also given an explanation of the principle underlying the solution (in this instance, finding the sides common to two squares and moving them so that they become the sides of only one square. In this way, the same number of elements can be used to make a smaller number of squares). The second group was more successful than the first when given new problems to tackle.

Corman (1957) took up the same question using the same problems, but he considered other variables at the same time including, in particular, what he called 'method' which consists of indicating the elements to be moved. He also tried to graduate the amount of information by using two types more or less explicitly presented. In view of the somewhat complicated nature of the experiment (it brings in various transfer problems and takes into account the mental ability of the subjects), it is difficult to draw absolutely clear conclusions, although information regarding principles was found to facilitate success.

The interaction of certain factors is nevertheless revealing. It is worthy of note that it is the most brilliant subjects who profit most from the most explicit information and that in some cases subjects can succeed without having been given any indications regarding the principle involved. We believe that this is due to the fact, which must not be overlooked, that the effectiveness of information depends on the subjects concerned and it may be useless to give information to someone incapable of profiting by it (cf. Crannell, 1956). Moreover, it is a matter of everyday observation that a suggestion can only be turned to account when the subject has assimilated the data of the problem sufficiently to enable him to integrate the new information. If it is supplied too soon, it is liable to appear merely as additional data and to complicate the situation rather than clarify it.

Marks (cf. page 65) obtained results that can be compared with those above. He found that subjects who had heard (admittedly three weeks before) a lecture on method in problem solving, in which the role of analysis was mentioned, succeeded no better than those who had not been present at the lecture. Furthermore, those who had been given a typed list in which the various possible causes were explicitly mentioned likewise fared no better!

*b) Verbal teaching and active method.* The sterility of verbal teachings and their lack of effectiveness in solving problems have often been denounced by educationalists, not on abstract grounds but from concrete observation of pupils. Hence the praise bestowed on active methods, by which the child is not merely given an outward knowledge but is made to put into practice notions which then become modes of action and patterns of response.

Szekely carried out experiments which fully justify this stand-

## Intellectual Activities

point. In one of these (1950 *a*), he showed that verbal knowledge of the principle of Archimedes is not sufficient to solve a simple problem in physics in which the metal, although in itself a heavy object, must be perceived as suffering in the same way as a light object the upthrust of the water which it displaces.

In his other experiment (1950 *b*) the subject must put into practice notions relating to momentum of rotation and inertia. The subjects receive instruction on this topic, some by the traditional method, namely a lecture followed by a demonstration with the aid of a torsion pendulum, the others by the modern method, in which the pendulum is presented to them and an attempt is made to indicate the effect of the position of the weights upon speed of rotation. (The torsion pendulum consists of a thread from which a bar bearing weights is suspended, so that the greater the separation of the weights, the slower the speed of rotation of the bar when displaced from its equilibrium position.) A few days later, a problem is set which involves the application of these notions. It concerns two metallic spheres of the same diameter and of the same total weight. One is made of light metal but is solid, while the other is of heavy metal but hollow. The subjects must state which is solid and which is hollow (the solution consists in making the two balls roll down an inclined plane: the hollow sphere having a greater momentum of inertia, will roll more slowly). Subjects in the modern group are significantly more successful than those in the traditional group (13 out of 20 as against 4 out of 20).

(An interesting methodological study of the kind of information used or sought after will be found in Rimoldi, 1955.)

### (D) METHOD

It seems obvious that working methodically leads to success more surely than working in a disorderly fashion (indeed it is a sign of development and of intellectual superiority). However, if one goes beyond the general meaning of the term (following an ordered course of action and continuing in one direction before proceeding in another, etc.), one must recognize that the nature of the method (like information) is largely conditioned by the particular problem that is put forward. A method that is effective with one type of problem is not necessarily so with others. This somewhat

*Pierre Oléron*

lessens the importance of method since, in extreme cases, it comes close to a response schema which is more or less specific to one task. Moreover, success, when there really is a problem, does not depend simply on putting a schema of this kind into automatic operation (otherwise the situation could hardly be called problematic) but on finding an effective schema or combination.

One aspect of the method which was brought out by Descartes in his famous *Discours de la Méthode* is to 'divide (split) difficulties'. The ways of doing this may be more or less rational, irrespective of the object to which the method is applied. Information theory has drawn attention to a form of division which consists in a succession of alternatives by which the range of possibilities is broken down each time into two mutually exclusive parts (the number of choices corresponding to the quantity of information received). The application of this procedure has the advantage of economy since for the first few choices at least, a wide range of possibilities can be eliminated in one operation. It is obvious that this aspect is valuable from the practical angle, since the time taken by a researcher or a technician to find the solution corresponds to money spent.

The method of dichotomic division or half-split[1] method is, however, applicable only to rather special types of problems where *all* the elements are simultaneously given and can be physically divided, and where there are implications and subordinations allowing inference from one element to another. The case *par excellence* seems to be the tracing of faults in mechanical or electrical systems (or of mishaps in the functioning of social or economic systems).

The method would apply, for example, to a system such as that shown in Fig. 21.

It is only if all the elements from A to H are in good working order that the apparatus can function. If each one is tested in turn, eight separate checks must be made. If the first test is carried out at point I, it serves to check the sub-assembly A–D. The next test (if the first suggests that the fault comes from that quarter) will be carried out at II and another (assuming the opposite case) at III. Thus, the fault can be located by means of only three operations. An approximately similar situation exists

---

[1] Translator's Note: Incorrectly referred to in the French text as the *split-half method*.

## Intellectual Activities

in the case of a typical car breakdown, when the engine fails to start. The range of possibilities can be divided into two. Either the fuel supply is responsible, or else the ignition. If the motorist observes that the plugs are sparking, he can eliminate the first set of possibilities. The fuel supply can be tested by splitting it into four points: tank, pump, filter, jet, and checking the half-way point. If the petrol comes out of the pump, the pump and the tank are eliminated and the failure must be due to the jet or the filter. This can be ascertained by a single test. If, on the other hand, the first test causes the ignition to be suspected, the same procedure can be applied. Check first the supply of current to the primary of the coil and then (for example) the coil itself or the sparking plug.

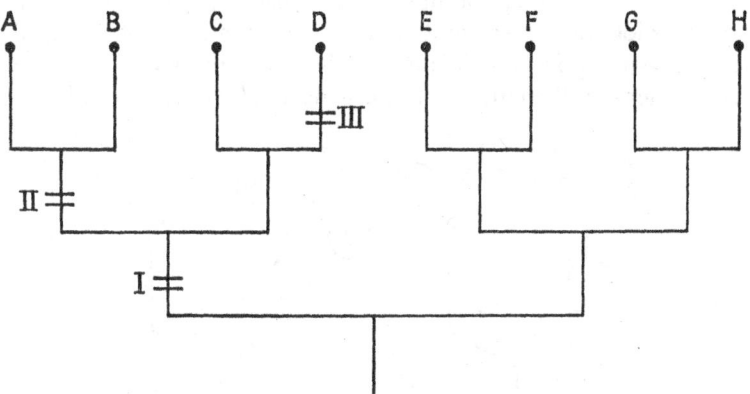

Fig. 21  HALF-SPLIT METHOD APPLIED TO A PROBLEM INVOLVING 8 ELEMENTS
See explanations in the text

These steps correspond to those indicated in the theoretical schema above, which can be taken to represent the elements of an engine.

Strict application of the half-split method is not always possible, however, even with systems of this type. There are various reasons for this.

First, not every assembly is necessarily divisible into two equal sub-assemblies. The choice of division, with one sub-assembly greater than the other and therefore requiring a greater number of tests, is then no longer a matter of indifferent option. Secondly, interdependence between the parts can assume complex forms, with ramifications that are irregular from the point of view of the logical schema. Likewise the fault may be due to temporal factors which are superimposed upon the spatial arrangement and do not form part of the schema (as when the engine fails to start because it has been 'choked' in the course of previous attempts at starting).

The half-split method implies that all elements are equivalent in all respects. However, one has only to consider the frequency with which faults may occur in each of the various elements to see that in fact this is rarely the case. Some develop faults more frequently than others and call for more frequent repairs (cf. Stolurow *et alia*, 1955). Is it possible to say that the repairer who begins by turning his attention to these elements is reasoning badly? This is not the opinion of Cronbach (in Quastler, 1955, 20). It is logical to test point A (Fig. 22) when the probability of the corresponding branch is .50; with a probability of .50 for the last element on the left, it is not unreasonable to test point B.

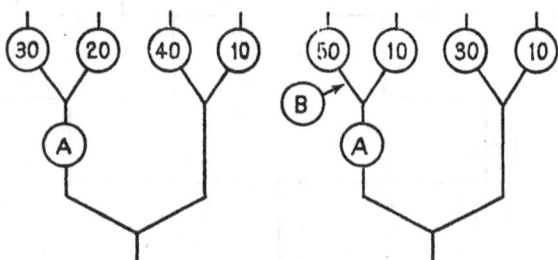

Fig. 22 APPLICATION OF THE HALF-SPLIT METHOD AS A FUNCTION OF THE PROBABILITY OF FAULTS

See explanations in the text. (Cronbach in Quastler, *Information Theory in Psychology*, Glencoe, Free Press, 1955, 20.)

Elements are not as a rule equivalent in yet another way. Testing costs are different. In a piece of apparatus, certain elements may take a long time to dismantle and there may be sequences of events which are very different from the logical sequence laid down by the method. It is not rational to neglect this and in fact it is profitable to turn first to the most easily accessible elements, disregarding the absolutely logical sequence.

So far, the method has been considered solely from the point of view of the object to which it is applied. One must also consider the subjects who are called upon to apply it. In other words, one must consider the steps involved and the corresponding abilities or more accurately the interaction between the subject and the object. Thus, Goldbeck *et alia* (1957) showed that the method led to a more rapid solution when dealing with simple systems but that this was not so when dealing with complex systems. Their experiment also brought out that the important thing is not so much the half-split method itself as the ability to reason and to infer at what points a split should be made. These two findings are in fact linked: easy problems are more easily solved because inference is easier and the relations between the parts are more easily grasped. But, and this too emerges from their research, additional practice can also play a part, enabling the subjects to apply the method more effectively. This seems quite normal to us. There is no 'natural method'. One learns methods as one learns specific procedures. Teaching may play a greater part in that methods can be, and should be, more systematic.

# Bibliography

ADAMSON R. E., 'Functional Fixedness as related to Problem Solving: a Repetition of Three Experiments', *J. exp. Psychol.*, 1952, **44**, 288–91

ANDREW, G. HARLOW, H. F., 'Performance of Macaque Monkeys on a Test of the Concept of Generalized Triangularity', *Comp. Psychol. Monogr.*, 1948, **19**, 1–19

ARCHER, E. J., BOURNE, J. E. Jr., BROWN, F. G., 'Concept Identification as a Function of Irrelevant Information and Instructions', *J. exp. Psychol.*, 1955, **49**, 153–64

ASCOLI, G., 'Comment l'enfant sait classer les objets', *Enfance*, 1950, **3**, 411–33

BARTLETT, F., *Thinking: an Experimental and Social Study*, London, Allen and Unwin, 1958

BERG, E. A., 'A Simple Objective Technique for Measuring Flexibility in Thinking', *J. genet. Psychol.*, 1958, **39**, 15–22

BILLINGS, M., 'Problem-solving in Different Fields of Endeavor', *Amer. J. Psychol.*, 1934, **46**, 259–72

BINET, A., *L'étude expérimentale de l'intelligence*, Paris, Schleicher, 1903

BIRCH, H. G., RABINOWITZ, H. S., 'The Negative Effect of Previous Experience on Productive Thinking', *J. exp. Psychol.*, 1951, **41**, 121–5

BOURNE, L. E. Jr., HAYGOOD, R. C., 'The Role of Stimulus Redundancy in Concept Identification', *J. exp. Psychol.*, 1959, **58**, 232–8

BOURNE, L. E. Jr., RESTLE, F., 'Mathematical Theory of Concept Formation', *Psychol. Rev.*, 1959, **66**, 278–96

BRUNER, J. S., GOODNOW, J. J., AUSTIN, G. A., *A Study of Thinking*, New York, Wiley, 1956

BULBROOK, M. E., 'An Experimental Inquiry into the Existence and Nature of Insight', *Amer. J. Psychol.*, 1932, **44**, 409–53

BURLOUD, A., *La pensée d'après les recherches de H. J. Watt, de Messer et de Bühler*, Paris, Alcan, 1927

BURT, C., 'The Development of Reasoning in School Children', *J. exp. Pedag.*, 1909, **5**, 1–17

BUSS, A. H., 'Reversal and Nonreversal Shifts in Concept Formation with Partial Reinforcement Eliminated', *J. exp. Psychol.*, 1955, **52**, 162–6

BUSS, S. H., 'A Study of Concept Formation as a Function of Reinforcement and Stimulus Generalization', *J. exp. Psychol.*, 1960, **40**, 499–503

CAHILL, H. E., HOVLAND, C. I., 'The Role of Memory in the Acquisition of Concepts', *J. exp. Psychol.*, 1960, **59**, 137–44

CHAPMAN, L. J., CHAPMAN, J. P., 'Atmosphere Effect Re-examined', *J. exp. Psychol.*, 1959, **58**, 220–6

# Bibliography

CHRISOF, C., 'The Formulation and Elaboration of Thought-Problems', *Amer. J. Psychol.*, 1939, **52**, 161–85

CLAPARÈDE E., 'La genèse de l'hypothèse', *Arch. Psychol.*, 1933, **24**, 1–154

COOK, T. W., 'The Relation Between Amount of Material and Difficulty of Problem-solving: II. The Disc Transfer Problem', *J. exp. Psychol.*, 1937, **20**, 288–96

CORMAN, B. R., 'The Effect of Varying Amounts and Kinds of Information as Guidance in Problem solving', *Psychol. Monogr.*, 1957, **71**

COWEN, E. L., 'The Influence of Psychological Stress on Problem Solving Rigidity', *J. abnorm. soc. Psychol.*, 1952, **47**, 512–19

CRANNELL, C. W., 'Transfer in Problem Solution as Related to the Type of Training', *J. gen. Psychol.*, 1956, **54**, 3–14

DATTMAN, P. E., ISRAEL, H. E., 'The Order of Dominance among Conceptual Capacities: an Experimental Test of Heidbreder's Hypothesis', *J. Psychol.*, 1951, **31**, 147–60

DELACROIX, H., 'Les opérations intellectuelles', in *Nouveau Traité de Psychologie* by Dumas, vol. V, part 2, Paris, Alcan, 1936

DETAMBEL, M. H., STOLUROW, L. M., 'Stimulus Sequence and Concept Learning', *J. exp. Psychol.*, 1956, **51**, 34–40

DUNCAN, C. P., 'Recent Research on Human Problem Solving', *Psychol. Bull.*, 1959, **56**, 397–429

DUNCKER, K., *Zur Psychologie des produktiven Denkens*, Berlin, Springer, 1935

EIDENS, H., 'Experimentelle Untersuchungen über den Denkverlauf bei unmittelbaren Folgerungen', *Arch. ges. Psychol.*, 1929, **71**, 1–66

ELLIS, W. D., *A Source Book of Gestalt Psychology*, London, Routledge and Kegan Paul, 1938

FIELDS, P. E., 'Study in Concept Formation: I. The Development of the Concept of Triangularity by the White Rat', *Comp. Psychol. Monogr.*, 1932, **9**, 1–70

FRAISSE, P., *Manuel pratique de psychologie expérimentale*, Paris, P.U.F., 1956

GELERNTER, H., 'Realization of a Geometry Theorem Proving Machine', in *Conférence sur le traitement de l'information*, U.N.E.S.C.O., Paris, 1960, 273–82

GELERTNER, H., ROCHESTER, N., 'Intelligent Behavior in Problem-Solving Machines', *I.B.M. J. Res. Developmt.*, 1958, **2**, 336–45

GELLERMANN, L. W., 'The Double Alternation Problem: II. The Behavior of Children and Human Adults in a Double Alternation Temporal Maze', *J. genet. Psychol.*, 1931 *a*, **39**, 197–226

'The Double Alternation Problem: III. The Behavior of Monkeys in a Double Alternation Box-apparatus', *J. genet. Psychol.*, 1931 *b*, **39**, 359–92

## Bibliography

GELLERMANN, L. W., 'Form Discrimination in Chimpanzees and Two-year-old Children', *J. genet. Psychol.*, 1933, **42**, 1–50

GENGERELLI, J. A., 'Mutual Interference in the Evolution of Concepts', *Amer. J. Psychol.*, 1926, **38**, 634–46

GLASER, R., SCHWARTZ, S. A., 'Scoring Problem-solving Test Items by Measuring Information', *Educ. psychol. Measurmt.*, 1954, **14**, 665–70

GOLDBECK, R. A., BERNSTEIN, B. B., HILLIX, W. A., MARX, M. H., 'Application of the Half-split Technique to Problem-solving Tasks', *J. exp. Psychol.*, 1957, **53**, 330–8

GOLDSTEIN, K., SCHEERER, M., 'Abstract and Concrete Behavior', *Psychol. Monogr.*, 1941, **53**, no. 239, 1–151

GOTTSCHALDT, K., 'Der Aufbau des kindlichen Handelns', *Beih. Z. ang. Psychol.*, 1933, **68**

GRANT, D. A., 'Perceptual versus Analytical Responses to the Number Concept of a Weigl-type Card Sorting Test', *J. exp. Psychol.*, 1951, **41**, 23–29

GRANT, D. A., JONES, O. R., TAILLANTIS, B., 'The Relative Difficulty of the Number, Form and Color of a Weigl Type Problem', *J. exp. Psychol.*, 1949, **39**, 554–7

GREEN, E. J., 'Concept Formation: a Problem in Human Operant Conditioning', *J. exp. Psychol.*, 1955, **49**, 175–80

GUILLAUME, P., 'L'appréhension des figures géométriques', *J. Psychol. norm. pathol.*, 1937, **34**, 675–710

— *La psychologie de la forme*, Paris, Flammarion, 1937.

GULLIKSEN, H. O., 'Studies of Transfer of Responses: I. Relative versus Absolute Factors in the Discrimination of Size by the White Rat', *J. genet. Psychol.*, 1932, **40**, 37–51

GYR, J. W., 'An Investigation into, and Speculations about, the Formal Nature of a Problem-solving Process', *Behav. Sci.*, 1960, **5**, 39–59.

HAMILTON, G. V., 'A Study of Trials and Errors in Animals', *J. animal Behavior*, 1911, **1**, 33–66

HANFMANN, E., KASANIN, J., 'A Method for the Study of Concept Formation', *J. Psychol.*, 1937, **3**, 521–40

HARLOW, H. F., 'The Formation of Learning Sets', *Psychol. Rev.*, 1949, **56**, 51–65

— 'Performance of Catarrhine Monkeys on a Series of Discrimination Reversal Problems', *J. comp. physiol. Psychol.*, 1950, **43**, 231–9

HARMS, E. (Ed.), 'Fundamentals of Psychology: The Psychology of Thinking', *Annals N.Y. Acad. Sciences*, 1960, **91**, 1–158

HEIDBREDER, E., 'An Experimental Study of Thinking', *Arch. Psychol.*, 1924, **73**, 1–175

— 'The Attainment of Concepts: I. Methodology and Terminology', *J. gen. Psychol.*, 1946 a, **35**, 173–89

— 'The Attainment of Concepts: II. The Problem', *J. gen. Psychol.*, 1946 b, **35**, 191–223
— 'The Attainment of Concepts: III. The Process', *J. Psychol.*, 1947, **24**, 93–139
— 'The Attainment of Concepts: VI. Exploratory Experiments on Conceptualization at Perceptual Levels', *J. Psychol.*, 1948, **26**, 193–216
HEIDBREDER, E., BENSLEY, M. L., IVY, M., 'The Attainment of Concepts: IV: Regularities and Levels', *J. Psychol.*, 1948, **25**, 299–329
HODGES, A., 'Double Alternation: A Measure of Intelligence', *J. consult. Psychol.*, 1956, **20**, 59–62
HOVLAND, C. J., 'A "Communication Analysis" of Concept Learning', *Psychol. Rev.*, 1952, **59**, 461–72
HOVLAND, C. J., WEISS, W., 'Transmission of Information Concerning Concepts through Positive and Negative Instances', *J. exp. Psychol.*, 1953, **45**, 175–82
HOWARD, H. K., GLUCKSBERG, S., KESTON, R., 'Perception and Mediation in Concept Learning', *J. exp. Psychol.*, 1961, **61**, 186–91
HULL, C. L., 'Quantitative Aspects of the Evolution of Concepts', *Psychol. Monogr.*, 1920, **28**, no. 123, 1–85
HUMPHREY, G., *Thinking*, London, Methuen, 1951
HUNTER, I. M. L., 'An Experimental Investigation of the Absolute and the Relative Theories of Transposition Behavior in Children', *Brit. J. Psychol.*, 1952, **43**, 118–28
— 'The Influence of Mental Set on Problem-solving', *Brit. J. Psychol.*, 1956, **47**, 63–64
— 'The Solving of Three-term Series Problems', *Brit. J. Psychol.*, 1957, **48**, 286–98
HUNTER, W. S., 'The Temporal Maze and Kinaesthetic Sensory Processes in the Rat', *Psychobiol.*, 1920, **2**, 1–18
HUNTER, W. S., BARTLETT, S. C., 'Double Alternation Behavior in Young Children', *J. exp. Psychol.*, 1948, **38**, 358–67
INHELDER, B., PIAGET, J., *The Growth of Logical Thinking from Childhood to Adolescence*, London, Routledge and Kegan Paul, 1958.
JACKSON, J., 'Transposition of Learning by Children', *J. exp. Psychol.*, 1940, **26**, 432–9
JACKSON, A. T., ECKHARDT, M. E., 'Studies on the Transposition of Learning by Children', *J. exp. Psychol.*, 1940, **27**, 302–17
JACKSON, A. T., JEROME, E., 'Studies in Transposition Behavior by Children: VI: Simultaneous vs. Successive Presentation of the Stimuli to Bright and Dull Children', *J. exp. Psychol.*, 1943, **33**, 431–9
JACKSON, T. A., STONEX, E., LANE, E., DOMINGUEZ, K., 'Studies in the Transposition of Learning by Children: I. Relative vs. Absolute

Response as a Function of the Amount of Training', *J. exp. Psychol.*, 1938, **23**, 578–600

JAMES, W., *The Principles of Psychology*, vol. 1, London, Macmillan, 1890

JOHN, E. R., 'Contributions to the Study of the Problem-solving Process', *Psychol. Monogr.*, 1957, **71**, no. 447

JOHN, E. R., MILLER, J. G., 'The Acquisition and Application of Information in the Problem-solving Process: An Electronically Operated Logical Test', *Behav. Sci.*, 1957, **2**, 291–300

JOHNSON, D. M., 'A Modern Account of Problem Solving', *Psychol. Bull.*, 1944, **41**, 201–29

— *The Psychology of Thought and Judgment*, New York, Harper, 1955
— *Psychology. A Problem Solving Approach*, New York, Harper, 1961 a
— 'Serial Analysis of Thinking', in Harms, *Fundamentals of Psychology, The Psychology of Thinking*, 1961 b

JOHNSON, D. M., LINCOLN, R. E., HALL, E. R., 'Amount of Material and Time of Preparation for Solving Problems', *J. Psychol.*, 1961, **51**, 457–71

JUZAK, T., 'The Effects of Praise and Reproof on the Generalization of Learned Concepts', *J. Psychol.*, 1955, **39**, 329–40

KATONA, G., *Organizing and Memorizing*, New York, Columbia Univ. Press, 1940

KATZ, D., 'Blendungsphänomene und Konnektive Hemmung bei Denkprozessen', *Theoria*, 1949, **15**, 141–54

KENDLER, H. H., 'Problems in Problem-solving Research', in *Current Trends in Psychological Theory: a bicentennial program*, Pittsburg, Univ. of Pittsburgh Press, 1961

KENDLER, H. H., D'AMATO, M. F., 'A Comparison of Reversal Shifts and Non-reversal Shifts in Human Concept Formation Behavior', *J. exp. Psychol.*, 1955, **49**, 165–74

KENDLER, H. H., KENDLER, T. S., 'Inferential behavior in Pre-school Children', *J. exp. Psychol.*, 1956, **51**, 311–14

KENDLER, T. S., KENDLER, H. H., 'Reversal and Non-reversal Shifts in Kindergarten Children', *J. exp. Psychol.*, 1959, **58**, 56–60

KENDLER, T. S., KENDLER, H. H., WELLS, D., 'Reversal and Non-reversal Shifts in Nursery School Children', *J. comp. physiol. Psychol.*, 1960, **53**, 83–88

KENDLER, H. H., MAYZNER, M. S., 'Reversal and Non-reversal Shifts in Card-sorting Tests with Two or Four Sorting Categories', *J. exp. Psychol.*, 1956, **51**, 244–8

KLÜVER, H., *Behavior Mechanisms in Monkeys*, Chicago, Univ. Chicago Press, 1933

KOCHEN, M., GALANTER, E. H., 'The Acquisition and Utilization of In-

formation in Problem Solving and Thinking', *Inform. Control.*, 1958, **1**, 267–88
KÖHLER, W., *The Mentality of Apes*, New York, Harcourt Brace, 1925
KÜLPE, O., 'Versuche über Abstraktion', *Ber. I. Kongress für exper. Psychol.*, 1904, 58–68
KURTZ, K. H., HOVLAND, C. J., 'Concept Learning with Differing Sequences of Instances', *J. exp. Psychol.*, 1956, **51**, 239–43
— *Les Attitudes, Symposium de l'Association de Psychologie Scientifique de Langue Française*, Paris, P.U.F., 1961
— *L'invention, Neuvième Semaine Internationale de Synthèse*, Paris, Alcan, 1938
LONG, L., 'Conceptual Relationships in Children: The Concept of Roundness', *J. genet. Psychol.*, 1940, **57**, 289–315
LUCHINS, A. S., 'Mechanization in Problem Solving: The Effect of Einstellung', *Psychol. Monogr.*, 1942, **54**, no. 248
LUCHINS, A. S., LUCHINS, E. H., 'The Einstellung Phenomenon and Effortfulness of Task', *J. gen. Psychol.*, 1954, **50**, 15–27
MAIER, N. R. F., 'Reasoning in White Rats', *Comp. Psychol. Monogr.*, 1929, **6**, 1–93
— 'Reasoning in Humans: I. On Direction', *J. comp. Psychol.*, 1930, **10**, 115–43
— 'Reasoning in Humans: II. The Solution of a Problem and its Appearance in Consciousness', *J. comp. Psychol.*, 1931, **12**, 181–94
— 'An Aspect of Human Reasoning', *Brit. J. Psychol.*, 1933, **24**, 144–55
— 'Reasoning in Children', *J. comp. Psychol.*, 1936, **21**, 357–66
MALTZMAN, I., 'Thinking: from a Behavioristic Point of View', *Psychol. Rev.*, 1955, **62**, 275–86
MALTZMAN, I., MORRISETT, L., 'Different Strengths of Set in the Solution of Anagrams', *J. exp. Psychol.*, 1952, **44**, 242–6
— 'The Effect of Single and Compound Classes of Anagrams on Set Solutions', *J. exp. Psychol.*, 1953, **45**, 345–50
MARKS, M. R., 'Problem Solving as a Function of the Situation', *J. exp. Psychol.*, 1951, **41**, 74–80
MCGEOCH, J. A., *The Psychology of human learning*, 2nd ed., New York, Longmans, Green, 1952
MONTPELLIER, G. de, *Conduites intelligentes et psychisme chez l'animal et chez l'homme*, Paris, J. Vrin, 1949
MOORE, O. K., ANDERSON, S. B., 'Modern Logic and Tasks for Experiments in Problem Solving Behavior', *J. Psychol.*, 1954, **38**, 151–160
MORGAN, J. J. B., MORTON, J. T., 'The Distortion of Syllogistic Reasoning Produced by Personal Conviction', *J. soc. Psychol.*, 1944, **20**, 39–59
MORGAN, W. J., MORGAN, A. B., 'Logical Reasoning with and without Training', *J. appl. Psychol.*, 1953, **37**, 399–401

## Bibliography

MUNN, N. L., *The Evolution and Growth of Human Behavior*, Boston, Houghton Mifflin, 1955

NATADZE, R., 'Das Erfassen wesentlicher Merkmale des Begriffs im Schulalter', *Z. Psychol.*, 1960, **165**, 226–34

— 'Beitrag zur Methode der Begriffsbildungsforschung', *Z. Psychol.*, 1962, **167**, 66–79

NEWELL, A., SHAW, J. C., 'Elements of a Theory of Human Problem Solving', *Psychol. Rev.*, 1958, **65**, 151–66

NEWELL, A., SHAW, J. C., SIMON, H. A., Report on a General Problem-solving Program in *Conférence internationale sur le traitement de l'information*, U.N.E.S.C.O., Paris, 1960

NICOLLE, C., *La biologie de l'invention*, Paris, Alcan, 1932

OLÉRON, P., 'Pensée conceptuelle et langage, Performance comparée de sourds-muets et d'entendants dans des épreuves de classements multiples', *Année psychol.*, 1951, **51**, 89–120

— 'Classement multiple et langage', *J. Psychol. norm. pathol.*, 1953, **46**, 299–315

— OLÉRON, P., *Recherches sur le développement mental des sourds-muets. Contribution à l'étude du problème 'langage et pensée'*, Paris, Édit. du C.N.R.S., 1957

— 'Étude sur l'appréhension des mots', *Psychol. franç.*, 1961 a, **6**, 21–31

— 'Qu'est-ce que le développement intellectuel?', *Rev. Neuro. Psychiatr. infant., Hyg. ment. Enf.* 1961 b, **9**, 325–36

— 'Le développement des réponses à la relation identité-dissemblance. Ses rapports avec le langage', *Psychol. franç.*, 1962, **7**, 4–16

OSEAS, L., UNDERWOOD, B. J., 'Studies of Distributed Practice: V. Learning and Retention of Concepts', *J. exp. Psychol.*, 1952, **43**, 143–8

OSGOOD, C. E., *Method and theory in Experimental Psychology*, New York, Oxford University Press, 1953

PIAGET, J., *The Child's Conception of Physical Causality*, London, Kegan Paul, 1930

— *The Child's Conception of the World*, London, Kegan Paul, 1929

— *The Psychology of Intelligence*, London, Routledge and Kegan Paul, 1950

PIAGET, J., and coll. *Études d'épistémologie génétique*, Paris, P.U.F., 1957

PIÉRON, H., 'Le problème de l'intelligence', *Scientia*, 1927, **42**, 337–48

— *Psychologie zoologique*, in *Nouveau Traité de Psychologie* by Dumas, vol. VIII, part 1, 1941

POINCARÉ, H., 'L'invention mathématique', *Bull. Inst. génér. Psychol.*, 1908, **8**, 171–87

QUASTLER, H., (Ed.), *Information Theory in Psychology, Problems and Methods*, Glencoe, Free Press, 1955

# Bibliography

RAAHEIM, K., 'Problem Solving and the Ability to find Replacement', *Scand. J. Psychol.*, 1960, **1**, 14–18

RAY, W., 'Complex tasks for Use in Human Problem Solving Research', *Psychol. Bull.*, 1955, **52**, 134–49

REED, H. B., 'The Learning and Retention of Concepts: I. The Influence of Set', *J. exp. Psychol.*, 1946, **36**, 71–87

— 'The Learning and Retention of Concepts: V. The Influence of Form of Presentation', *J. exp. Psychol.*, 1950, **40**, 504–11

REID, J. W., 'An Experimental Study of "Analysis of the Goal" in Problem Solving', *J. gen. Psychol.*, 1951, **44**, 51–69

RÉVÉSZ, G., 'Recherches de psychologie comparée. Reconnaissance d'un principe', *Arch. néerl. Physiol.*, 1923 a, **8**, 1–13

— 'Expériences sur la mémoire topographique et sur la découverte d'un système chez des enfants et des singes inférieurs', *Arch. Psychol.*, 1923 b, **18**, 323–42

REY, A., *L'intelligence pratique chez l'enfant*, Paris, Alcan, 1935

RICHARDSON, J., 'Retention of Concepts as a Function of the Degree of Original and Interpolated Learning', *J. exp. Psychol.*, 1956, **51**, 358–64

RICHARDSON, J., BERGUM, B. O., 'Distributed Practice and Rote Learning in Concept Formation', *J. exp. Psychol.*, 1954, **47**, 442–6

RIMOLDI, H. J. A., 'A Technique for the Study of Problem Solving', *Educ. psychol. Measurmt.*, 1955, **15**, 450–61

— 'Problem Solving as a Process', *Educ. psychol. Measurmt.*, 1960, **20**, 449–60

RITCHER, M. N. Jr., 'The Theorical Interpretation of Errors in Syllogistic Reasoning', *J. Psychol.*, 1957, **43**, 341–4

ROBINSON, E. W., 'A Preliminary Experiment on Abstraction in a Monkey', *J. comp. Psychol.*, 1933, **16**, 231–6

ROMMEITVEIT, R., 'Stages in Concept Formation and Levels of Cognitive Functioning', *Scand. J. Psychol.*, 1960, **1**, 115–24

ROSENBAUM, G., 'Stimulus Generalization as a Function of Level of Experimentally Induced Anxiety', *J. exp. Psychol.*, 1953, **45**, 35–43

ROSENSTEIN, J., 'Cognitive Abilities of Deaf Children', *J. Speech Hear. Res.*, 1960, **3**, 108–19

RUDEL, R. G., 'Transposition of Response by Children Trained in Intermediate Size Problems', *J. comp. Psychol.*, 1957, **50**, 292–5

SARGENT, S. S., 'Thinking Process at Various Levels of Difficulty', *Arch. Psychol.*, 1940, no. 249

SAUGSTAD, P., 'An Analysis of Maier's Pendulum Problem', *J. exp. Psychol.*, 1957, **54**, 168–79

— 'Problem-solving as Dependent on Availability of Functions', *Brit. J. Psychol.*, 1955, **46**, 191–8

## Bibliography

SAUGSTAD, P., 'Availability of Functions. A Discussion of some Theoretical Aspects', *Acta psychol.*, 1958, **14**, 384–400

SAUGSTAD, P., RAAHEIM, K., 'Problem-solving and Availability of Functions', *Acta psychol.*, 1957, **13**, 263–78

SCOTT, J. P., *Animal Behavior*, Chicago, Chicago Univ. Press, 1958

SELLS, S. B., 'The Atmosphere Effect: an Experimental Study of Reasoning', *Arch. Psychol.*, 1936, no. 200

SELLS, S. B., KOOB, H. F., 'A Classroom Demonstration of "Atmosphere Effect" in Reasoning', *J. educ. Psychol.*, 1937, **28**, 514–8

SHAKLEE, A. B., JONES, B. E., 'Distribution of Practice prior to Solution of a Verbal Reasoning Problem', *J. exp. Psychol.*, 1953, **46**, 424–34

SIGEL, I. E., 'The Dominance of Meaning', *J. genet. Psychol.*, 1954, **85**, 200–8

SMOKE, K. L., 'An Objective Study of Concept Formation', *Psychol. Monogr.*, 1932, **42**, no. 191

— 'Negative Instances in Concept Learning', *J. exp. Psychol.*, 1933, **16**, 583–8

SPAET, T., HARLOW, H. F., 'Solution by Rhesus Monkeys of Multiple Sign Problems Utilizing the Oddity Method', *J. comp. Psychol.*, 1943, **35**, 119–32

SOLLEY, C. M., SNYDER, F. W., 'Information Processing and Problem Solving', *J. exp. Psychol.*, 1958, **55**, 384–7

SPEARMAN, C. E., *The Abilities of Man; Their Nature and Measurement*, London, Macmillan, 1927

SPENCE, K. W., 'The Differential Responses in Animals to Stimuli varying within a Single Dimension', *Psychol. Rev.*, 1937, **44**, 430–44

STAATS, A. W., 'Verbal and Instrumental Response-hierarchies and their Relationship to Problem-solving', *Amer. J. Psychol.*, 1957, **70**, 442–6

STEVENS, S. S., *Handbook of Experimental Psychology*, New York, Wiley, 1951

STEVENSON, H. W., ISCOE, I., 'Overtraining and Transposition in Children', *J. exp. Psychol.*, 1954, **47**, 251–5

STOLUROW, L. M., BERGUM, B., HODGSON, T., SILVA, J., 'The Efficient Course of Action in "Trouble Shooting" as a Joint Function of Probability and Cost', *Educ. psychol. Measurmt.*, 1955, **15**, 462–77

STONE, C. P., *Comparative Psychology*, 3rd ed., New York, Prentice Hall, 1951, 189

STÖRRING, G., 'Experimentelle Untersuchungen über einfache Schlussprozesse', *Arch. ges. Psychol.*, 1908, **11**, 1–127

SWEENEY, E. J., *Sex Differences in Problem Solving*, Stanford, Stanford Univ., 1953

SZÉKELY, L., 'Knowledge and Thinking', *Acta psychol.*, 1950 a, **7**, 1–24

— 'Productive Processes in Learning and Thinking', *Acta psychol.*, 1950 b, **7**, 388–407
TERRELL, G. Jr., KENNEDY, W. A., 'Discrimination Learning and Transposition in Children as a Function of the Nature of the Reward', *J. exp. Psychol.*, 1957, **53**, 257–60
THISTLETHWAITE, D., 'Attitude and Structure as Factors in the Distortion of Reasoning', *J. abnorm. soc. Psychol.*, 1950, **45**, 442–58
TRESSELT, M. E., LEEDS, D. S., 'The Einstellung Effect in Immediate and Delayed Problem Solving', *J. gen. Psychol.*, 1953, **49**, 87–97
UNDERWOOD, B. J., 'Studies of Distributed Practice: XV. Verbal Concept Learning as a Function of Intralist Interference', *J. exp. Psychol.*, 1957, **54**, 33–40
UNDERWOOD, B. J., RICHARDSON, J., 'Some Verbal Materials for the Study of Concept Formation', *Psychol. Bull.*, 1956 a, **53**, 84–95
UNDERWOOD, B. J., RICHARDSON, J., 'Verbal Concept Learning as a Function of Instruction and Dominance Level', *J. exp. Psychol.*, 1956 b, **51**, 229–38
VAN DE GEER, J. P., *A Psychological Study of Problem-solving*, Harlem, De Toorts, 1957
VIAUD, G., *L'intelligence. Son évolution et ses formes*, Paris, P.U.F., 1946
VINACKE, W. E., *The Psychology of Thinking*, New York, McGraw Hill, 1952
VINCENT, M., 'Rôle des données perceptives dans l'abstraction', *Enfance* 1956, **9**, 1–20
— 'Sur le rôle du langage à un niveau élémentaire de pensée abstraite', *Enfance*, 1957, **10**, 444–64
— 'Les classifications d'objets et leur formulation verbale chez l'enfant', *Psychol. franç.*, 1959, **4**, 190–204
WALLON, H., *De l'acte à la pensée*, Paris, Flammarion, 1942
— 'La pensée précatégorielle chez l'enfant', *Enfance*, 1952, **52**, 97–101
WEIGL, E., 'Zur Psychologie sogenannter Abstraktionsprozesse: I: Untersuchungen über das "Ordnen"', *Z. Psychol.*, 1927, **103**, 1–45
WELCH, L., 'A Behavioristic Explanation of Concept Formation', *J. genet. Psychol.*, 1947, **71**, 201–22
— 'The Transition from Simple to Complex Forms of Learning', *J. genet. Psychol.*, 1947, **71**, 233–51
WERTHEIMER, M., Uber Schlussprozesse im produktiven Denken, 1925, in ELLIS, W. D., *A Source Book of Gestalt Psychology*, London, Routledge and Kegan Paul, 1938
— *Productive Thinking*, New York, Harper, 1945
WHITFIELD, J. W., 'An Experiment in Problem Solving', *Quart. J. exp. Psychol.*, 1951, **3**, 184–97

## Bibliography

WODINSKY, J., BITTERMAN, M. E., 'The Solution of Oddity-problems by the Rat', *Amer. J. Psychol.*, 1953, **66**, 137–40

WOODWORTH, R. S., SELLS, S. B., 'An Atmosphere Effect in Formal Syllogistic Reasoning', *J. exp. Psychol.*, 1935, **18**, 451–60

WOHLWILL, J. F., 'The Abstraction and Conceptualisation of Form, Color and Number', *J. exp. Psychol.*, 1957, **53**, 304–9

YOUNG, M. L., HARLOW, H. F., 'Generalization by Rhesus Monkeys of a Problem involving the Weigl Principle using the Oddity Method', *J. comp. Psychol.*, 1943, **36**, 201–6

— 'Solution by Rhesus Monkeys of a Problem involving the Weigl Principle using the Oddity Method', *J. comp. Psychol.*, 1943, **35**, 205–18

# Chapter 23

## Mental Images

### Jean Piaget and Bärbel Inhelder

The evolution of ideas concerning mental images is perhaps the clearest demonstration of the stages through which experimental psychology has passed. During the first stage, at the height of associationism, images were considered both *a*) as a direct product not only of perception but of sensation, of which they were allegedly the residual trace and *b*) as one of the two fundamental elements of thought, conceived as a system of association between images. In 1897, it was still possible for Alfred Binet to write a whole work on *The Psychology of Reasoning*, in which he expressly defended the thesis that reasoning is based on a succession of associations linking images.

There followed a second stage, beginning around 1900, during which the same Alfred Binet in *L'Etude expérimentale de l'Intelligence* (1903) and also Marbe, Külpe and the *Denkpsychologie* of the Würzburg school discovered the existence of 'imageless thought' (affirmations and negations, relations, the act of judgment itself) and concluded that images cannot be considered as an element of thought but at the most as an auxiliary. Less emphasis was given to the analysis of images. Indeed it was relegated to the background without there having been any real experimental investigation, except in the field of memory and memory-images (or 'eidetic' images, the nature of which is still a matter of controversy). In this connection, the distinction between memory consisting in recognition, which appears earlier and is independent of images, and memory consisting in evocation, which implies images, tends to suggest that there is little that is primitive in the genesis of images.

In the third stage, which brings us to the present day, we have witnessed three kinds of progress which directly affect our knowledge of images. The first remains theoretical in nature: images are no longer interpreted as an extension of perception but tend (as Dilthey had foreseen) to acquire the status of a symbol (see the fine chapter by I. Meyerson, 1932). The second contribution comes from a set of psychophysiological studies and psychopathological observations that have helped to reveal some of the conditions governing the production of imaged representation. What they tend to stress particularly in the formation of images is the role of motor activity whereby an act is reproduced in outline. The third contribution comes from child psychology. It is twofold. First, it enables us to work out approximately the stage at which images are formed (beginnings of the symbolic function with language, symbolic play and deferred imitation). Second, it helps us to trace the development of imaged representation, especially in its multiple relations with the evolution of operations (independence, opposition, subordination, etc.).

## 1 Statement of Problems

We propose in this chapter to describe some typical experiments concerning images and to point out the gaps that remain in our knowledge. It is not our ambition to give an exhaustive summary of what exists, nor do we propose to undertake a complete theoretical restatement. Nevertheless, no good experiment is ever initiated except in answer to a question and a question cannot be properly asked unless it is correctly situated in relation to a number of other problems. We shall therefore begin by examining these problems, and we hope to present each experiment in its proper perspective in relation to them.

Images are an instrument of knowledge and therefore depend on cognitive functions. These present two distinct aspects according to a fundamental dichotomy which must be recognized if problems are to be correctly stated. Indeed, we have already encountered this dichotomy in Chapter 18 in connection with perception.

## Mental Images

### 1 Figurative and operative aspects of cognitive functions

The aspect to which mental images are referable is what we shall call the *figurative* aspect. It characterizes the forms of cognition which, from the subject's point of view, appear as 'copies' of reality although, from the objective point of view, they offer only an approximate correspondence to objects or events. But this correspondence relates to the figural aspects of reality, that is to configurations. It is possible to distinguish three fundamental varieties of figurative knowledge: perception, which functions exclusively in the presence of the object and through the medium of a sensory field; imitation in the broad sense (by means of gestures, sounds or drawing, etc.), functioning in the presence or absence of the object but through actual or manifest motor reproduction; and mental images, functioning only in the absence of the object and by internalized reproduction.

The other aspect of cognitive functions, which does not directly concern images, but to which we shall sometimes be obliged to refer, is the *operative* aspect. This characterizes the forms of knowledge which consist in modifying an object or an event so as to grasp the actual transformations and their results, and not merely as before the static configurations corresponding to the 'states' linked by these transformations. These forms of knowledge include *a*) sensori-motor actions (except imitation), the only instruments of the sensori-motor intelligence which becomes organized before language; *b*) internalized actions which are an extension of the above. They first appear at the pre-operational level (age two to seven); and *c*) operations that are properly attributable to intelligence. These are actions which are internalized, reversible and co-ordinated into integrated structures bearing on transformations (see Chapter 24).

We are speaking, for the moment, merely of two 'aspects' of cognitive functions and not of two categories, for it is obvious that at a certain level of development one is capable of imagining some, if not all, transformations figuratively, as well as the states or configurations linked by these transformations. The two aspects of cognition, figurative and operative, thus become complementary. Whether this is so at all levels or whether mental images are at first too limited or too static to succeed in figuring transformations remains an open question.

*Jean Piaget and Bärbel Inhelder*

## 2  Meaning and symbolic function

Another dimension of cognitive functions to which we must refer from the beginning in order that we may properly envisage the problems raised by images, is the dimension relating to the structure of meanings. All cognition implies meaning or signification and signification for its part supposes a significant and a significate. But there exist several categories of significants and of significates and it is necessary to distinguish between them in order to understand the questions which mental images raise in connection with them.

It is first of all necessary to distinguish between significants which are differentiated from what they signify and those which are not. The latter consist of 'indices' or cues and the former of 'symbols' and 'signs'. An 'index' or cue is an undifferentiated significant in the sense that it consists in a part or an aspect of the significate. For instance, a perceptual cue such as the apparent diminution of an object, which indicates its distance from the point of observation, is only one aspect of the perceived complex 'apparent magnitude × distance' in which distance could in its turn act as a cue in helping to estimate apparent magnitude. Sensori-motor cues called I.R.M. (innate releasing mechanism) by K. Lorenz, such as a particular arrangement of colours reminiscent of the mother's beak and releasing the instinct to follow her,[1] remain undifferentiated in the sense that they are simply borrowed from the characteristics of the significate. They thus give a partial perception of it. Symbols and signs, on the contrary, are differentiated from what they signify in a way that must be accurately defined if one wants to be clear about the position of images.

But first let us note that signs and symbols also differ from one another and thus we have a second distinction: signs are 'arbitrary', as linguists say of verbal signs or words, meaning that there is no family relationship or likeness between the thing signified and the significant; in other words, they are purely conventional and thus social in nature. Symbols, on the contrary, are 'motivated', that is, they present a relationship or likeness between the significant and the significate.

Signs are thus significants that differ from what they signify;

[1] In the young of the grey lag goose (*Anser anser*).

this goes without saying since they are arbitrary: thus, words are at once conventional and clearly differentiated from the thing named. In the case of symbols, however, such as we find even in the simplest of children's symbolic games (for instance pretending to be asleep just for fun), how can one assess the difference between the significant (pretending to be asleep—with appropriate gestures) and the significate (really sleeping) since the gestures concerned are similar and, in the event, almost identical? The criterion is as follows: the deferred imitative gesture (pretending to sleep) is not a part or an aspect of the significate (really sleeping), but an evocative copy, thus differing from its model. A perceptual cue, on the other hand, is not a copy but a part of actual perception, with no representative evocation. As for the I.R.M. mentioned above, even if one replaces the colours of the mother's beak by artificial signals reproducing the same colours and releasing the same reaction, there is actual perception of the substitute of the usual perceptual cue and of a substitute *fused* with it but not evoking it by a distinct mental representation. The same applies to signals occurring in conditioning, which we therefore also class as cues.

Signs and symbols are thus considered to differ from what they signify because they require an *evocation* not just a perception of it. In view of this, we shall term *symbolic function*[1] the ability to evoke objects or situations not actually perceived at the time, by the use of signs or symbols. As mental images are clearly a product of evocation and not of perception, two problems will arise, that of determining the links between images and the symbolic function and that of establishing whether images are significants or significates, or whether they partake of both functions.

Before specifying the problems, however, let us point out once again the possible overlap between what was said under *1* about the figurative and operative aspects and what we have just seen concerning meanings. The operative aspects of knowledge are definitely not significants but significates. As to the figurative aspects, it is necessary to distinguish between the various levels.

---

[1] We say 'symbolic function' in order to conform to usage (Head, etc.) but it would be preferable to use the term 'semeiotic function' (which we propose to adopt) in view of the fact that symbols are only one instance and that signs are another. By using 'semeiotic' we can refer to both at once.

## Jean Piaget and Bärbel Inhelder

In perception there are both significants and significates but the latter consist only in undifferentiated 'cues'. Imitation itself includes several stages and the higher stages are probably orientated towards the constitution of symbolic significants (deferred imitation). Thus, another problem will arise: that of understanding the role of this evolution in the constitution of images. We shall now classify the various problems and suggest methods of solving them.

## 3 Classification of problems

The main questions arising from what we have so far discussed are, broadly speaking: *a*) to explain the formation of images within the series of figurative structures: are they a direct extension of perception or do they proceed from imitative behaviour with its components of motor reproduction? *b*) to establish whether the development of images constitutes an independent evolution, thus conferring a relative autonomy on imagery, or whether on the contrary it is subject to increasingly important contributions from outside (from operative mechanisms in particular). On the answer to these two questions assuredly depend all interpretations of the structure and the meaning of images, considered as a form of symbolism or as a constituent element of thought. In trying to formulate these questions in detail, one is led to the nine following problems:

1) Leaving aside for the moment the question of genesis, and thus from a purely synchronic standpoint, one can try to determine whether images are by nature *motor* or *sensory* or both. Does an image of any content consist only in a kind of internal picture similar to, although less 'real' than, a perceptual picture in its sensory aspect or does it also imply a motor reproduction, at least in outline? Such a problem belongs to the psychophysiological and psychopathological spheres, both of which can offer decisive data. While the motor character of images can thus be established, their *mode of formation* remains to be determined. This is a problem of a general character and as such it can be subdivided into questions 2 to 4, to which different methods apply.

2) It is first necessary to define the *genetic level* at which images are formed. This calls for systematic observation of children's

*Mental Images*

behaviour. One can begin by showing why there do not seem to be any mental images during the initial stage, throughout which perception nevertheless develops under relatively complex forms —a fact which tends to dissociate images from perception. In the second place, the emergence of new forms of behaviour enables us to establish approximately the level of formation of images. This appears to coincide with the constitution of the symbolic function (defined in Section 3, 2).

3) The next step is to try to determine the *relations between images and imitation*, again by means of genetic observation: in this respect imitation seems to be both the instrument of transition leading from the sensori-motor stage to the symbolic and the very source of images, which would thus be deferred and internalized imitation.

4) Passing from observation to experimentation, we can try to determine the relations between images and imitation within the more limited sphere of *relations between images and drawing* (considered as graphic imitation). In this connection, experiments that have proved instructive (with children aged from 4 to 7) are those relating to the reproduction of lengths (parts of straight lines) in various situations which are apt to modify the mental image and to have repercussions on the graphic image.

Next comes the general problem of the *development of images* with age, which can be subdivided into two questions:

5) The first requirement is to draw up a *classification of images*, so as to establish more or less general stages in the evolution of mental imagery or, at least, an *order of succession* which could then be verified. We are thinking less of a classification by contents (visual images, auditory images, etc.) than of a hierarchy based on degrees of complexity: images occurring in direct reproduction (copy), in the reproductive evocation first of static configurations and then of kinetic configurations and finally anticipatory images. The method takes the form of experimental tests allowing performances to be seriated.

6) Once the various types of images have been distinguished, the central problem consists in establishing whether there is an *autonomous evolution* of images, that is, whether images of a higher level $n+1$ derive directly from images of $n$ or $n-1$ level. By 'derive directly', we mean that images of $n+1$ level are constructed by means of the same mechanisms as those of earlier

levels or by means of mechanisms extending them by differentiation. The reverse hypothesis would be that images of $n+1$ level succeed those of prior levels only through the intervention of new mechanisms, that is, of contributions outside imagery and figurative functions in general: these contributions could in particular come from intellectual operations, which are capable of directing the construction of new images. (They have a similar guiding influence on perceptual activities as we saw in Chapter 18, Section 3, 4.)

Problem 6 may be solved by recourse to experimental situations in which one can observe the transition from initially static and reproductive images to anticipatory images and where one can judge the possible intervention of operations that lie outside images.

7) The preceding problem leads back to a question that has become classic since the work of Binet and the Würzburg School, that of the *relations between images and thought*. The question, however, no longer consists in establishing whether thought can exist without images. We now know that the aspect of thought which extends beyond images is none other than the operational aspect (action-schemata and operations), especially in the form of operations proper. The question which remains, however, is to know whether and in what sense images prepare or at least encourage the functioning of these operations.

The most suitable experimental technique for dealing with question 7 consists in going back to certain operational tests (particularly those referring to conservation) but asking subjects to anticipate everything by images (actual transformations and their results), then comparing the solutions based on imagination with those that follow perceptual perusal of the data.

8) A particularly instructive problem concerning the relations betweeen images and operations is that raised by *spatial images*. It is a purely psychological problem but it corresponds closely to the problem of *geometrical intuition* raised by mathematicians in connection with the epistemology of their science: why is it that imagery, beyond a given level of development, is particularly apt to duplicate spatial operations? Experimentation in the genetic field is particularly fruitful here.

9) Finally, there are two more problems which should be discussed. They are distinct but have a common feature in that

*Mental Images*

they extend beyond the framework of normal images. The first is the problem of *eidetic images*, discovered by Jaensch and the second is that of the role of images in *hallucination*. But, in both cases, the phenomena in question are not general since the first has been observed only in a minority of otherwise normal subjects while the second is pathological. We are therefore obliged to refrain from discussing them, as lying outside the scope of this work. We mention them, however, since one might well ask whether their very existence does not contradict the conception of images which will be suggested by the experiments described in this chapter.

2 Psychophysiological data and the problem of whether images are sensory or motor

Psychology turns to neurology for the answer to two distinct though probably related problems concerning images.

*1 Quasi-sensory character of images*

The first refers to their sensory or quasi-sensory character. A visual image gives with varying approximations the shape, dimensions and colour of the object evoked. In individuals of a visual type the sensory qualities of images can sometimes attain a surprising degree of precision. However, as Lotze had already remarked, 'images do not light up'; they lack the character of present and living reality found in perception. Similarly, a sound image can render a melody and in individuals of an auditory type it will reproduce it in some detail. Nevertheless the subject will not turn his head to see where the sound is coming from as in the case of perception. The first problem is therefore that of the physiological mechanism of quasi-sensory evocation and it is being solved experimentally by neurosurgical techniques (partial ablation and above all electrical stimulation) evolved by Foerster and remarkably developed by Penfield and his collaborators. When the cortical projections of the optic or auditory tracts are stimulated, one obtains sensory states which, according to Penfield, have nothing in common with hallucinations (therefore even less with images) and are purely sensations. On the other hand, temporal lobe stimulation leads to memory states which can be graduated according to the nature of the images involved and their vividness. Kubie (1952) divides these experimental states into three groups: *a*) states of which the content seems present and immediate, but where the subject nevertheless has the impression of being at once an actor and a spectator (as sometimes happens in dreams to which images in this group are closely related, according to Kubie); *b*) states that are also quite vivid but evoked as past (according to Kubie these have a quality of imagery comparable to that of images occurring in dozing (hypnagogic reveries) ); *c*) non-vivid memories, without sensation. According to de Ajuriaguerra and Hécaen (1960, p. 436) the sensory systems play a part in the first two groups and, at the level of the temporal lobe, it would be easy to admit the joint action of sensory and memory mechanisms.

Concerning the mechanism of evocations, Penfield (1960, pp. 1444–5) specifies that 'the temporal cortex has some sort of selective connection with a detailed flash-back record of the past, most of which has been forgotten as far as the individual's ability for voluntary recall is concerned'. These flash-backs provoked by electrical stimulation unfold at the former rate of speed as long as the electrode is held in place. An example is hearing a musical theme to which the subject listened some years before. He sees at the same time the orchestra and the singer and is conscious once again of the emotion he felt during the actual performance.

But Lhermitte (1960) specifies that it is not yet possible to locate the seat of the mechanisms enabling us 'not only to imagine but to image'. All that we know is that efferent impulses from the occipital region link up with the 'centrencephalic system and also with the diencephalon'. In addition, Oscar Wyss, quoted in the discussion of Lhermitte's report, specifies that artificial stimulation of the diencephalon can provoke in animals behaviour which causes one to infer the existence of visual hallucinations (1944).

## 2 The role of motor activity

A second problem arises in connection with the first: do images consist only in quasi-sensory evocation or are they in part an active reconstruction expressing itself through the necessary

## Mental Images

intervention of motor activity? It is this second question which has received most attention, for the following reason. In the days when images were conceived merely as a residual extension of perception (a tradition to which can be attributed the defective use of the word 'image' in the expression 'after-image'), their quasi-sensory character could encourage the illusion that there was no problem, since they were considered as a weakened form of perception. Yet, even then, authors who believed that movement played a part in perception, were trying to discover movement in the functioning of imaged representation. Thus, Jackson stressed that it contained a motor element in addition to the sensory element and Ribot laid stress on the presence of movements of the eyes and even of the limbs, in analogy with perception.

The problem of the role of motor activity in images takes on its full meaning once images have been recognized as something other than residual perception. Thanks to modern techniques, it has been possible to deal with this problem by direct experimentation bearing in particular on the representation of a movement of one's own body. On this point, the alternative is quite plain: either the representative evocation of the movement is something other than the movement itself and consists in 'imagining' it like a picture detached from the action, or else this process of imagining the movement rests on the motor adumbration of the movement itself. Electroencephalographic and electromyographic techniques can give valuable information on this point by making it possible to compare the electrical modifications occurring during the act itself and during its representation. For example, Gastaut (1954), using electroencephalograms, observed the same beta waves during the mental representation of the act of flexing the hand and during actual flexing. At the same time, Allers and Scheminsky (1926), followed by Jacobson (1931, 1932) detected, with electromyograms, the existence of a slight peripheral muscular activity during a representation of arm movements. This slight activity is parallel to that which occurs when the act in question is actually being performed. Conversely, one of Foerster's patients (1936) could neither imagine nor perform the required movements after section of the sensitive posterior roots.

A. Rey (1948) showed the impossibility of imagining one's

forefinger tracing a given figure while it is performing a simple rhythmical flexing movement. Either the real movement is well performed but there is no representation of the figure (e.g. a circle) or else representation is possible, but the rhythm is disturbed as seen from the instrument recording the flexion. A. Rey also found (1947) that the time required for the internal representation of a movement is equal to or greater than the time required actually to perform it.

A. Rey also noted, in the case of visual representations of hand movements, that eye movements partly reproduced those of the hand. Complex oculo-manual co-ordinations are thus established. They serve to reinforce the precision of the image and, in our opinion, already show the character of imitative schemata found in images. We shall have occasion to stress this character later.

In short, imaged representation of a movement of one's own body does not rest on simple evocative pictures external to the movements, but implies an internalized imitation by which they are reproduced in outline, complete reproduction being held back by inhibition.

## 3 Eye movements

The analysis of visual images led F. Morel (1947) to similar conclusions. He began by observing a patient with protruding eyes which made it easier to observe his eye movements. When the patient was asked to shut his eyes and imagine a table, a round garden pond, etc., it was possible, by laying a finger on his eyeballs, to follow movements reproducing the shape of the objects he was imagining. Morel then constructed with Schifferli an apparatus to record eye movements by photographing projections of a light ray on the cornea. Schifferli (1953) compared eye movements during perception and during imaged representation and was able to make the following observations. Regarding perception, his results corroborated the classical discovery that it consists of jerky explorations, with alternating fixations and movements. At the same time, he was able to establish the existence of varied and relatively stable individual types of oculomotor exploration. Regarding mental images, he again found the same types of movements in the same subjects as if the subjects followed in their imagination the contours of objects in a way comparable to that occurring in perceptual exploration. It would however be profitable, we feel, to check these results by making sure that they persist when the oculo-motor investigation of the image does not immediately follow that of perception, so as to avoid possible perseveration and above all involuntary suggestion arising from the instructions: 'And now try to picture or to imagine etc., what you have just seen' (or some similar instruction). For instance, if a patient has perceived a square with black lines, he should next be shown a circle drawn in red, and only then should he be asked to imagine the 'black figure' (so as to avoid suggestion from the word 'square') which preceded the 'figure in red'; etc.

Several recent studies have also shown the existence of eye movements during dreams, thus confirming a hypothesis put forward as early as 1892 by G. Trumball Ladd. In 1955, Aserinsky and Kleitmann distinguished two types of eye movements during sleep, the rapid type accompanied by a heightening of cardiac and respiratory activity and by a typically slow E.E.G. voltage in the frontal and occipital areas and sometimes by vocalizing on the part of the subject. These authors therefore assume that the rapid movements bear a relation to the visual imagery of dreams. In 1957, Dement and Kleitmann, and in 1958, W. Dement and E. Wolpert attempted to verify this hypothesis by a twofold technique which they applied to adult subjects. They measured differences in potential during eye movements, taking every precaution to avoid artifacts. They also woke the subjects during each eye-movement period and obtained accounts of dreams (including as a control some external stimuli, such as a doorbell). Dement and Wolpert concluded that the rapid eye movements thus recorded do not occur haphazardly during sleep or even dreams but that they are specific instruments of the dreamer's visual activity. These eye movements appear to be controlled by cortical centres different from those which control the majority of other movements, since these are not brought into play during sleep.

However, in connection both with the possible role of eye movements in dream images and with the observations of Morel and Schifferli on the motor analogies between visual images and perception, there are a number of points that we wish to make. In doing so, we hope to show that what has been said is not simply a reversion to former ideas whereby images were conceived as mere extensions of perception. We should remember first of all (see Chapter 18 of the present work) that perception takes place on two or more distinct planes: there are those elements that result from the perceptual and are independent of motor activity (at least once they have been established) and there are perceptual activities such as exploration, transportation, etc., dependent on motor activity. If an analogy between images and perception exists, it must be between images and perceptual activities, in contrast to primary perception, which merely provides the prototype for the sensory substance of images. As to the analogy with movements of structuring exploration, it in no way implies that images merely 'extend' perceptual activity in the way in which an automatized habit is an extension of the early phases of that habit. The analogy rests, on the contrary, on the two following circumstances: 1) Exploratory activity is already a kind of imitation, since exploratory perceptual activities follow the contours of the object and serve only to favour the 'figurative' aspect of perception (and not to modify the object like 'operative' actions); 2) the mental image which follows perception (in Schifferli's technique, etc.) is not a residual perception, but results from an active reproduction of perceptual movements and thus constitutes an imitation of them (to the second power), just as we saw that the representation of a movement of one's own body amounts to tracing the movement by internalized imitation.

## 4  Auditory images

Finally, we come to auditory images. These have been studied less and we shall confine ourselves to the following remarks. Taking verbal images first, we find that they consist in 'hearing' a word belonging to internal language and therefore there is a trace of articulation proper:[1] there is proof of this in the fact that it is impossible to speed up an auditory evocation beyond a certain limit (especially in the case of a difficult word, such as 'peripatetic' or 'anacoluthon'). This limit coincides with the time required actually to say the word. Taking musical images next, we find that they are clear and distinct only in so far as one is

---

[1] In deaf-mutes, who use sign language, Max observed that dreams are often accompanied by movements of the fingers.

capable of producing an approximate imitation. As to the orchestral background that accompanies the recollection of a melody after a concert, it is more in the nature of a sound continuum—sensible but not very structured—than of detailed evocation. Thirdly, if we take auditory images of odd noises (thunder, breaking china, tractors, aeroplanes, etc.) we find that they are remarkably vague and abstract, compared to images of sounds heard less frequently but which can be imitated (birdsong, for example).

3   Genetic Data concerning the stage at which and the manner in which images are formed: images and imitation

---

Although psychophysiological data bring out the fact that images contain an element of active reconstruction, and consequently of motor activity, this in itself is not entirely sufficient to dissociate images from perception, for it is still possible to wonder to what extent similar factors enter into perceptual activities as opposed to sedimented and automatized field effects. The study of genetic data yields supplementary information which, added to the former, seems decisive.

*1   Level at which images appear*

It is indeed extremely instructive to note that although perception develops from the earliest months in forms that are already complex (perceptual constancies begin to emerge at least as early as five to six months), mental images do not appear to play any part in children's behaviour until the middle of the second year. It is admittedly impossible to prove once and for all the non-existence of a phenomenon, especially one as difficult to pin down as mental images. Nevertheless, a number of convergent reasons make it possible at least to affirm that all the behaviour observed up to that level can be explained without recourse to 'representation'.

One set of facts concerns the evolution of behaviour destined to play a part in the formation of the symbolic function: play and imitation. Symbolic or imaginative play (such as slowly moving a small white object while saying 'miaow') leads to images or even already implies them. During the first year of life, however, games are merely practice games or functional games (repeating for the fun of it an action which is otherwise not playful) and symbolic play does not begin until the second year. (It is true that K. Groos (1896) attributed it to young mammals but this was an abuse of the term and there is absolutely no need to attribute imaged representation to a kitten pretending to bite its mother or to run after a marble.) In the same way, 'deferred' imitation (of the kind which starts only in the absence of the model) may lead to images or already suppose them. It also does not appear until the age of about thirteen to fourteen months. All earlier forms of imitation are learnt in the presence of a model and through sensori-motor adjustments based on various signals or perceptual cues and there is no need to invoke imaged representation.

A second set of facts concerns behaviour relating to objects that have disappeared from view. Here again, images play a part beyond a certain level, when the subject has to recall a series of successive displacements or reconstitute non-perceptible displacements. In this case too, such behaviour appears late and it is not until approximately the age of nine months that the infant even becomes capable of finding an object which has just been covered by a screen before his very eyes. What is more, if the object is first hidden and then found beneath a screen A (to the child's right), then hidden again, still under the child's eyes, under screen B (to his left), he will go back first of all to A without taking any notice of the second displacement (Piaget, 1955). In short, the search for objects that have disappeared is subject to a particularly slow and complex development and one is obliged to conclude that if the child had from its first year the ability to form mental images, this evolution would be at once much shorter and simpler.

A third set of facts is concerned with the beginnings of representation in intelligent acts. One observes from the age of fourteen to eighteen months (but not before) the ability to solve problems through internalized co-ordinations of action; for example, in trying to open a box of matches that is nearly shut, the subject gropes for a while, then pauses, looks attentively at the aperture which has to be made bigger opening and shutting his mouth as

## Mental Images

he does so until finally he puts his finger in the slit and thus solves the problem. It is probable that there is in this a beginning of representation (and the presumably imitative movement of the mouth is perhaps a tentative evocation of the goal to be reached). The point is that such behaviour is not encountered before the age of twelve to fourteen months and all previous intelligent acts are the result of 'step by step' adjustment and trial and error, with nothing to suggest representative evocation.

It is therefore not incautious to locate the formation of the first mental images at the level at which the symbolic function is constituted, that is, towards the middle of the second year. While the facts that have gone before lead us to dissociate the genesis of images from perception, the data that will now follow allow us to link it to a process that is at once general and clearly characterized, namely the internalization of imitation.

## 2 Symbolic function and imitation

Around the age of fourteen to eighteen months, one observes the first manifestations of the symbolic function in the form of differentiation between significants and significates (Section I, 2). This fundamental transformation is shown in four activities which develop more or less simultaneously: 1) the acquisition of language; 2) the emergence of symbolic play following mere practice games; 3) the beginning of deferred imitation (once the different varieties of direct imitation have been systematically mastered); 4) the first manifestations of representation in intelligent acts (internalized co-ordinations in the sense indicated above).

Without claiming to solve all the problems (in particular the neurological problems) raised by these correlative transformations, it is at least possible to extract a basic factor which accounts for the emergence of the individual forms of symbols and, in a general way, for the figurative aspect (Section I, *1*) of thought: we refer to the development of imitation.[1] Indeed, in symbolic play (which provides young children with an individual way of

---

[1] From 1936 onwards (English edition: *The Origins of Intelligence in the Child*, 1953, pp. 354–356), we have stressed the part played by imitation as a transition between the sensori-motor and the representative levels. H. Wallon developed the same idea in 1942 in a brilliant chapter in *De l'acte à la pensée*.

expressing personal experiences as opposed to the impersonal system of language) all the symbolism is supplied by imitation. Deferred imitation represents the culmination of all previous sensori-motor imitation. Finally language, which is of social and not of individual origin, is also acquired in a context of imitation. If it was acquired merely as a result of conditioning, it would appear much earlier.

In a general way, sensori-motor imitation which develops very early (from the age of three to four months) already constitutes a kind of representation in action, allowing in particular a correspondence to be set up between the non-visible parts of one's own body (face, etc.) and the visual spectacle of someone else's body, etc. Thereafter, imitation has only to acquire the faculty of extending itself in 'deferred' forms to pass from the state of a direct sensori-motor copy to that of evocations which still consist of gestures but are already symbolic. Subsequently, in accordance with the general laws of internalization of behaviour and in particular of social behaviour (cf. internal language, etc.), we find that imitation, which can already be deferred (and thereby enriched) begins to extend also to internalized imitations. It is in the establishment of these that we can find the starting point of imaged representation and of images themselves in their capacity of motor reproductions.

In conclusion, there is no doubt that genetic data (by putting the evolution of images so much later than that of perception and by relating images to symbolic processes proper, which govern representation in general) throw considerable light on psycho-physiological facts. But these genetic hypotheses, of which certain consequences have yet to be verified by experiment, naturally explain only the beginnings of specifically reproductive images. There remains the whole problem of the subsequent development of images, particularly in their anticipatory form.

## 4  Experiments on elementary reproductive images

Before attempting to classify the different varieties of images according to development (which supposes rather more complex experiments than those of which we are about to speak), we must

*Mental Images*

justify the preceding hypothesis by analysing what might almost be called copy-images. These are images of an object constructed in its presence. For instance, the object of the image may simply be displaced (without the displacement being in any way difficult to understand). In such cases, either the image merely prolongs perception, which would contradict our hypotheses, or else it differs from it and it will be necessary to examine to what extent it comes close if not to internal imitation (a reality which unfortunately it is difficult to penetrate) at least to external imitation, in the form of gesture or drawing.

*1 Reproductive image of a rod*

We began by conducting with B. Matalon the following experiment on one hundred and ten children aged from five to eleven and sixty adults. A black and rigid rod A, made of wire and measuring 20 cm. in length and 1·8 mm. in diameter is presented to the subject and placed on a sheet of paper perpendicularly to the sagittal axis (henceforth referred to as the 'horizontal' position), but on the left half of the sheet of paper. Then the subject is told that the rod is going to be rotated (showing him an actual rotation of 180°) until it reaches position $A^1$, a direct prolongation of the first position. He is then asked (Question 1) to draw the rod A to the exact length that it will be in position $A^1$. While he does so, the rod is left in its original position. Question 2 consists in picturing (again with a drawing) the length of rod A as it will be in $A^1$ after it has been displaced by a simple movement of translation, which is also physically performed before returning A to its original position so that the subject continues to have it before his eyes while drawing. Question 3 simply consists in drawing rod A in $A^1$ reproducing the exact length, A remaining where it is and no mention being made of displacement. One can see that in all three cases the task consists in drawing the same rod A, perceptually present, in the same position $A^1$, the only difference between the three questions being that the rod A is supposed to move by rotation or translation in questions 1 and 2 and to remain motionless in question 3. The results obtained were as shown in Table 1 overleaf.

It can be seen that 1) young children of 5 produce shorter drawings after imagining a displacement (with no significant differences between rotation and translation) than when making a direct copy (there is a very significant difference between drawings in this category and those in the other two.[1] 2) These underestimations diminish with age and are not found in adults. 3) The copy itself is subject to underestimation by young children and this too disappears with age.

TABLE I

Errors in drawings of the length of a 20 cm. rod when subjects are first asked to imagine rotation and translation, or simply to make a direct copy (averages as a percentage of 20 cm.)

|  | Rotation | Translation | Copy |
|---|---|---|---|
| Age 5 (30 subjects) | | | |
| % | −20·5 (15·9 cm.)* | −19·0 (16·2 cm.) | −13·5 (17·3 cm.) |
| σ | 2·8 | 2·2 | 1·7 |
| Age 7 (20 subjects) | | | |
| % | −20·5 (15·9 cm.) | −17·0 (16·6 cm.) | −10·5 (17·9 cm.) |
| σ | 2·9 | 2·2 | 1·8 |
| Age 11 (60 subjects) | | | |
| % | −5·0 (19·0 cm.) | −4·5 (19·1 cm.) | −8·5 (18·3 cm.) |
| σ | 1·7 | 1·2 | 1·0 |
| Adults (60 subjects) | | | |
| % | +3·5 (20·7 cm.) | −2·5 (19·5 cm.) | +2·0 (20·4 cm.) |
| σ | 1·5 | 1·2 | 1·1 |

* 15·9 = Mean of the actual length of the rods drawn.

Underestimation of length when copying proved very general in all the drawings of straight lines produced by children of five to six. This is decidedly interesting from the point of view of images themselves, since it shows that the simple graphic reproduction of a line implies a previous schema which precedes the act of drawing. We shall therefore come back to it in a moment when comparing graphic reproductions with reproductions by

[1] The three values all differ significantly from 20. Taking into account the fact that the three measures were recorded for the same subjects, we find for Student's $t$ that $t = 1·29$ (not significant) between rotation and translation and $t = 3·65$ or $3·14$ (highly significant) between rotation or translation and copy.

*Mental Images*

means of gestures. But it can be said at once of this 'anticipatory sketch' that, even if it does not lead to a complete mental image of the line to be drawn (complete in the sense of containing a quasi-sensory element, as discussed in Section 2, *1*) it is related to images considered as motor 'sketches'. This explains what happens in questions 1 and 2, when young subjects are asked to draw in the same position $A^1$ the same rod A, clearly visible in front of them. They make it even shorter simply because they first imagine a displacement on request. That they do this is a clear indication that there exists an imitative or quasi-imaged anticipatory motor schema before the process of drawing begins (since the difficulties in drawing are identical in all three cases, and reduced to the minimum); furthermore, it is proof that this imitative motor anticipation is partially inhibited as soon as the subject tries to imagine something further. What happens is not that subjects are distracted by their effort to imagine the rotation in detail, for we shall see that they are hardly capable of doing so. Nor is it simply that a curb is put upon the movement of the hand in drawing for although this factor probably plays a part (particularly in the underestimation that occurs during direct copying), it does not explain the significant differences between the drawings following rotation or translation and direct copies. Finally, it cannot be ascribed either to non-conservation of the length of the rod in the case of rotation or of translation, such as occurred in the operational test based on the overlapping parallel sticks[1] since there is no overlap in this instance: 78 per cent of the subjects examined affirmed conservation in these cases (against 25 per cent of the same subjects in the case of the overlapping sticks).

## 2 *Graphic and digital estimations*

Let us now return to the underestimation of lengths found in direct graphic copying, as compared with reproductions by means of simple digital indication. We feel that these phenomena

[1] Test of conservation of length. Two equal rods measuring 15 or 20 cm. are presented to the subject and their equality is demonstrated by putting them together. Then, one of the rods is moved under the child's eyes until it overlaps the other by 5 to 7 cm. (allowing a gap of 3–5 cm. between the rods to facilitate comparison). Until about the age of 7 or 8, children consider one of the rods to be longer than the other because it overlaps it.

are important in that they can help us to understand reproductive images, in particular when they are compared with transformational images and anticipatory images, which will be considered in Section 5.

The child is presented with a cylindrical rod 15 cm. in length and 1·8 mm. in diameter, resting horizontally on a 33 cm. square sheet of paper. The child has a sheet of the same size on which to draw. The model is placed slightly nearer the top of the sheet (to the left or to the right), the child faces midway between the two sheets. Results for right and left were found to be identical, whereas when the model is placed level with the drawing to be made, underestimation, while still evident, is a little less marked. The tests are as follows: *a*) copying the rod in the horizontal position (after attempts have been made in the sagittal and the oblique positions); *b*) choosing from drawings measuring 13, 14, 15, 16 and 17 cm. in length, the one that appears equal to the model rod (when the children indicate several, it is worth asking in the case of each one whether it is too big, equal or too small). While questions *a*) and *b*) are being asked, and also while the next is being asked, the model rod is taken away and replaced each time to avoid possible error concerning the standard. (cf. Chapter 18, Section 2, *1*); *c*) Digital evaluation: the child is asked to reproduce with his two forefingers the extremities of the model rod, on a similar blank sheet measuring 33 × 33 cm.

The results obtained with 53 subjects by F. Frank and T. Bang were as shown in Table 2.

There is a clear contrast between digital indication, which begins by an overestimation (whereas motor copying or indication by gestures is similar to drawing, according to research to be published elsewhere), choice among ready-made drawings (slight underestimation) and the graphic image itself. Controls have been applied showing that the phenomenon persists independently of the actual length of the lines and also operates in the case of closed figures (such as a square). It is essential to note, moreover, that subjects of 5 or 6 draw with a single stroke. Adjustments and corrections are not really made until the age of 7. (Table 2 deals only with the initial drawings but spontaneously amended drawings continue to show marked underestimation.) It would appear, therefore, that underestimation, while specific to graphic images, has a bearing on mental images. It indicates that in order to make even the most immediate copy, there must be an anticipatory sketch or pre-image and that it is this sketch which is

## Mental Images

TABLE 2

Copies of the length of a 15 cm. rod
(errors as %)

|  | Drawing | Choice | Digital evaluation |
|---|---|---|---|
| Age 5–6 (22 subjects) | −22% (=11·7 cm.) | −4·9% (=14·2 cm.) | +9·3% (=16·4 cm.) |
| Age 7–8 (18 subjects) | −14·0% (=12·9 cm.) | −4·6% (=14·3 cm.) | +10·2% (=16·5 cm.) |
| Age 9–10 (20 subjects) | −14·0% (=12·9 cm.) | −3·0% (=14·6 cm.) | +3·7% (=15·6 cm.) |

perturbed when the subject is at the same time required to imagine rotation or translation as in Table 1. In the majority of cases this anticipation, which already plays a part in reproductive images, is accompanied by a process of restructuring (we shall see an example of this in the following section, Table 3). We wanted to show the difference between images and perception from the outset, and in order to do this, we felt that it was useful to establish that even in a simple graphic copy, the movement is planned since errors are not distributed at random. This anticipation is at once motor and representative (since the gesture concerned is intended as a copy and is not merely an idle movement). It contains, in an as yet indistinct form, an element of internal imitation which will emerge in an explicit form in all the varieties of images. These we must now classify.

## 5 Classification of images as a function of their development

Images can be classified according to their content (visual, auditory, etc.) or according to their structure, and it is this second standpoint alone that will concern us here. The problem that arises takes the following form. A normal adult is capable of imagining static objects (a table), movements (the swing of a pendulum), known transformations (dividing a square into two equal rectangles). He can even imagine in anticipation a transformation that is new to him (thrice folding a square sheet in two, cutting off the point of intersection of the folds with scissors and imagining before unfolding the paper that he will see two holes and not just one, as when the paper is only twice folded in two). It is clear, however, that these various images are not all equally easy to build up and that there exist, therefore, hierarchic levels of images, possibly corresponding to stages in development. Unfortunately, research has not yet progressed far enough for us to be able to identify any such stages. Indeed, this is one of the main problems that remain to be solved but we felt that we should mention its existence. On the other hand, it is already possible to outline a structural classification of images and to base this classification on restricted studies showing that, in a given limited experimental situation, a particular category of images is formed before another particular category. We are now going to demonstrate this.

To make it easier to understand Section 5, we shall begin by setting out the proposed framework, which we shall later show to be justified by the facts. We must first of all establish a dichotomy between *reproductive* images (R), consisting in the evocation of objects or events that are already known and *anticipatory* images (A) which represent in imagination an event not previously perceived. Reproductive images themselves fall into three categories. They are *static* (RS) if they evoke a motionless object or configuration and *kinetic* (RK) if they evoke a movement. Finally they may consist of images reproducing a *transformation* (RT), if they figure a transformation that is already known (such as the transformation of an arc into a straight line in the case of subjects who have already had experience of this with a piece of wire, etc.). Anticipatory images may also be *kinetic* (AK) or may refer to *transformations* (AT). This simple framework is not sufficient, however, and two further subdivisions must be introduced for the following reasons. In the first place, it may be of interest for genetic reasons to distinguish in the case of static reproductive images (RS) and kinetic reproductive images (RK) between images produced by immediate copy (RSC and RKC) and deferred images (RSD and RKD). Secondly, transformational images (RT and AT), to which this distinction cannot apply, nevertheless comprise two very different levels according to whether the subject imagines only the result or product P of the transformation (hence RTP and ATP) or forms clear images of (and could for instance draw) the stages of the transformation itself, with all its successive modifications M (hence RTM and ATM).

## 1 Kinetic reproductive images

We shall naturally not examine each of these classes of images but simply give a few typical examples (in this paragraph and in Section 6). Taking *static or kinetic reproductive images* first, we find that Table 2 has already shown the need to distinguish between deferred images and the kind of image or pre-image occurring in immediate copy. The following experiment is instructive from this point of view, but it concerns kinetic images only. Having observed with Lambercier the difficulty experienced by young subjects in reproducing the movements perceived in the configurations used by Michotte to study causality, we took up the problem with A. Etienne, in the following form. Two 1 cm. cubes (one red, one blue) are moved along a 75 cm. trajectory according to various patterns: 'entraining' (the first cube starts from the beginning of the trajectory, joins the second, which is standing still in the middle, and carries it along by contact to the end of the trajectory;) launching (*id*. but the second moves alone after the impact); crossing (both cover the whole trajectory but in opposite directions to one another); simultaneous displacements (the first covers half the trajectory while the second covers the other half in the same direction); symmetrical movements (each starts from one end, touches the other at the half-way point and goes back in the opposite direction) and partly symmetrical movements (one makes the two half-journeys while the other starts from the middle and goes to the opposite end). The subject is given two similar cubes which he moves by hand on a table (but under a screen to avoid visual checks) and is then asked to reproduce the movements perceived, either during actual perception or immediately after the model has stopped moving. The results are as shown in Table 3 overleaf.

In considering failures in simultaneous reproduction, allowance must naturally be made for difficulties arising from the perceptual structurization of the model and for those in motor co-ordination,[1] etc. But what interests us here is that there is a gap between simultaneous imitation and consecutive reproduction, which is very wide at the age of three to four and which narrows with age.

[1] In the case of asymmetrical models (these being the most difficult), subjects err particularly in the direction of 'good motor forms', i.e. symmetrical movements.

## Table 3

Comparison of successes (as % of number of subjects) in the simultaneous and consecutive reproduction of pairs of movements

|  | Simultaneous reproduction | | Consecutive reproduction | |
| --- | --- | --- | --- | --- |
|  | Immediate | Progressive* | Immediate | Progressive |
| Age 3 (7 subjects) | 38 | 64 | 0 | 0 |
| Age 4 (21 subjects) | 64 | 81 | 15 | 35 |
| Age 5 (12 subjects) | 77 | 97 | 58 | 93 |
| Age 6 (10 subjects) | 100 | 100 | 80 | 100 |

* Progressive successes (which include immediate successes) are obtained by reproducing the experiment several times and therefore owe something to learning (practice effects).

Table 2 also shows us that the simultaneous copy itself implies a pre-imaged motor sketch which becomes automatic with age. Taken together, these two facts show the complexity already present in ordinary static or kinetic reproductive images. We must therefore expect a much greater difficulty when we come to transformational images. In particular we shall find that they follow much clearer stages of development.

## 2 Anticipation of the rotation of a rod

Between kinetic reproductive images and those that reproduce transformations, we find all the intermediate forms, since a movement may be considered as a transformation of positions. It is only in the case of changes affecting at least orientation itself (co-ordinates) that we shall speak of transformations, however. We shall now give a typical example of the initial difficulty that subjects experience in reproducing by means of images the simplest and most commonly encountered transformations. It concerns merely the transition from the vertical to the horizontal position of a rigid rod pivoting on its lower extremity (research carried out with F. Paternotte).

*Mental Images*

The experimenter presents to the child a black vertical rod of which the base is fixed and he shows with a quick gesture how it passes from this original position to the final horizontal position. The subject is then asked to represent these two extreme positions and some of the intermediate positions. There are four ways of reaching the mental images of the child and although, naturally, none of them yields the internal image itself, it is possible by comparing the results obtained with each method to arrive at a relative approximation: 1) Subjects are required to draw the vertical and horizontal positions (and are told that the rods must be pivoted about the same point, if they begin by leaving a space between the two lines). They must also show 'how the rod will fall' from one position to the other; 2) they are asked (but not immediately after making their drawings, which are not left on the table) to choose the best of several ready-made drawings which include correct drawings mixed with others reproducing the children's most frequent errors; 3) they are asked to imitate by gestures, using the rod itself, the actual movement that it describes: 4) finally, verbal commentaries can be useful in cases, admittedly rare, where the child considers his drawing an inadequate expression of his representation.

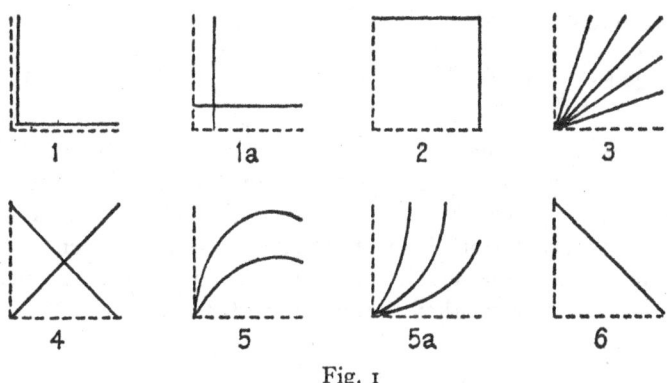

Fig. 1

Results are so disconcerting before the age of 7 or 8 that one may well wonder whether the question put before the children is not a matter of comprehension and of geometrical operations rather than of images as such. Yet they are not asked to make a judgment but only to evoke an everyday situation, physically recalled at the beginning of the experiment. We shall distinguish two main classes of inadequate images, in addition to entirely negative reactions (no representation): I: Trajectories inscribed in a square, either parallel to the extreme positions (1 and 2, Fig. 1) or correctly oblique but with the extremities inscribed in a square (3). II: Random trajectories (4), curved trajectories (5) or others that merge with the trajectory of the tip of the rod (6), which trajectory is represented by a straight line.

The results are as follows:

TABLE 4

Drawings, choice among figures or imitation by gesture, of the trajectories of a rod falling from the vertical position to the horizontal position

|  | Correct Drawings | Errors I | Errors II | Choice | Imitation |
|---|---|---|---|---|---|
| Age 4–5 (18 subjects) | 23 | 54 | 18 | 21 | 7 |
| Age 6 (17 subjects) | 47 | 29 | 24 | 46 | 43 |
| Age 7 (17 subjects) | 65 | 6 | 29 | 81 | 87 |
| Age 8–9 (11 subjects) | 82 | 9 | 9 | 82 | 82 |

It is clear that there is satisfactory concordance between the results of the three techniques, except that the imitation of trajectories in space is more difficult at the age of 4 to 5 than their graphic representation. Also, at the age of 7 drawing seems to be slightly behind choice and imitation. Choosing among ready-made drawings is no better than the drawings themselves.

## 3 Interpretation and control experiment

One might be tempted to conclude from these facts that before the age of 7, children have inadequate reproductive images of transformations simply because they have not noticed these transformations. A subject who has never paid attention to the increment or the decrement of the moon cannot be expected to

## Mental Images

have an image of its transformation! In other words, it would follow that this experiment teaches us nothing about images, but only about the boundaries of the area of reality which can be evoked by images. Things are not so simple, however, as the fact remains that *a*) this type of reproductive image is relatively good from the age of 7 or 8, thus from the level of the first 'geometrical operations'. This raises the question whether these two acquisitions are related; *b*) if the construction of the image is due solely to the fact that the transformation of which the child was hitherto unaware (although it corresponds to a common experience) is finally noticed, then we must try to find out how a reality must be 'noticed' in order to be translated into an adequate image. Is it sufficient to look at it, in accordance with the hypothesis that images are an extension of perception, or must it be imitated? In the case of transformations, this would suppose a more complex imitation than with static or even kinetic images, assuming that such imitation is partly a matter of comprehension and amounts to a figurative symbolization of the operation itself.

To clarify this question of the path through which a vertical rod falls,[1] we undertook a control experiment with B. Matalon. The experimenter asks the child to draw a rod that 'falls a little way', at the same time tracing the direction on the paper with his finger, thus accentuating the 'reproductive' aspect of the images

TABLE 5

Drawing of oblique lines following indication of direction
(as % of number of subjects)

|  | No Drawing | Straight lines in wrong direction | Curves | Correct Drawings |
|---|---|---|---|---|
| Age 4–5 (18 subjects) | 12 | 6 | 22 | 50 |
| Age 6 (17 subjects) | 12 | 16 | 12 | 60 |
| Age 7 (17 subjects) | 0 | 12 | 0 | 88 |
| Age 8–9 (11 subjects) | 0 | 0 | 0 | 100 |

[1] We used many other controls besides. It goes without saying that if one obliges the subject (but this is a kind of intentional artifact) to maintain the fixity of the fulcrum, results are better than those given in Table 4. Even so, one finds that only 66% of the subjects succeed at the age of 5 or 6, as in Table 5.

concerned. Besides drawings correct except as regards length, one still finds straight lines drawn in the wrong direction or curves.

It can be seen from Table 5 that results are a little better but still inadequate before the age of 7. We made a separate study with F. Paternotte of the image of the trajectory not of the whole rod but of its tip, on which we fixed a pearl or a pin surmounted by a pearl. Again, it was found that the image is adequate only from the age of 7 or 8. The same applies to drawings of the whole rod when its lower and upper halves are shaded in two distinct colours.

Returning to the problem of the structural classification of images, we thus find that 1) an important distinction must be drawn, from the point of view of development, between static or kinetic reproductive images and transformational images; 2) where the latter are concerned, there is probably not as clear-cut a difference between reproductive and anticipatory images as there is in the case of kinetic images (to which we shall return in Section 6). This is because in order to reproduce a transformation by images, it seems necessary to understand it and thus be capable of anticipating it. We must therefore return to the question of anticipatory images in general, both those referring to movements (kinetic) and those referring to transformations. In particular we must continue our discussion of the relations between the formation of images and the area of reality to which they correspond, since that is the problem which dominates the whole question of the evolution—whether autonomous or not—of the different types of imaged representation.

## 6  Mechanism of the evolution of images

### 1  Introduction

In studying the development of intellectual operations (Chapter 24 of this work), one finds an evolution which can be described as autonomous in the sense that, despite the complexity of the factors involved (maturation, physical experience, social interactions and equilibration), there occurs a progressive structurization

## Mental Images

which begins at the level of sensori-motor actions and ultimately extends to the higher operations. This structuring applies only to the operative aspect of the cognitive functions since this aspect progressively dominates the figurative aspect without being determined by it. On the contrary, the development of one of the main figurative mechanisms, that is, perception (Chapter 18), appears progressively subordinated to the intervention of external factors, operative in origin: first the whole action and finally operations. We consequently feel that the main question concerning the evolution of images is to determine upon which of these two kinds of development it depends.

The method to be followed, in studying a question of this kind, consists in analysing anticipatory images, the existence of which was hinted at in Section 5, and in discovering to what extent they derive in direct line from an earlier level of reproductive images or at what point they begin to imply the intervention of new mechanisms which lie outside images. It goes without saying that we shall then again come across the question that was raised in connection with the trajectory of rods (Table 4): what makes an image appear? Is it simply the discovery of the objects which it evokes and is there therefore a progression whereby the first images to be formed are those of static objects, followed by those of movements etc., and finally of operations (in the case of anticipatory images)? The image itself would not change in character but its content would simply grow richer. Could it be, on the contrary, that the process of internalized imitation, which constitutes the image, undergoes a transformation according to the type of behaviour to be imitated (namely perceptual exploration in the case of static forms, but operations in the case of transformations to be imagined in anticipation)? Is the structure of the image thus modified according to what is to be represented?

## 2 Transformation of an arc into a straight line

Starting with the study of images which anticipate a transformation, one of the simplest possible modifications—so simple that one could at first take it to be only a question of perceptual evaluation—is the transformation of an arc into a straight line or *vice versa*. The images required of the subjects may refer only to the result of the transformation (compared lengths of the straight line and of the arc) or to its stages (intermediate figures between the original and final configurations).

The child[1] is given three arcs measuring 10, 13 and 24 cm. (arcs of a circle with a circumference of 26 cm.), made of flexible wire, and he is asked 1) to copy these and also straight lines of the same length (this preliminary question is intended to assess the general underestimation inherent in the drawings of young children; it is given to a separate group of subjects, so as not to influence the remainder of the experiment); 2) to draw (reproducing their exact length) the straight lines that will result from drawing out the arcs (the transformation of an arc into a straight line is demonstrated with the aid of another piece of wire); 3) to indicate with his two forefingers (symbolism here takes the form of gesture and not of drawing) the length of these straight lines, while looking at the corresponding arcs; 4) to run his finger along an arc and to trace with his finger a straight line of equal length; 5) to choose straight lines equal in length to the arc among ready-made drawings or straight pieces of wire; 6) to draw the stages of the transformation by which the arc becomes a straight line (with a minimum of three drawings, two of which show the extreme positions and one—or more, if possible—shows an intermediate position); 7) to choose among ready-made drawings those which best represent these stages in the transformation.

All these questions are also asked about the transformation which results from bending a straight piece of wire into an arc. In addition, it is useful to have information about the level of understanding attained by the child concerning the conservation of length. He is therefore asked whether two straight lines of 11 cm., which are shown side by side, remain the same length if one of them is transformed into an arc. Finally, again for the sake of information, he is shown an arc with a chord and asked (with the drawing still before him) whether the chord is equal to the arc, or longer or shorter.

We shall report only three of the many findings which we obtained with this technique. The first is that the straight lines resulting from drawing out arcs are at first heavily underestimated (and this even in relation to the mean of the underestimations found in copies) and that this systematic error diminishes with age, while the arcs resulting from bending straight lines are greatly overestimated and this error likewise is corrected with age (see Table 6).

The second finding was the discovery that children are not

---

[1] This research was carried out with Françoise Frank.

*Mental Images*

able, until about the age of 7, to picture, even by approximate images, the intermediate stages between the arc of a circle and the straight line that results from drawing it out, or *vice versa*.

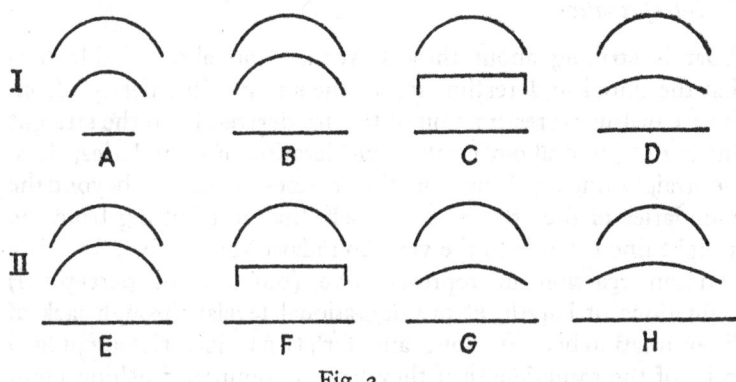

Fig. 2

Rather than enter into statistical detail, we shall simply give the eight types of drawings that we obtained showing the transformation of an arc into a straight line, a transformation which was in fact suggested to the child by pulling symbolically the two ends of an arc made of wire. Yet, among the drawings obtained (Fig. 2), series I (A–D) shows no increase in length (cf. Table 6) and drawing A even shows a decrease. Moreover, only drawings C and D show a flattening of the arc, but C does so in a discontinuous fashion and D correctly but without increase in length. In series II, where the increase has been achieved (E–H), only H is

TABLE 6

Estimation of the results
of the transformation of an arc into a straight line
(Mean of errors as %)

|  | Age 5 (*10 subjects*) | Age 6 (*9 subjects*) | Age 7 (*10 subjects*) | Age 8–9 (*10 subjects*) |
|---|---|---|---|---|
| Transformation of an arc into a straight line | −34 | −22 | −8 | −11 |
| Inverse transformation | +29 | +8 | +7 | +7 |

correct, while E–G present discontinuities either in the curve or in its extension.

## 3  Interpretation

What is striking about these drawings and about Table 6 is that the initial underestimation of the straight line derived from the arc or the overestimation of the arc derived from the straight line are brought about by the consideration of boundaries; thus, the straight line resulting from the arc does not extend beyond the boundaries of the arc and conversely the arc resulting from the straight line extends to the very boundaries of the line. This is a common reaction in representative (but not in perceptual) evaluations of length, at pre-operational levels: through lack of differentiation between 'long' and 'far', two trajectories are judged to be of the same length if they have a common finishing point irrespective of their starting points.

One could perhaps object that, in these initial reactions, the child's mental image does no more than express his notion and presents nothing special or interesting as an image. But where does this notion come from? First of all from the initial primacy of ordinal over metrical considerations, and this initial primacy is indeed notional in character and unrelated to images. To this must be added, however, that 1) these relations of order apply in the first place only to the finishing points; 2) 'far' does not replace 'long' through mere semantic misunderstanding but through lack of differentiation between them and 3) the consideration of boundaries that are not to be overstepped plays a general rather than a purely ordinal role, as we shall see in a later experiment. Our interpretation is therefore as follows: ordinal relations of a notional character are not the only factor responsible for initial reactions, indeed their excessive hold on the child comes precisely from the fact that they are linked to images. The characteristics peculiar to pre-operational thought could therefore largely be explained by the fact that it rests on images. Thus, we are once more led back to images. It is therefore by comparing them to the operations that begin at the age of about 7 or 8 that we must try to find the reason for the preceding reactions.

The solution can be sought in the following direction. The operation which is responsible for the transformation of an arc

## Mental Images

into a straight line, or *vice versa*, is essentially an 'act' which has two characteristics: *a*) it brings about the transformation in a continuous fashion, and *b*) it conserves the fixed length throughout the transformation. However, conservation of length is accepted by only 15 per cent at the age of 5 and it begins to be recognized only at the age of about 6 or 7; as to continuity, Table 6 and Figure 2 clearly show what conclusions we must draw. It is easy to see that, even at the operational level (and in adults even, no matter how mathematically inclined they may be) no mental image is sufficient to symbolize the operation adequately. No matter how adequately we try to visualize the transformation of an arc into a straight line or *vice versa*, our images proceed in jumps and do no more, according to Bergson's famous phrase, (which was in fact a criticism of imaged representation and not of intelligence as revealed in operations!) than to take instantaneous 'snapshots' amid the continuum, instead of attaining it as a transformation. What is more, none of our images, although in themselves static, give us the least assurance of conservation.... Thus, images cannot exhaust the operation and there are gaps, which are particularly numerous at the pre-operational level. The results are: inability to anticipate in imagination, inadequate intermediate images and (through failure to imagine the transitions symbolizing continuity) evaluation based only on the starting and finishing points and on the preferred character of boundaries. At the operational level, on the other hand, there appears a new type of image based on symbolic imitation of these operations which succeeds in multiplying 'snapshots' to stimulate a continuum and in anticipating approximately the continuation of the sequence thus evoked.

### 4   Images of a somersault

Another experiment shows equally clearly the link between anticipatory images and the constitution of operations. It consists in imagining the trajectory of a cardboard tube somersaulting in the air, with a rotation of 180°. Again drawings and gestures are used, but with the addition of verbal description. A 15 cm. cardboard tube is used. It projects over the edge of a spring-board so that one has only to press the free end with a forefinger to produce a somersault and to make the tube drop on the table with its ends reversed. At the outset, the front half of the tube is red and the back blue. When it comes to rest the colours are therefore reversed, in a way that is clearly perceptible to the subject.

The tube is first placed on the spring-board and the child is told to look carefully at what is going to happen as he will have to draw it. There follows the somersault and the tube is removed immediately after its fall. The child is then asked to draw the tube as it was on the 'box' and as it comes to rest on the table. He is next asked to draw intermediate stages. ('Draw the tube as it was soon after leaving the box; a little after that;' etc.) Then the tube is given back to the child who is asked, while holding it in his hand, to reproduce the movement it described (as slowly as possible). It is therefore not a matter of reproducing the somersault, but of following its course in slow motion holding the tube from beginning to end. The subject is also asked for a verbal description if he has not given one as he went along. Finally he must draw the trajectory of the two ends of the tube, one in red and the other in blue.

The following table gives the results for drawing, gesture and verbal description but does not take into account the degree of graphic success of the drawings. Eighty children were examined with E. Siotis, ranging in age from 4 to 7.

TABLE 7

Imagining the somersault performed by a tube
(rotation of 180°)
(Successes as % of number of subjects)

|  | Drawings of intermediate positions | Imitation | Verbal description | Trajectory of the ends | |
|---|---|---|---|---|---|
|  |  |  |  | One correct | Both correct |
| Age 4 (4 subjects) | 0 | 25 | 25 | 0 | 0 |
| Age 5 (18 subjects) | 0 | 23 | 59 | 0 | 0 |
| Age 6 (19 subjects) | 18 | 42 | 64 | 28 | 0 |
| Age 7 (20 subjects) | 42 | 45 | 75 | 30 | 5 |
| Age 8 (19 subjects) | 60 | 70 | 100 | 30 | 60 |

*Mental Images*

The verbal description was judged correct as soon as the idea of rotation was expressed in some way: 'It fell over backwards', 'It turned over', 'This side (the back) came to the front,' etc. We are thus concerned with global comprehension, which does not imply detailed determination of the trajectory in all its continuity, but which does include the notion of the final state seen as the outcome of the transformation. It is instructive to observe that this comprehension precedes imaged representation. It is better than reproduction by imitative gesture, which in its turn is better than drawing.

## 5 Reversal of the ends

As to the permutation of the coloured ends following rotation, we tried to establish 1) whether it was noticed and 2) whether it can be imagined. In order to answer the second question, we gave other subjects a white tube and asked them, after drawing the starting and finishing positions, to assign a distinctive colour to each of the ends in the starting position, and then to show how these are placed after the somersault. The results were as follows:

TABLE 8

Permutation of colours
(as % of successes)

|  | *Age 5* | *Age 6* | *Age 7* | *Age 8* |
|---|---|---|---|---|
| Coloured tube | 47 | 50 | 66 | 100 |
| White tube | 50 | 60 | 71 | 100 |

It is first of all apparent that what might be called copy-images (cf. Section 5 and below, paragraph 7) are no better than anticipatory images, since they refer to the result of a transformation and in this sphere adequate observation calls for a measure of comprehension. Next, it is apparent that these results are better than those in Table 7, except where verbal description is concerned. This again shows that operational comprehension is ahead of representation or of images portraying the details of the transformation. But it shows, above all (and that is why we kept Tables 7 and 8 separate) that it is easier to imagine the result of a

## Jean Piaget and Bärbel Inhelder

transformation (i.e. the new order of colours) than the transformation itself (i.e. the permutation as a reversal of order resulting from rotation). This is because the result of a transformation is only a state and a static image is all that is needed to represent it. This accounts for the simplicity of the images which we referred to as RTP and ATP at the beginning of Section 5. The transformation itself, however, is a dynamic continuum and imagining the successive stages (RTM or ATM in our notation) remains much more symbolic and subordinate to the operation. Yet, despite the greater simplicity of the image of the result (cf. the figure of 100 per cent at age 8 as against 60 or 70 per cent in Table 7), it is only at about the age of 7 or 8 that it rises to 75 per cent because it is subordinate to operational comprehension. Thus, although the result of the transformation is only a state, it is a state that is imagined and even observed only in so far as it is produced by the transformation, and this presupposes that the latter is 'understood' even if it cannot yet be represented by adequate images.

## 6 The displacement of a square

In view of the fact that anticipatory images relating to the change in shape or rotation of an object are so late in appearing, what of the anticipation of a transformation which is no more than the simple displacement (translation) of one of the elements of a figure in relation to another? We studied this with F. Frank and T. Bang.

Two 5 cm. square cards, one above the other and touching (Fig. 3, A) are presented to the child and the experimenter checks first that the child can draw this configuration. Then the child is asked to make a drawing anticipating what the figure will look like after the top square has been slightly pushed from left to right while the lower square remains where it is (Fig. 3, H). Once the child's drawing has been obtained, he is asked to choose the correct figure among ready-made drawings. It is necessary to take the usual precautions with the youngest subjects: showing only a few drawings at a time and, if several are said to be correct, asking which is the best. As the choices appeared to be affected by the perseveration of the anticipations that had preceded them, we finally decided to study anticipations and choices with separate groups. As a final question, the children are asked to copy the correct figure (H) to make sure that such a drawing

*Mental Images*

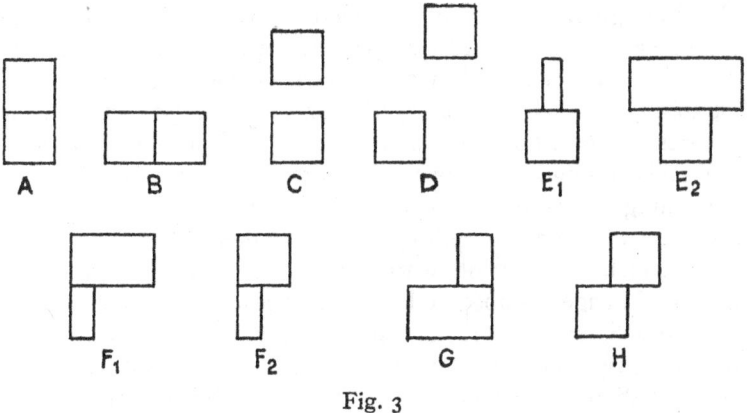

Fig. 3

is possible. Several other controls were carried out: the same tests were administered but with non-contiguous squares separated by a space of 1 cm., or with contiguous squares of different colours, or varying the instructions by saying that both squares would move at once in opposite directions.

TABLE 9

Graphic anticipations of the displacement of a square (in % of solutions) and choice among ready-made drawings (in brackets)

| Figures drawn | A–D | $E_1$–$E_2$ | $F_1$–$F_2$–G | H (Correct) |
| --- | --- | --- | --- | --- |
| Age 4 (13 subjects) | 55·5 (41·4) | 11·1 (6·9) | 5·6 (24·2) | 27·8 (27·5) |
| Age 5 (21 subjects) | 29·0 (33·3) | 4·0 (9·8) | 33·0 (23·5) | 34·0 (33·3) |
| Age 6 (21 subjects) | 7·0 (12·6) | 7·0 (6·3) | 40·0 (28·2) | 53·0 (53·0) |
| Age 7 (10 subjects) | 0·0 (0·0) | 7·0 (7·0) | 15·5 (15·5) | 77·5 (77·5) |

Choices among ready-made drawings, representing the possible solutions given in the anticipations, are except at the age of 4 remarkably in agreement with individual anticipations. This already provides an answer to the possible objection that the scarcity of correct solutions among young children is due to difficulty in drawing figure H and not to difficulty in visualizing it as an image. However, as we have already said, a control was carried out by asking the subjects to make a direct copy of figure

H. Although an exact copy was made by only 32 per cent of the 19 subjects at age 4 and by 48 per cent of the 23 subjects at age 5 to 5·5, it was achieved by 79 per cent of the 19 subjects at age 5·6 to 5·11. Let us also note that when a space is left between the squares, one still finds errors of the type A–C but mostly figures of type D. Using squares of two colours does not improve results. Imagining the simultaneous displacement of two squares in opposite directions complicates the solutions.

To conclude, it is interesting from the point of view of the theory of images to observe how static they remain until the age of 7 and 8, even in such a simple case as a straightforward relative displacement. The subject may very well show by gestures the displacement of the top square but this is a global image. As soon as it comes to visualizing detail, either the top square becomes detached from the bottom square (drawings B to D) or the child begins to imagine the spatial shift, but pictures it as symmetrical ($E_1$ and $E_2$) or else visualizes a projection to one side but a block at the other boundary (F, G).

## 7 Kinetic anticipatory images

We must now mention another type of experiment, relating to purely kinetic anticipatory images, that is, not to a transformation where a possible displacement is imagined but to the simple continuation of a movement of which the beginning is perceived. We have in this connection resumed with E. Siotis earlier research on the notion of speed which had brought to notice the role of 'overtaking' (cf. Chapter 24, Section 4, 4). In an experiment where we used two moving objects travelling at unequal speeds, and where one was about to overtake the other before they both stopped, we had been struck by the fact that young subjects either did not anticipate the continuation of these movements or else took into account only the order of the finishing points with no regard to the movements themselves. Here, then, is a field to be explored from the point of view of anticipatory images.

> The moving objects used as models follow two rectilinear and parallel courses 90 cm. long, the last third of which is through a tunnel. Before reaching the tunnel, the two cars, one red, one yellow, go through the following motions (with carefully regulated synchronism over 1½ seconds and with respectively constant speeds): *a*) over-

taking (just before entering the tunnel); *b*) catching up (at the exact moment of entry); and *c*) partial catching up. The points of departure are always staggered, one of the cars is always quicker than the other (but sometimes it is the one, sometimes the other) and both stop in the tunnel. The child is placed facing the half-way mark and looks down perpendicularly on the courses. He has a strip of paper 1·80 m. long, without a tunnel (but the part corresponding to the tunnel is coloured blue like the tunnel); every 10 cm. there are little strokes dividing the strip into equal segments (so that the experimenter can see whether the subject varies the intervals between the cars). The only two questions that interest us here are: *a*) reproducing the movements perceived (after the model cars have stopped inside the tunnel and so without a visible finishing point), and *b*) anticipating (immediately after the reproduction called for in question 1) the continuation of the movements perceived, on the understanding that the respective speeds are maintained (that 'they go on travelling as before'). These questions are then followed by a verbal question *c*) on the speeds involved, to determine the operational level of the subject but this does not concern us here, except indirectly. Finally *d*) the tunnel is removed and the subject is asked to reproduce the relative movements of the two cars (and not merely the starting and finishing positions).

It will be observed that the two questions (*a* and *b*) do in fact concern only mental images, reproductive in the case of (*a*) and anticipatory in (*b*). The subject is not asked to estimate speeds but exclusively to reproduce what he has seen, then to prolong it through anticipation. One could almost suspect, where success proves general, that such anticipation is no more than simple perseveration. The interest of the results obtained with 161 children aged 5 to 11 lay precisely in showing that, even where there is correct reproduction, anticipation does not result from it by way of a simple prolongation, but implies new and original contributions.

Let us begin by noting, but without dwelling on the fact since the problem was already mentioned in Section 5, that the reproduction of movements is far from being perfect and does indeed confirm what was said at the beginning of Section 6, 3 about the difference between images and operations from the double standpoint of continuity and conservation: in young children, reproduction of movement proceeds in jerks, without conservation of speed, thus with noticeable acceleration before catching up and temporary increase in the interval between the moving objects after overtaking. It is only towards the age of 8 that subjects realize that in order to reproduce movements accurately it is necessary to see the objects move, that is, to take into account the kinetic continuum (with conservation) and not merely the finishing points, or starting and finishing points. Here are the results of the final reproductions (question *d*).

TABLE 10

Reproduction of the movements of two cars (with no tunnel) (in % of number of subjects)

|  | Age 5 (*30 subjects*) | Age 6 (*30 subjects*) | Age 7 | Age 8 | Age 9 | Ages 10–11 |
|---|---|---|---|---|---|---|
| Overtaking | 20 | 35·2 | 64·7 | 73·6 | 100 | — |
| Catching up | 13·3 | 11·7 | 41·1 | 63·1 | 100 | — |
| Partial catching up | 0 | 5·8 | 47 | 42·1 | 60 | 81 |

Regarding anticipation, we shall distinguish three categories of reactions: 1) no anticipations, not even of the ordinal type; 2) purely ordinal anticipations, that is, taking into account only the order (before and after) of the cars and not the extent of the spatial intervals between them; 3) 'hyperordinal' anticipation (taking the term in the same sense as Suppes), which foresees that the spatial interval between the cars increases progressively. The results computed in the absolute and also in relation to the number of subjects who gave a good reproduction are given overleaf (Table 11).

The conclusion to be drawn from this experiment is thus clear and confirms those of the three preceding experiments. In the first place, one observes that while hyperordinal consideration of increasing and decreasing intervals plays a fundamental part in the perception of speed,[1] it does not play a decisive part in anticipatory images (72–77 per cent) until the age of about 10 or 11, when the ordinal operations of speed (overtaking) give way to metrical operations ($v = s/t$). One then observes that ordinal anticipations only gradually assert themselves (approximately

[1] See Piaget, Feller and McNear, *Arch. Psychol.* (Rech. XXXVI).

TABLE II

Ordinal anticipations (O) and hyperordinal anticipations (Ho) in relation to the number of accurate reproductions
(in brackets O + Ho as absolute %)*

| | Overtaking | | | Catching up | | | Partial catching up | | |
|---|---|---|---|---|---|---|---|---|---|
| | Ho | O | (Ho±O) abs. | Ho | O | (Ho±O) abs. | Ho | O | (Ho±O) abs. |
| Age 5 (29 subjects) | 10.6 | | (31.5) | 0.0 | 50.0 | (18.0) | 0.0 | 15.3 | (7.0) |
| Age 6 (30 subjects) | 23.3 | | (53.2) | 10.0 | 60.0 | (46.6) | 16.6 | 58.3 | (43.2) |
| Age 7 (24 subjects) | 40.0 | | (70.7) | 22.2 | 53.3 | (49.9) | 25.0 | 25.0 | (21.6) |
| Age 8 (25 subjects) | 43.8 | | (72.0) | 10.5 | 57.8 | (56.0) | 15.3 | 53.8 | (52.0) |
| Age 9 (34 subjects) | 50.0 | | (76.4) | 27.2 | 45.4 | (50.0) | 38.8 | 55.5 | (51.5) |
| Ages 10–11 (19 subjects) | 76.5 | | (89.4) | 72.2 | 16.6 | (84.1) | 77.0 | 23.0 | (81.2) |

* The O column refers to the anticipation of straightforward overtaking in cases where only catching up or partial catching up are visible. In the case of visible overtaking, relative ordinal anticipation has no meaning and merges with accurate reproductions.

between the ages of 6 and 8) linked this time with ordinal operaations. Briefly, whereas reproductive images proceed in static and discontinuous 'snapshots', images can only become anticipatory when directed by operations, by dint of multiplying 'snapshots' and orientating them according to a new mode of comprehension, based on continuous transformation and no longer exclusively on the reproduction of configurations.

## 8   The evolution of images

The conclusion of Section 6, like the evolution of images, is not independent, in the sense that the anticipatory images which characterize the later stages do not simply derive from the reproductive images of earlier stages. Like perception (Chapter 18), the activities of which are framed by the whole action and then by intelligence, images do not develop in an autonomous fashion and this appears to be a general characteristic of the figurative forms of cognitive activity; imitation also, in which images seem to be a product of internalization, cannot be achieved without the assistance of operative intelligence[1] since the child, like the chimpanzee, imitates only what it can at least partially understand. Images therefore begin at pre-operational levels by being reproductive only and attached to configurations (including kinetic configurations) rather than to transformations. Proceeding as they do by discontinuous and static 'snapshots', they long remain incapable of symbolizing transformations. But following the constitution of intellectual operations, whose role is precisely that of grasping these transformations through acts of dynamic comprehension, there appears a new type of image based on the imitation of these operations. Now, the imitation of an operation is not an operation, for it fails to capture the continuity of the operation as well as the unique synthesis of invariances and transformations, but it imitates these new characteristics by multiplying 'snapshots' of the internal movement of the operational act. In this it allows itself to be guided by the movement itself and achieves the illusion of continuity by a diffuse consciousness of the jumps leading from each snapshot to the next.

[1] The reader is reminded that we use the term 'operative' to refer to that aspect of intelligence which embraces actions (physical or internalized) and operations. This is by opposition to the term 'operational', which refers to operations alone.

# 7 Images and thought: the role of images in the preparation and functioning of operations

## 1 Introduction

Binet and the Würzburg School showed the existence of 'thought without images', although it would be better described as thought distinct from images, since as I. Meyerson (1932) stresses, it may be that all thought, even when distinct from images, needs imaged symbolic support besides the system of linguistic signs. We now know that this aspect of thought, distinct from images, is operational in nature. An operation is, in fact, unrepresentable in itself, being an act which is apt to become 'pure' in the sense in which one speaks of 'pure mathematics', that is, independent of any object. Thus, a number does not carry with it any image, except in a symbolic capacity: if one tries to imagine the number 4, one can 'see' four apples, or the sign 4, etc., but the number as such is something quite different and is defined by the bi-univocal correspondence between all sets of the same power. This correspondence in turn may also be symbolized, for example by spatial rows linked term-for-term, but in generalizing to 'all' one no longer imagines anything. That type of reasoning which, after verifying that a property is true at O and that it is also true for $n+1$ if it is true for $n$, concludes that it is true of 'all' numbers, may rest at the outset on more or less distinct imaged 'intuitions'. These symbolize among other things the succession of whole numbers, but these images provide an evocation that is ridiculously restricted in relation to the infinite.... If we turn to the child, we find that he long denies all conservation. Eventually he comes to admit that when the shape of an object is changed, the quantity of substance remains invariant, because increase in one dimension is offset by decrease in another. The point here is that the child's image may well 'symbolize' an approximate compensation but it cannot of itself represent exact conservation or compensation even though operational thought recognizes these to be necessary.

Nevertheless, it is unlikely that we ever carry out an operation without imaged symbolic support and the most abstract mathematicians recognize that even if 'intuition' has no demonstrative value, it remains indispensable as a tool for further discovery. This presents a problem and it remains for us to try to establish how far reproductive or anticipatory images contribute to the formation or at least to the functioning of nascent or higher operations. But, here again, the answer cannot come from theoretical discussion. Experimentation alone is instructive.

The method consists in going back to a number of known operational tests (see Chapter 24) and asking the subjects to anticipate by means of images some of the data and the products of particular transformations. This they must do prior to the manipulation and actual transformation of the objects concerned. This method has proved a fruitful one for in many respects it enables us to establish that images are ahead of operations, at least apparently. This forwardness must be interpreted and confronted with the apparently contrary results set out in Section 6, concerning the tardy formation of anticipatory images and their dependence on operations.

## 2 Anticipation of the seriation of lengths

An easily reproduceable experiment concerns the seriation of lengths.

> The child is presented with ten little strips of wood ranging from 10 to 16·5 cm., placed in random order on a table, and he is asked to sort them into a 'staircase', starting with the shortest and ending with the longest. Following the usual technique, which is not directed at the problem of images, the child is allowed to manipulate the elements from the beginning and one thus obtains three levels from the operational standpoint (for results in figures, see Chapter 24, Table 8).
> 
> There is first of all the failure level where the child proceeds in pairs or small series which bear no ordered relation to each other. Next there is a level of pre-operational success where the child arrives at the correct series, but by trial and error and empirical corrections. Finally there is the operational level (age 7–8) where the child tries first to find, by paired comparisons, the smallest of all the elements, A, and having found it sets it down first; secondly the smallest of those that are left, B, which he puts in second place; thirdly the next smallest, C, etc. This level is called operational because the child uses a systematic and exhaustive method and because this method implies comprehension of the fact that a particular element, E, is at once bigger than those preceding it ($E > D, C, B,$

*Mental Images*

A) and smaller than those following (E < F, G, ...), which implies reversibility by reciprocity.[1] To analyse the possible role of images, one will then proceed as follows:

1) instead of allowing immediate manipulation of the strips of wood, the subject will be asked to imagine the result of seriation and, for instance, to draw in advance with a black crayon the 'staircase' to be achieved. We shall call this 'global anticipation' and it can also be symbolised by gestures; 2) strips of distinctive colours will be used and the child will be offered crayons of corresponding colours (with a few extra colours) and will be asked (before any manipulation) to make a coloured drawing of the series to be constructed, observing the correspondence between colours and lengths: this we shall call 'analytical anticipation'.

The results obtained are very clear as to the distinction between global and analytical anticipations:

TABLE 12

Percentage of graphic varieties of anticipation of seriation

|  | Age 4 (19 subjects) | Age 5 (33 subjects) | Age 6 (19 subjects) | Age 7 (10 subjects) | Ages 8–9 (7 subjects) |
|---|---|---|---|---|---|
| Failure in anticipation | 89 | 42 | 5 | 0 | 0 |
| Global anticipation | 11 | 55 | 73 | 20 | 0 |
| Analytical anticipation | 0 | 3 | 22 | 80 | 100 |

It is evident from this that global anticipation is found much earlier than operational seriation (see Chapter 24, Table 8). This amounts to saying that a large number of subjects are perfectly capable of drawing the series in advance (in black or without taking the order of colours into account), but cannot for all this construct it by an operational method (they are content to make successive groping attempts until they arrive at a configuration that conforms to their internal model). Analytical anticipation, on the other hand, is at least as difficult as operational seriation.

[1] This operational solution is achieved by 6% of the 5-year-olds (the same children as will be mentioned in connection with images), 22% of 6-year-olds, 80% of 7-year-olds and 85% of 8-year-olds. For more extensive statistical results, see Chapter 24, Table 8.

*Jean Piaget and Bärbel Inhelder*

## 3 Interpretation

The reason for these facts seems clear. As global anticipation is not sufficient to give rise to the operation (there is a two years' time lag), it cannot be interpreted as a preparation for the operation, nor even as an anticipatory image, for a series of elements of uniform gradation is perceptually a 'good form' and its evocation amounts to no more than a reproductive image copying this perceptible form. The fact of achieving a drawing without blurs does not imply operational reversibility, since this is a one-way action. It is much easier to produce pencil strokes of increasing length (since these are freely decided) than to find among disordered objects those which obey a law of regular increment. Analytical anticipation, on the other hand, supposes that the subject orders the objects themselves, since in this case he must assign to each pencil stroke a colour corresponding to that of the object differentiated according to its size. Anticipation thus presupposes genuine seriation, by combination of percepts and images, but the overall image which is thus genuinely anticipatory rests *ipso facto* on the operation. In fact it merges with the 'draft' or plan of the actual operation.

Another variety of anticipatory image was studied by A. Rey who showed that it was based on the operation of seriation. It enables us to confirm these two interpretations. Rey (1944) had the ingenious idea of presenting to children a square sheet of paper with a square drawn in the middle and asking them to draw on the same sheet 'the smallest possible square'[1] next to the square already drawn (or alternatively 'the largest possible square' that can be drawn on the sheet). From the age of 8, subjects succeed in drawing a square of $1-2$ mm$^2$. (or, in the opposite case, one closely following the edges of the paper), while the youngest subjects, despite their efforts at reducing or increasing the scale continue for a long time to produce squares scarcely smaller and scarcely larger than the original square. Rey correctly interprets this failure of small children as due to a lack of anticipation. They are not able to rely on operations of seriation

---

[1] The original square in the middle of the sheet was drawn by the child himself. He is then told: 'Now draw, next to it, the smallest square that can be drawn; draw a square so small that it couldn't be any smaller.' If the child fails, he is asked whether he can't make an even smaller square, etc.

*Mental Images*

but from the age of 7 or 8 the handling of this operational structure makes it possible to clear in one leap the series of intermediate squares between the one given and the one required. One then sees why it is that this anticipatory image, even if the question asked does not explicitly call for an operation, is of late development. It is because, like the analytical anticipation of drawings in colour, it rests in fact on seriation as an operation, whereas global anticipation does no more then evoke in advance the required configuration, which could be the product of an operation but is not necessarily so (unlike Rey's largest and smallest possible squares), since it is also simply a good perceptual form.

## 4 Anticipation of conservation

A second experiment, itself the prototype of a series of others, has yielded similar results. It shows that images are partly ahead of operations and it also shows the use made of images in operations and the final subordination of states or configurations to transformations which cannot be represented figuratively in an adequate fashion.

Former observations (see Chapter 24, Section 2, 5) had taught us that if one transfers a liquid from a glass A, to a glass B which is narrower and taller than A, or into a glass C which is wider and lower, a child of 5 to 6 does not believe in the conservation of the quantity of liquid transferred. At the age of 5 (see Chapter 24, Table 4) one obtains only 4 per cent total success, at 6, 18 per cent and at 7, 74 per cent (as against 85 per cent total failure at 5, 40 per cent at 6, and 4 per cent at 7, the other reactions being intermediate). We therefore asked ourselves with S. Taponier: 1) whether children of 5 to 6 would imagine conservation or the reverse when the transfer was not physically performed (or else performed behind a screen so that only the outline of glasses B and C could be seen) but simply anticipated in thought; 2) what anticipatory image they would have of the levels reached by the liquid in the course of these imagined transfers; 3) how they would imagine the levels reached by two equal quantities ( = the same amount 'to drink') in glasses A and B.[1]

The results are very decisive. Out of 44 + 30 subjects (the

[1] Independently, therefore, of any transfer.

latter with six glasses instead of three), 4 categories of responses were found (*a* to *d*). First, we should note that the levels were correctly anticipated (for 3 glasses: question 2) by 25 per cent of the subjects at age 4 and 5, 38 per cent at age 6, 63 per cent at age 7 and 72 per cent at age 8.

*a*) First there are the subjects who anticipate conservation (question 1); they also imagine that the levels will be maintained despite differences in shape and size between the glasses (question 2), they assign equal levels to equal quantities (question 3) and therefore no longer believe in conservation when the liquid is actually transferred at the end of the experiment.

*b*) Then there are subjects who anticipate the levels correctly (question 2), but who do not anticipate any conservation (question 1), because they believe that equal quantities mean equal levels (question 3). They therefore continue to deny conservation when the liquid is actually transferred.

*c*) There are subjects who foresee conservation, who correctly anticipate the levels (questions 2 and 3) and thus maintain their opinions when the liquid is transferred at the end.

*d*) Finally there are a few aberrant subjects who postulate conservation (through simple identity) without being able to predict the levels.

If one calculates the relation between anticipation of levels (question 2) and final conservation (after actual transfer) one finds that

*a*) 30 per cent fail to imagine levels and final conservation;
*b*) 23 per cent succeed in imagining the levels but fail in the final conservation;
*c*) 42 per cent succeed in imagining the levels and succeed with the final conservation;
*d*) 5 per cent fail to imagine the levels but succeed with the final conservation.

It therefore seems that in cases where levels are accurately imagined prior to any notion of conservation (category *b*), there is only a reproductive image based on acquired experience. Every child may have occasion to pour liquid from a wider to a narrower container! It is also evident that the image of levels is not sufficient in itself to give rise to operations of compensation, which are the source of the notion of conservation. This is shown by the fact that subjects in this category (*b*) think that two identical

*Mental Images*

quantities of liquid poured into two different glasses A and B will give the same levels (question 3) as if quantity was measured by level alone!

The conclusions to be drawn from this type of experiment, as from the previous type (see Section 7, 2) are therefore first that operations transcend images, while making use of them; and second that, once brought into play, operations direct images and even determine them almost entirely in some cases. That is why in order to imagine the inequality of levels in glasses A, B, and C, given equal quantities of liquid, it is necessary to introduce an operational system of compensation;[1] since the image of the levels is here a function not of a transfer to be anticipated but of an equality to be achieved between two distinct quantities of liquid. In a general way, in fact, no image of compensation can acquire any true degree of approximation without relying on a system of operations, deductive or metrical.

8 Spatial images and 'geometrical intuition'

---

It is true in a general way that images constitute symbols which are relatively adequate when they represent static configurations but which become less and less adequate when they attempt to represent increasingly complex operational transformations. Nevertheless, there exists a whole category of images that have remarkable relative adequacy, even concerning transformations. We refer to spatial images, the source of what mathematicians call geometrical intuition. The psychological problem raised by these images consists in establishing whether their particular adequacy is due to an autonomous development of imagery itself, or whether it results from the progressive intervention of operations, indeed of specifically spatial operations. If it is to be attributed to these operations, there is no doubt that their specific character would account for the fact that they can be represented by adequate images.

---

[1] The relations between question 3 and the final conservation are: 42% succeeding in both, 54% failing in both and 4% succeeding in conservation but failing question 3.

## Jean Piaget and Bärbel Inhelder

### 1 Distinctive character of spatial images

The particular position of spatial images is due to the relations between their form and content, and it is necessary to specify this point in order to understand the experiments that will follow. The 'form' of an image is spatio-temporal in character, since images are an internalized imitation of objects and events as they appear in space (visual images, etc.) and in time (auditory images). When images have as their 'content' (that is to say tend to refer to) logical or arithmetical operations, these operations usually possess spatio-temporal points of reference. This makes it possible to have an image of their results (except in the case of purely formal operations, not applied to concrete objects). On the other hand, these logico-arithmetical operations remain acts of transformation, which cannot be represented by images because they have nothing to do with spatial configurations. It is possible to imagine a sequence of numbers as a row of little strokes, etc., or to imagine classifying operations by means of circles (Euler circles) or of compartments that can be inserted or taken out. These images, however, provide only very approximate symbolism (except where there is isomorphism between certain algebraic and topological structures). What they do, in fact, is merely to translate non-spatio-temporal transformations into imaged, and therefore spatialized, forms. In the case of spatial images, on the other hand, the contents to be represented are spatial like the imaged forms which represent them and spatial operations (displacements, projections, etc.) are again figurative transformations and so, in a sense, figures in space. There is then more or less complete homogeneity between form and content and this is enough to account for the privileged character of spatial images.

From this particular homogeneity, there follow two fundamental consequences. The first is that spatial images are the only images in which the symbolizing form tends to complete isomorphism with the symbolized content. The image of a number or a class is not a number or a class but an image of numbered or classified objects, while the image of a square is approximately square and the image of a straight line, while having width, may be considered as a sheath of parallel straight lines. The second consequence is that the field of spatial images is the only one

*Mental Images*

where images of transformations are situated on the same plane as static images and anticipatory images on the same plane as reproductive images. Given sufficient practice, geometrical intuition can thus enable one to 'see in space' the transformations themselves, even at times the most complex and the furthest removed from common physical experience. This is because the image rests on a spatialized imitation of operations which are themselves spatial.

## 2 Images of development[1]

It is of vital interest to the theory of images to establish whether images of transformation, and in particular anticipatory images, derive simply from internal progress and the progressive flexibility of reproductive images or whether the development of geometrical 'intuition' depends necessarily on that of operations. To solve this question, one might be tempted to keep to the experiments described in Sections 4 to 6, since most of these already refer to spatial images. It is more interesting, however, to study areas which correspond, on the one hand, to familiar observations concerning particular aspects of the child's spontaneous graphic images (evolution of drawing) and, on the other, to the possible intervention of certain well defined geometrical operations, the development of which is already known to us. Among the many examples available, we shall mention only one, which is particularly striking: that of so called 'rotations' in children's drawings, so well described by Luquet, which we shall consider in conjunction with truly geometrical operations of development. The question lies in establishing whether or not imagery occurring in the former can lead to anticipatory images giving an adequate visual representation of the transformations involved in the corresponding operations.

We do in fact know that children's drawings are commonly characterized by a phenomenon which we shall call 'pseudo-rotation' and which Luquet aptly described as a 'mixture of viewpoints'. In one of the examples which he quotes, a horse is drawn in profile pulling a cart which is not represented in the

[1] Translator's Note: 'Development' is used here in a technical sense: '*Geom.* The action of unrolling a cylindrical or conical surface, the unbending of any curved surface into a plane, or of any non plane curve into a plane curve.' (O.E.D.)

same perspective but shown in plan view from above. As for the wheels, they are all four on the same horizontal plane which supposes a rotation of 90° in relation to the floor of the cart.[1] In fact, therefore, three distinct viewpoints are mixed and juxtaposed. One can wonder whether subjects who are capable of thus dissociating viewpoints, will succeed in anticipating by images the result of the unfolding of cardboard cubes, cylinders or cones, of which all the elements are developed on a single horizontal plane. The analysis of reactions, by age groups, gives two results contrary to this hypothesis: *a*) imagining the result of true developments goes far beyond the level of spontaneous pseudo-rotations, since it supposes a *co-ordination* of viewpoints (and not simply a random mixture), hence an operational factor based on the action of unfolding itself; *b*) correct images of these developments result from an internal imitation of the actions of unfolding and of their results and are not a mere extension of perceptions or of the spontaneous pseudo-rotations occurring in drawing. The latter merely express the diversity of possible perceptions (each imitated separately as a reproductive image), but the capacity for anticipation resulting from operational co-ordinations is lacking.

Three stages have been observed (bearing in mind that standardization of the test is not yet complete). During the first stage (until about the age of 6, that is, at the ages corresponding to pseudo-rotations in drawing) children are not yet capable of imagining any true development. They draw the whole object without transformation.

During the second stage, fruitless efforts are made to imagine development and the drawings express these attempts in a symbolic form. The side of a tube to be rotated is, for instance, drawn with a line indicating the direction of the rotation; or again, a slit is put in to symbolize the beginning of the action required to unfold the side, etc.

During the third stage (from the age of 7 or 8) development is at last imagined and drawn, but in progressive stages according to an order of hierarchy among objects; first cylinders and cones, then cubes—a little more difficult because of their six sides—and finally pyramids.

---

[1] Two of the wheels are shown below the floor of the cart, as if they were situated in the same perspective as the horse, but the other two are drawn above, which therefore shows a general rotation of 90° for the four wheels, without relation to the position of the horse.

*Mental Images*

In short, this example like all the others so far observed seems to show that although geometrical intuition really is the preferred sphere of mobile and anticipatory images, there is no question of a capacity present at all ages nor of a product purely of mental imagery. Such 'intuition' is in fact essentially operational and images play their essential part only when guided and informed by operations.

## 9  Conclusion

At the close of this survey of the problems relating to mental images, we should like to recall briefly the questions set out in Section 1, 3 to find out how far the facts we have reported assist in providing a solution and above all how much remains to be done before proceeding to verifications that are properly demonstrative.

1) Concerning the role of motor activity in the production of images, psychophysiological data already offer a partial demonstration, but we have as yet no reliable data concerning centres and pathways. Apart from this, we do not as yet understand the link between the motor aspect of images and their quasi-sensory aspect: is it a matter of partial sensory reafferent impulses, of a simple symbolic evocation or of a special mechanism ensuring Penfield's flash-back?

2) Concerning the stage of development at which images appear, what we have said owes a lot to conjecture. Psychoanalysts date back imaged symbols to well before the level of the second year, which is where we ourselves situated it (with symbolic play and deferred imitation). The discussions which one of us (Piaget) had on this subject at the Menninger Foundation at Topeka (U.S.A.) led to the conclusion that the most appropriate verification at this stage would be to apply to infants at various levels of development the techniques used by Dement and Wolpert to record eye movements during sleep. There is no doubt, indeed, that dreams begin before the age of 12 to 16 months. But are they motor dreams (as is probably the case in dogs, who bark while they are asleep) or symbolic dreams? Dr. Riley Gardner has undertaken to pursue research in this direction at Topeka.

3) Concerning the supposed relationship between images and material imitation which is subsequently internalized, a choice field which would perhaps admit of decisive verifications would be that of the development of the body schema. It seems very probable that its genesis is closely linked to the development of imitation and that it is also accompanied by the formation of images. The extraordinary thing is that we do not yet have detailed scales concerning the evolution of the body schema and reference should therefore be made to the experiment by J. Bergès and I. Lézine on the imitation of gestures from the ages of 3 to 6 (1963).

4) Concerning the relations between images and drawing, we once made a qualitative study of stereognosis (or haptic perception) from this standpoint to determine to what extent and how directly drawings produced by the child as visual correspondents of objects which he touches without seeing express his movements of exploration. Detailed standardization has yet to follow. In a general way, it would be instructive to extend further the analysis of relations between drawing, copying by gesture and mental images (as revealed, for example, by choices among prepared drawings).

5–6) Concerning the classification and evolution of images, our results seem to indicate that there is a fairly systematic difficulty in passing from reproductive to anticipatory images and that, in the course of this transition, it is necessary to introduce operational factors foreign to images. But these results refer only to averages irrespective of all typological considerations. The fact is that the diversity of imagery in adults has always been recognized. Some people are particularly visual, others mainly motor, auditory, etc. It would be very interesting to study the question from a genetic angle and where one finds early typological diversity, to select a few particularly visual or particularly non-visual subjects in order to re-examine with both types problems relating both to the transition from reproductive images to anticipatory images and to the relations between images and operations.

7–8) With reference to the relations between images and thought, it is probable that the last word has yet to be said, for if one accepts the proposed distinction between the operative and the figurative aspects—and we shall need many more facts before we can decide whether such a distinction is fundamental or arti-

## Mental Images

ficial—it follows that images are at once necessary to represent states but insufficient to understand transformations, and this somewhat modifies the terms of a classical problem. It is probable that more detailed analysis of geometrical intuition in pure geometry and in the geometrical representation of phenomena will supply the key to these questions. Although we can nowadays study the beginnings of geometrical intuition, we are strangely at a loss regarding all that concerns both its functioning and the respective parts played by images and operations in the thought processes of scientists who make a daily and creative use of this 'intuition'. One of us (Piaget) was the pupil of a great tectonician who had founded 'alpine embryology' and who was gifted with extraordinary vision in space, as shown for instance by his work on the overthrust of folds: 'I can see them moving,' he would say, looking at a chain of mountains of which he had made a particular study. What lessons could not be drawn from a close analysis of the play of images in the thought of such men? Yet no research of this kind is known to have been undertaken.

9) One day a connection will be established between genetic studies of the integration of functions and the psychopathological study of their disintegration. Had this already been done, it would probably have been impossible to write a chapter on images without recourse to the theories concerning hallucination. The fact that it has not been so clearly shows the extent of the field which remains to be explored before we can master in their most general forms the laws of images in their relations to the laws of thought.

# Bibliography

AJURIAGUERRA, J. de, HÉCAEN, H., *Le cortex cérébral. Étude neuro-psychopathologique*, 2nd ed., Paris, Masson, 1960

ALLERS, R., SCHEMINSKY, F., 'Ueber Aktionsströme der Muskeln bei motorischen Vorstellungen und verwandten Vorgängen,' *Arch.f.d. ges. Physiol.*, 1926, **212**, 169–82

ASERINSKY, E., KLEITMAN, N., 'Two Types of Ocular Motility Occurring in Sleep', *J. appl. Physiol.*, 1955, **8**, 1–10

BERGÈS, J., LEZINE, I., *Test d'imitation de gestes*, Paris, Masson, 1963

BINET, A., *The Psychology of Reasoning*, London, Kegan Paul, 1899

— *L'étude expérimentale de l'intelligence*, Paris, Schleicher, 1903

DEMENT, W., KLEITMANN, N., 'The Relation of Eye Movements during Sleep to Dream Activity', *J. exp. Psychol.*, 1957, **53**, 339–46

DEMENT, W., WOLPERT, E. A., 'The Relation of Eye Movements, Body Motility and External Stimuli to Dream Content', *J. exp. Psychol.*, 1958, **55**, 543–53

FOERSTER, O., BUMKE, O., *Handbuch der Neurologie*, VI, Berlin, 1936

GASTAUT, H., TERZIAN, H., GASTAUT, Y., Etude d'une activité électroencéphalographique méconnue: le rythme rolandique en arceaux, *Marseille Med.*, 1952, **89**, 1–16

GASTAUT, H., BERT, I., 'EEG changes during cinematographic presentation', *EEG clin. Neurophysiol.*, 1954, **6**, 433–44

GROOS, K., *Die Spiele der Tiere*, Iéna, 1896; English translation: *The Play of Animals: a study of animal life and instinct*, London, Chapman and Hall, 1898

JACOBSON, E., 'Electrical Measurements of Neuromuscular States during Mental Activities. V. Variation of Specific Muscle Contracting during Imagination'. *Amer. J. Physiol.*, 1931, **96**, 115–21

— 'The Electrophysiology of Mental Activities', *Amer. J. Physiol.*, 1932, **44**, 677–94

KUBIE, L., 'Discussion on Penfield Memory Mechanisms', *Arch. Neurol. Psychiat.*, 1952, **67**, 191–4

LHERMITTE, J., Les hallucinations dans leurs relations avec les lésions du lobe occipital, in ALAJOUANINE T., *Les grandes activités du lobe occipital*, Paris, Masson, 1960

LORENZ, K., Comparative Behaviourology in TANNER J.M., INHELDER, B., (Ed.) *Discussions on Child Development*, Tavistock Publications, London, vol. 1, 108–31

LUQUET, G. H., *Les dessins d'un enfant*, Paris, Alcan, 1913

MEYERSON, I., Les images in DUMAS, G., *Nouveau traité de Psychologie*, vol. II, Paris, Alcan, 1932

MOREL, F., *Introduction à la psychiatrie neurologique*, Paris, Masson, 1947
PENFIELD, W., Neurophysiological Basis of the Higher Functions of the Nervous System, *Handb. of Physiol.*, sect. I, vol. III, Washington, 1960
PIAGET, J., *The Origins of Intelligence in the Child*, London, Routledge and Kegan Paul, 1953
— *The Child's Construction of Reality*, London, Routledge and Kegan Paul, 1955
— *Play, Dreams and Imitation in Childhood*, London, Heinemann, 1951
PIAGET, J., INHELDER, B., *The Child's Conception of Space*, London, Routledge and Kegan Paul, 1956
PIAGET, J., FELLER, Y., MCNEAR, E., 'Essai sur la perception des vitesses chez l'enfant et l'adulte', *Arch. Psychol.*, 1958, **36**, 253–327
REY, A., 'Le problème psychologique des "quantités limites" chez l'enfant', *Rev. suisse Psychol.*, 1944, **11**, 238–49
— 'Sur la durée de l'acte réel et de l'acte représenté mentalement', *Arch. Sciences nat.*, Geneva, 1947, **64**, 65–70
— 'L'évolution du comportement interne dans la représentation du mouvement (image motrice)', *Arch. Psychol.*, 1948, **32**, 209–34
— 'Dimension des images mentales visuelles', *Arch. Sciences nat.*, Geneva, 1953, **6**, 413–21
— *Les images mentales en psychophysiologie*, Dialectica, (Zurich), 1958, **12**, 130–45
SCHIFFERLI, P., 'Étude par enregistrement photographique de la motricité oculaire dans l'exploration, dans la reconnaissance et dans la représentation visuelles', *Rev. mens. Psychiat. neurol.*, 1953, **126**, 53–118
WALLON, H., *De l'acte à la pensée*, Paris, Flammarion, 1942
WYSS, O., 'Effets moteurs et réactions affectives provoquées par la stimulation et la destruction dans le diencéphale du chat', *Confinia neurologica*, 1944, **6**

## Chapter 24

## Intellectual Operations and their Development

## Jean Piaget and Bärbel Inhelder

Compared with the other fields of mental life, the field of intellectual operations has given rise to a relatively limited number of experimental studies. And yet, in so far as all behaviour simultaneously comprises cognitive and affective aspects, one would think that the operations which alone make it possible to distinguish the true from the false would have attracted the attention of researchers at every phase of scientific psychology. The fact that this has not been the case is probably due to two reasons. There is also a third reason which is fundamental.

The first reason is that everyone (including, sometimes, psychologists), believes that he has adequate insight into his own intellectual operations. As introspection is linked to verbal habits and to socially acquired notions, it has naturally encouraged the belief that the descriptions of thought mechanisms given by philosophers and by classical logic are adequate (the analyses of modern logic have failed to attract attention partly because of their technical character). Thus, the tests proposed by Toulouse and Piéron in 1911 contained as yet no other means of measuring intellectual operations than a set of syllogisms. The premises were given and the subjects had to deduce the conclusion.

The second reason is that in so far as experimental psychologists have attempted to give a fresh interpretation of intellectual operations, they have begun by giving in to 'reductive' tendencies, hence the effort made by associationism to reduce these operations to a mere play of associations between images, etc. Finally there was a reaction against reductionism, strongly evident in the Würzburg school but resulting in a return to logicism.

The main reason that experimental work on intellectual

## Intellectual Operations and their Development

operations has not flourished must be sought elsewhere. These operations are linked in normal adults to complex structures which escape introspection and which in the analysis of behaviour (in problem solving techniques, etc.) either still pass unnoticed or else give rise merely to descriptions. The only really fruitful method consists in studying their genesis and this implies different techniques. That is why experimental psychology has taken so long to approach the central problem in this field: that of the progressive construction of operational structures in the course of development from birth to maturity.

It is therefore fitting to begin this chapter with a brief historical survey indicating the main methods that have been adopted and showing why recourse to the genetic dimension is necessary. Following this, it will be sufficient to describe some typical experiments, taking each level of mental development in turn so as to show how the main operational structures become organized. Finally a retrospective study will assist us in adopting a position on several general problems. It would be unwise to discuss and even to state these before examining the facts, for in a field so fraught with philosophical reminiscences, it is essential that the psychologist should learn to avoid every *a priori* interpretation. He should pose problems only in so far as he is led to do so in following the development of genetic processes.

Caution is very necessary as misunderstandings can arise from the language that one is led to use. When describing the results of a particular experiment, concerning perception or factor analysis, etc., the mathematical language used is unlikely to lead to confusion, since it is relatively easy to dissociate the mathematical form of the expressions from their psychological content (although the famous discussions between C. Spearman and G. Thomson on the role of such and such a 'factor' already showed that not everyone views the dissociation in the same way). When it comes, however, to describing the structure of particular intellectual operations from the qualitative angle independently of their measurable (or metrical) performance, one has no option but to use, as a language, the general theory of structures which in mathematics goes by the name of general algebra and which includes the algebra of modern logic. In a case of this kind, one must naturally remain on one's guard to avoid a confusion between the psychological content (which in a sense constitutes a logic, since it concerns the intellectual operations of the subject, hence his logic) and the form used to describe it (which is also a logic, but of the kind formulated by algebraists). It would be unreasonable at this point to accuse the psychologist of dealing with logic and not with psychology. He is simply using a precise language, as he may be led to do in statistics, and no one would ever think of saying that calculating a correlation is mathematics and not psychology. The discussion between Spearman and Thomson shows that with more advanced probabilistic analyses, things are not always straightforward. Similarly, the description of operational structures in terms of qualitative algebra requires constant care in order to avoid interference between the intellectual operations of the observed subject (e.g. the child at such and such a level), those of the psychologist who is observing him and above all those which are involved in the language used by the psychologist, when it is that of logical or algebraic structures generally.

1  Historico-critical survey

The proof that this is not an imaginary danger is that on comparing the various experimental studies on the psychology of thought, it becomes apparent that for want of genetic perspective they either simply ignore the existence of operational structures or merely employ those used in classical logic. It is only by systematic genetic study that it has been possible to reveal the existence of structures that had not been noticed until then, some presenting a certain amount of psychological interest but little logical interest[1] (cf. the 'grouping' structure: Section 3), others both a logical and a psychological interest (cf. the 'INRC group': Section 5).

It is striking to note that even studies which have not arrived at the notion of operational structures offer glimpses, under various names, of the reality of 'operations'. This is very significant since one could wonder whether the concept of 'operation' is an authentic psychological reality or merely a term borrowed from logi-

---

[1] Because they are not general enough.

cians.[1] The only studies which have long remained totally foreign to the idea of operation are those inspired by classical or contemporary associationism. But, as we shall see, the very history of these studies, taking into account their recent transformations and especially the 'conversions' which they have brought about, points to certain notions which are definitely operational in character.

## 1 From associationism to 'strategies'

Thus, Binet, after having admitted in *The Psychology of Reasoning* (as we recalled in Chapter 23 in connection with images) that inferences are due to simple associations between images later stressed in his *Étude expérimentale de l'intelligence* the specific character of affirmations and negations, of judgments expressing relations, etc.—in short of what we shall term 'operations' as against imaged representations. In so doing, he resolutely left behind him his original associationism.

Similarly, modern associationism has led, particularly in the case of Hull and those who followed him, to an interpretation of the acquisition of notions (number, etc.) which is based on the stimulus-response schema, on generalizations of stimuli or of responses, on external reinforcements and on the hypothesis of habit-family hierarchies. One of Hull's successors, D. Berlyne, recognized as a result of personal experience the cogency of our distinction between representation of states or configurations and operations referring specifically to transformations. He added to Hull's conception by introducing a new duality: he distinguished between copy-responses, relating to states and transformation-responses which modify the former and thus correspond to our 'operations' (Berlyne, 1960).

Above all, within the context of 'behaviour theory' on which are based the many American conceptions of learning, a particular technique for analysing intellectual mechanisms has developed. It is known as the problem-solving method. It consists in setting the subject a problem that is new to him and which may be of any

[1] Let us note here that apart from certain exceptions (Curry's combinatorial logic and Lorenzen's operational logic), logicians avoid the notion and even the term of 'operation' and speak of 'functors', etc. Couturat used to accuse the notion of operation of being 'manifestly anthropomorphic', in other words of being psychological!

## Jean Piaget and Bärbel Inhelder

level (ranging from sensori-motor intelligence to the higher thought processes). His behaviour sequence up to the discovery and consolidation of the solution is then analysed. Although most interpretations of this kind of data have begun by being linked to associationism and thus foreign to the idea of operation, the most remarkable achievement arising from the use of this method is a definitely anti-associationist work: *A Study of Thinking* (1956) by J. Bruner, J. J. Goodnow and G. A. Austin, which opens up new perspectives. According to these authors, the successive steps taken by a subject as he grapples with problems are not 'associations' simply determined by previous experience. They are 'decisions' made by the subject as he comes to grips with, or matches himself against, objects or events. The appropriate language in this case is that of 'strategies' used in game theory and one sees at once the kinship between these decisions or strategies and what we call operations (as J. Bruner himself indicates).

### 2 Claparède's 'implication'

Although research arising out of associationism (as a continuation or as a reaction against it, but using the methods arising from it) has not led to an analysis of operational structures, it has nonetheless arrived on several occasions at notions close to that of operation. This is also true of an allied standpoint which however lays more stress on the subject's activities. It tends to reduce acts of intelligence to a succession of groping attempts which may be actual physical attempts, in the form of trial and error with selection arising from the pressure of facts, or internalized attempts in the form of 'hypotheses', controlled by acquired consciousness of relations. This interpretation, inspired by the work of Jennings and Thorndike, was adopted by Claparède. He proceeded to devise an ingenious method for analysing acts of intelligence. This method, known as 'spoken reflection', consists in observing the successive steps taken by subjects who have previously been trained to think aloud while solving everyday problems (such as finding the caption of a cartoon or the end of a story).

In his fine study *La genèse de l'hypothèse*, in which he recorded the results obtained by this method, Claparède went beyond his original views on groping and arrived at a fundamental conclusion. Groping, he tells us, is never purely random, but is to some extent directed from the beginning by certain connections. Furthermore, it is not the most elementary form of behaviour but appears only when a number of primitive connections have been invalidated. What are these connections which precede groping or impose a direction upon it? They are not associations, according to Claparède, but connections asserting themselves with a sort of internal necessity. These he calls 'implications'. That is how 'cat' implies 'miaowing' even to a baby, once he has simultaneously seen and heard a cat. At the level of acts of thought, every act of comprehension relies on such implications and, in the case of actual research, all groping is directed or framed by implications.

Although Claparède did not yet regard implication as the product of operational or pre-operational activities (since he believed that it was due to a kind of elementary syncretism), it is nevertheless easy to show that this interpretation necessarily follows. As one of us[1] remarked after the publication of Claparède's studies, it is not at the first perceptual contact that 'cat' implies 'miaowing'. The cat miaows and this is no more than a fact. But from the second contact, when the baby recognizes a cat, he can infer that it will miaow. Implication is thus subordinated to an act of assimilation. Assimilation means construction of schemata (implication in the broad sense is in fact the expression of these schemata) and it is this schematization which probably constitutes the point of departure of operational activities and of their structurizations (cf. 6, 4).

## 3 Spearman's 'noegenesis'

From a totally different standpoint, the studies carried out by C. Spearman culminated, even more clearly, in the recognition of operations, but without involving as yet the recognition of integrated operational structures. It is well known that Spearman's work on intelligence evolved on two planes: a probabilistic analysis of 'factors' on the one hand, and a qualitative analysis of 'noegenesis' on the other. The factor analysis of intelligence led to nothing further than a distinction, to which the great English psychologist attached great importance, between general

[1] Piaget, 1936, pp. 404–412 (English edition, 1953).

intelligence and particular factors. He did not reconstitute the actual genesis of general intelligence by directly studying mental development but was content to retrace an ideal genesis as it were. This is nevertheless of undoubted interest because, despite his empiricism, Spearman in part revealed the operational nature of acts of intelligence. He believed that intelligence develops in three stages: the 'apprehension of experience', the 'eduction' of relations and the 'eduction' of 'correlates'. As all knowledge is supposed to be drawn from experience and from experience alone, there is as yet no question of 'structuring' experience, but only of 'apprehending' it. Similarly, relations are not constructed but simply 'educed', that is drawn from an experience that contains them in advance. As for 'correlates', that is, relations between relations, (e.g. feathers are to birds what hair is to mammals), Spearman considers that they are also drawn from reality by 'eduction', but this is incorrect since it goes without saying that in reaching this degree of complexity, eduction assumes the form of a genuine operation. It amounts in fact to a multiplicative co-ordination of relations, corresponding to a matrix or table of double entry.

Spearman, however, did not become altogether conscious of the operational character of his 'eductions'. He omitted to ask himself whether those he had observed did not necessarily require to be completed by others and especially whether collectively these possible operations did not obey the general laws governing structures. It is nonetheless highly significant that the inventor of factor analysis should have come so close to an operational conception of intelligence. Indeed it was probably only his empiricist underestimation of the part played by the subject's activities that prevented Spearman from formally elaborating this conception.

## 4 'Gestalt' structures

With the *Gestalt* psychologists came the discovery of integrated structures. With Wertheimer in particular, they begin to take on an explicitly operational character. The Gestaltists, it is true, were willing to recognize only one type of structure (the *Gestalt* in the particular sense ascribed to the term). In spite of this, their discovery was far-reaching in that, for the first time, logical

## Intellectual Operations and their Development

structures made an appearance in psychology not because they had been postulated in advance but as a result of a general interpretation based on experimentation.

It is well known that the theory of Form has renewed our knowledge of perception. It began as a field hypothesis and went on to refute atomic associationism. W. Köhler, Meili, Duncker and Metzger viewed problem solving as a restructuring of perceptual data, passing from a less good to a better form and obeying the same laws as the *Gestalt*, that is laws of totality according to which the whole is distinct from the sum of its parts and appears as an organization with properties of its own by virtue of being a totality. The decisive moment in the assimilation of the structures of intelligence to *Gestalt* laws came when Wertheimer began to study higher acts of intelligence: the solving of mathematical problems or of deductive problems in general. According to Wertheimer, deductions like these are simply restructurizations such as Koehler had already claimed to have found in the sphere of practical intelligence. In a syllogism of the type 'All B's are C's, A is a B, therefore A is a C', the act of thought consists only in fusing into a new whole AC the partial wholes AB and BC, by 'recentering' A in C after dissociating it from its one original link B. In his posthumous work (1945), when Wertheimer wanted to describe the successive acts of this process of restructuring, he used the term 'operation' which we ourselves had used to describe the construction by the child of his first concrete logical structures (1941, A and B). Thus he also regards these operations as bound up with integrated structures.

A difficulty remains concerning the nature of these. The notion of *Gestalt* brings together into a single concept: 1) the idea of a whole whose properties are those of a total system and are thus distinct from those of the parts, and 2) the idea of a whole differing from the sum of its parts (non-additive composition). Logico-mathematical structures possess the first of these characteristics in that their properties are those of integrated systems. They do not possess the second, however, since they are rigorously additive. The series of whole numbers, for instance, is an admirable integrated system which has laws *qua* system (laws of 'groups', of 'sets', of 'rings', of 'lattices', etc.) and yet $2+2$ are rigorously 4 and not a little more or a little less as in probabilistic or perceptual compositions. Logico-mathematical structures are thus not *Gestalten*, as these are of a non-additive and therefore irreversible nature. To define operations, it is necessary to go beyond the category of *Gestalten* and to conceive the existence of other psychological integrated structures, which are reversible.

## 5 'Thought psychology'

A solution that is simpler than the *Gestalttheorie*, while also in reaction against associationism, was outlined as early as the beginning of the century and could be drawn upon to overcome the above difficulty; it is that of the German *Denkpsychologie*. Having discovered at the same time as Binet the existence of imageless thought, the Würzburg school then tried to characterize it. They used a method of induced introspection (for instance subjects were asked to produce supraordinate associations, such as bird → animal or plum-tree → tree and to describe the accompanying states of consciousness). From the very beginning, Marbe, failing to find states of consciousness corresponding bi-univocally to the act of judgment, introduced a logical factor claiming that it was at once causal and 'non-psychological' as if a logical structure could play a part in the mental context and could modify it without resulting from it! Those who followed him, Messer, Watt and especially Bühler, renounced this position with its dangerous methodology, but turned towards a kind of logico-psychological parallelism. According to this, there exists a correspondence between certain well-defined states (that have indeed been very subtly described, as for instance K. Bühler's *Regelbewusstsein* or 'consciousness of rules') and given logical structures. Finally, the main heir to this tradition, O. Selz (whose work breaks away from induced introspection and seeks instead to analyse, in behaviour itself, the process of 'reproductive' and of 'productive' thought) regarded thought with all its interconnections as a 'mirror of logic'.

But this point of view, which seems at first sight to avoid all conflicts by adopting a cautious principle of parallelism in fact fails to resolve anything, for two reasons. The first is that there is nothing to prove the existence of isomorphism between the subject's logic, with which the psychologist is concerned, and that of the logician, which goes far beyond it. Even if there is partial isomorphism, nothing proves that the function of thought is to reflect a logic that has appeared out of the blue. It is much more likely that logic is in fact an axiomatization of the forms of equilibrium that characterize thought, an autonomous axiomatization, it goes without saying, but one which, like all axiomatizations, serves to formalize preliminary data. Thereafter, the data are of no further concern in logic but fall within the province of the corresponding concrete science (in this instance, the psychology of thought). Secondly, if *Denkpsychologie* was content with a somewhat facile parallelism between logical structures and acts of thought, this was because it confined itself to the analysis of adult thought. In considering the child and his development, the real problem is to discover how structures are constructed and not how they appear when completely formed. More exactly, knowledge of the final states can only arise out of knowledge of how they come to be constructed.

## 6 Method to be followed

The lesson that we learn from these two observations is that for our methods to be sound, we must not refer to any pre-existing logical structure (although we may use the instruments of the logician to describe with precision what we observe, but that is another question, affecting the language adopted and not the facts themselves). We must first try to find out whether spontaneous intellectual operations exist or whether such operations are only learnt socially, or again whether the term 'operation' is of interest only to logicians and embraces a psychological complexity too great to serve as a natural psychological unit. We must then establish whether operations develop in isolation (along similar lines to Spearman's 'eductions') or whether they are always bound up with integrated structures. Finally it is most important that we should determine whether these operations and their integrated structures are present at all levels of development or, if not, when and how they are constituted, which amounts to asking of what they consist.

In order to solve these problems we must use material studied by American psychologists under the heads of *problem solving* and *concept formation*. A combination of data from both areas is necessary since a problem that is really new to the subject demands an elaboration of concepts. These studies need to be supplemented by a systematic study of concept formation from birth to adolescence. Only then do we discover the essentials and find that the laws of progressive structurization reveal the simultaneous formation of operations and of their integrated structures.

Our genetic studies, of which we shall give a few examples, have been going on for forty years. The main finding has proved different from what our knowledge of the psychology of adult thought and of logistic axiomatization would have led us to expect. It is that, underlying language and at a level far below conscious reflection, there exists a logic of co-ordinations of actions, if one rates as logical the relations of order, inclusion etc., which regulate actions as they are later to regulate thought. The notion of operation is thus psychologically natural. This is so not only if one calls by that name internalized actions (uniting, dissociating, ordering, etc.) which can be performed in both directions (reversibility)[1] but also if one characterizes internalized actions by their most specific genetic property which is that they are abstracted from the most general co-ordinations of actions. Operations are thus only a higher form of regulations, and that is enough to guarantee their psychological authenticity, despite their convergence with what are known as operations in mathematics and logic. Logico-mathematical activities are thus to be conceived psychologically as an inexhaustibly fruitful prolongation of the co-ordination of actions. The second fundamental characteristic of operations, which follows directly from the first, is that they are always structured in integrated systems. Here again, genetic analysis has produced unexpected results in that 1) the large structures described in general algebra (groups and lattices, with their derivatives) are led up to, from the time of concrete operations (which provide a bridge between co-ordinations of actions and formalizations of thought), by much more elementary structures. These, however, are already mixed in character and we shall call them 'groupings' (see Section 3), 2) the transition from these concrete structures to abstract structures is made possible by a group of four transformations. There are many manifestations of these at the pre-adolescent and adolescent levels (see Section 5) yet the part they play in adult

---

[1] For example, the action of uniting (addition) can be inversed into an action of dissociating (subtraction), etc.

## Intellectual Operations and their Development

thought had escaped logicians. We ourselves owe the discovery of the existence of this group of transformations entirely to our genetic studies.

## 2 Notions of conservation

### 1 Introduction

Let us assume for a moment that there is a researcher who doubts the existence of operations as experimental facts and considers that they belong to a type of interpretation which goes beyond psychology. He will ask that they should be shown to him as observable processes, spontaneous activities, modes of functioning that 'really' play a part when the subject is presented with a stimulus and makes a response.

We have just assumed, however, that operations are a higher form of regulations of action. This amounts to saying that the reversibility characterizing operational structures is in fact the culmination of the approximate compensations appearing in regulations. A regulation cannot be observed directly, but its effects are recorded objectively in 'responses' to given stimuli. In the field of sensori-motor or perceptual regulations, there is a particularly famous example which several Gestaltists (Katz, etc.) have compared to a form of homeostasis: it is the constancy of magnitude, form, colour, etc. In such cases, it is true that one cannot follow regulations in detail but one can see when they occur (for instance with the colours of figures), and when they do not (for instance with background colours: experiment by Kardos). One can also assess their degree of effectiveness. Can it be said that all this is only a measure of performances and not an analysis of functioning? One can pass from the consideration of performance to that of functioning by analysing the factors, by measuring for example (at various levels of development) the estimation of apparent magnitudes, of distances and of real magnitudes. All this will give a preliminary approximate idea of the functioning of constancy of magnitude (see Chapter 18, Section 4).

The example of perceptual constancies is a remarkable prefiguration, at the level of elementary regulations, of the manner in which operations appear at the level of thought. There is one difference in that when regulations have become operational they reveal themselves not only by their performances—judgments of conservation corresponding to evaluations of constancy—but also in their actual functioning, since the subject is able to justify in part the reasons for his affirmations and thus to describe the process of reversibility.

The best criterion of the emergence of operations at the level of concrete structures (towards the age of seven) is, in fact, the constitution of invariants or notions of conservation. Observation shows, as we shall see from several examples, that a child who can internalize an action or imagine its result is not necessarily able to visualize *ipso facto* the possibility of performing the same action in reverse and thus cancelling the result. In other words, an action does not at once transform itself into a reversible operation. There are a number of intermediates such as imagining reversal, but on request or as a new action distinct from the first and not implied by it (this we shall call 'empirical reversal'). It is therefore not easy to recognize in the subject the beginnings of reversibility as such, except by its results. Yet, one has only to listen to what the subject says once he has mastered the notion of reversibility, to obtain an expression of reversibility and consequently of operations (internalized actions that have become reversible) which is remarkably simple and exact. Moreover, it coincides with the best of logical definitions: an operation is that which transforms a state A into a state B leaving at least one property invariant throughout the transformation and allowing the possibility of return from B to A thereby cancelling the transformation. It so happens—and this time diagnosis is easy—that at pre-operational levels the transformation is conceived as modifying all the data at once, without any conservation. This of course makes it impossible to return to the point of departure without a new action transforming the whole once more (re-creating what has been destroyed, etc.) and consequently differing from the first instead of remaining the same action but inversed. That is why we feel that tests dealing with conservation give the best indication of the natural, and not merely the logical, reality of operations. We shall therefore begin with these.

## 2 The ball of clay

Let us now examine the first of the forms of non-conservation followed by conservation which we observed.[1] The results have been re-examined and controlled by various authors (Vinh-Bang, 1959; Lovell and Ogilvie, 1960 and 1961; Elkind, 1961; Laurendeau and Pinard, in preparation).

The subject is shown a ball of clay and asked to make another ball of the same size and weight. One ball, A, is left on the table as evidence and the other is transformed into a sausage, a pancake, a number of pieces, etc. The subject is asked first whether there is still the same amount of substance in B as in A and why. The procedure is the same whether the child answers 'yes' or 'no'. In either case, his answer and the reason that he gives (for instance, in the case of the sausage: 'There is more stuff because it is longer') serve to prompt further modifications of the object (in this case, making the sausage longer or shorter). This is done to see whether he will continue to reason in the same way or will change his opinion. The stage that the child has reached is noted (no conservation of substance, ungeneralized and uncertain conservation, or necessary conservation) and also the kind of arguments he uses (see below). One then passes to the conservation of weight, but if possible not immediately afterwards, so as to avoid verbal perseverations. Questions are asked about the same transformations as in the case of substance (sausage, etc.), but the child is asked whether or not the weight remains the same. To make the questions more concrete, he is given a balance with two scales and the ball is put on the first scale. He is asked to anticipate what will happen when the other (modified) object is placed on the second scale. Finally, the same questions are asked about the conservation of volume, but it is not sufficient to use the terms 'large', 'big', etc., as these remain ambiguous in relation to the amount of substance (it took us a long time to realize that, to the child, substance is not equivalent to volume.) The ball of clay A is therefore immersed in a narrow[2] cylindrical jar three quarters full. The child is asked whether the sausage,

[1] Piaget, 1937; Piaget and Inhelder, 1941, Chapters I–III.
[2] A narrow jar is used so that the change of level may be sufficiently perceptible. In addition, to dissociate the action of volume from that of weight (often wrongly adduced by the child), the ball of plasticine A is replaced by a metal ball of the same volume but of greater weight.

etc. B will take up 'as much room in the water and will make the water rise' to the same level in another container identical with the first.

## 3  Qualitative and quantitative results

Three kinds of results were obtained. In the first place, three successive stages can be observed in the case of each of the notions studied. At first there is lack of conservation when the object is modified. This is followed by transitional reactions (conservation is assumed but without certainty and in the case of some transformations only). Finally conservation comes to be affirmed and regarded as evident throughout the various transformations of the ball of clay.

Secondly, we find that three arguments are advanced by the child on reaching the third stage and these are characteristic of an operational approach. Longitudinal analysis carried out by one of us (Inhelder) in collaboration with G. Noelting on 12 subjects who were examined every three months, has shown that these three arguments do not correspond to three sub-stages but are interdependent and do not always appear in the same order. The first is based on simple reversibility: there is in B as much (substance, weight or volume) as in A because the ball A can be remade from B. The second rests on a more subtle kind of reversibility[1] based on compensation: object B is longer but thinner, etc. (composition of two seriations in inverse order: longer × thinner = same quantity). The third argument appears less sophisticated and is simply based on identity: the quantity (or the weight, etc.) does not change 'because it's the same stuff', 'because it has only been rolled', 'because it has only been flattened' or 'because nothing has been taken away or added'. The remarkable character of this identity is that it ranks as an argument of conservation only when the other two arguments have been discovered. Young children at the pre-operational level also knew that it was the 'same stuff' and that nothing had been taken away or added, but did not conclude from this that there was conservation. It therefore seems clear (chronologically and functionally) that the arguments are interdependent and that they lead to the construc-

[1] Or reversibility through 'reciprocity', as distinct from simple reversibility or reversibility through 'inversion'.

tion of an integrated operational structure, of the 'grouping' type (cf. Section 3) in which conservation constitutes the invariant.

In the third place, the results obtained at Geneva and at Saint-Gall show a time-lag between the child's acquisition of the notion of the conservation of substance (towards the age of 8), of weight (age 9–10) and of volume (age 11–12). At least, that is what we had observed in the past in the course of clinical analysis (Piaget and Inhelder, 1941). One of us (Inhelder, 1943) found when studying 159 mental deficients ranging in age from 7 to 30 that conservation of weight was never present without that of substance, nor conservation of volume without that of weight. This did not apply the other way round.[1] In their standardization of operational tests, Vinh-Bang and Inhelder obtained the following percentage with 25 subjects per age group:

TABLE I

Percentage success in tests on the conservation of substance, weight and volume*

| Ages | 5 | 6 | 7 | 8 | 9 | 10 | 11 |
|---|---|---|---|---|---|---|---|
| *Substance* | | | | | | | |
| Non-conservation | 84 | 68 | 64 | 24 | 12 | — | — |
| Transitional | 0 | 16 | 4 | 4 | 4 | — | — |
| Conservation | 16 | 16 | 32 | 72 | 84 | — | — |
| *Weight* | | | | | | | |
| Non-conservation | 100 | 84 | 76 | 40 | 16 | 16 | 0 |
| Transitional | 0 | 4 | 0 | 8 | 12 | 8 | 4 |
| Conservation | 0 | 12 | 24 | 52 | 72 | 76 | 96 |
| *Volume* | | | | | | | |
| Non-conservation | 100 | 100 | 88 | 44 | 56 | 24 | 16 |
| Transitional | 0 | 0 | 0 | 28 | 12 | 20 | 4 |
| Conservation† | 0 | 0 | 12 | 28 | 32 | 56 | 82 |

\* Each of the 175 subjects underwent the three tests, but on different days so as to avoid verbal perseverations.

† Out of the numbers given for conservation, 12 per cent of the seven-year-olds, 12 per cent of the eight-year-olds, 16 per cent of the nine-year-olds, 28 per cent of the ten-year-olds and 26 per cent of the eleven-year-olds foresaw that the displacement of water would be the same with the ball that has been pulled out of shape as with the round ball but attributed this to the conservation of weight.

[1] Inhelder also showed that the conservation of volume is found only in

## Jean Piaget and Bärbel Inhelder

### 4  American and English controls

As a control, here are the results obtained in the United States by D. Elkind (1961) with 25 subjects per age group:

TABLE 2

Percentage success in tests on the conservation of substance, weight and volume
(according to D. Elkind, U.S.A.)

| Ages | 5 | 6 | 7 | 8 | 9 | 10 | 11 |
|---|---|---|---|---|---|---|---|
| Substance | 19 | 51 | 70 | 72 | 86 | 94 | 92 |
| Weight | 21 | 52 | 51 | 44 | 73 | 89 | 78 |
| Volume | 0 | 4 | 0 | 4 | 4 | 19 | 25 |

Elkind stresses the fact that 70–75 per cent of the subjects show a definite time lag between acquiring the notion of the conservation of weight and that of substance. In the case of volume, there is still no conservation at the age of eleven with most subjects. This last result, according to him, is to be explained by a slight difference in technique: he himself asked whether the two objects (ball and sausage, etc.) took up the same amount of *space* in the water. When the question is worded (as ours was) in terms of displacement of water level, the problem is more quickly solved.

Lovell and Ogilvie (1960 and 1961) obtained the results shown in Table 3 concerning substance and weight in four primary school classes in Leeds, in which the children's ages ranged from 7–8 to 10–11.

It is clear that evolution is broadly the same, with the same time-lag between weight and substance (and between volume and weight, but the authors used a different test for volume). On the other hand, Laurendeau and Pinard (in the press) found scarcely any inversion in the order: substance, weight and volume (12 aberrant cases out of 441) but observed that their Canadian

---

subjects suffering from retarded development and never in true mental deficients (probably because the notion of volume implies the notion of proportion and this is attained by formal operations—see below, paragraph 5—of which th are incapable).

subjects acquired the notion of the three conservations in a much shorter space of time, particularly in the case of weight and volume. This interesting result seems linked in part to the techniques which they used. According to one technique, each of the five transformations of the ball (into a ring, a cube, a sausage,

TABLE 3

Percentage success in tests on the conservation
of substance and weight
(according to Lovell and Ogilvie)

| Tests | Substance (322 subjects) | | | Weight (364 subjects) | | |
|---|---|---|---|---|---|---|
| | Non-conservation | Transitional | Conservation | Non-conservation | Transitional | Conservation |
| Class I (age 7-8) | 31 | 33 | 36 | 91 | 5 | 4 |
| Class II (age 8-9) | 20 | 12 | 68 | 29 | 36 | 36 |
| Class III (age 9-10) | 11 | 15 | 74 | 32 | 20 | 48 |
| Class IV (age 10-11) | 5 | 9 | 86 | 13 | 13 | 74 |

a filament and finally ten rounded pieces) was followed by questions on volume, weight and substance in turn. In our technique, these three aspects were dealt with in separate questionnaires and each questionnaire referred to the modifications of the ball as a whole. Laurendeau and Pinard followed this pattern with their other technique, but with no interval between the three questionnaires. It is therefore probable that systematic transfers occurred and it is all the more remarkable that subjects who attained the notion of conservation in the case of all the transformations studied retained the order of succession: substance, weight and volume, the last two being acquired earlier.

## 5 Transfer of liquids or beads

A second example of initial non-conservation followed by operational conservation, among the dozens that we could mention, is to be found in the transfer of liquids or beads from a container A to containers B or C of a different shape from A. We have chosen this particular example for two reasons. The first is because there is complementary information on this subject in the chapter on images (Chapter 23). The second is because it differs from the previous example in the following way. With the ball of clay, we find that if the child is asked to anticipate the effects of its transformation into a sausage before the transformation actually takes place, he expects general non-conservation. In the case of the transfer of beads or liquids, however, he anticipates a kind of general conservation (or invariance) of the quantities involved, including the conservation of levels, despite the difference in shape between glasses A, B and C. Most probably the reason for this is that a ball seems to be modified in itself if its shape is changed while a liquid or a heap of beads assumes the shape of the containers. They do not appear to change in quantity unless the child foresees, by exact imaged representation, that the level will rise or fall in passing from A to B or C. When this happens, the unexpected perceptual configuration following the actual transfer leads to belief in non-conservation until such time as operations of compensation, etc., enable the child to substitute a necessary or true conservation for the pseudo-conservation or invariance that was at first anticipated.

The experiment is as follows. Two cylindrical glasses of the same size, $A_1$ and $A_2$ are presented to the child. He is asked to pour as much liquid in $A_1$ as in $A_2$, or as many beads (in this case putting a red bead in $A_1$ with one hand every time he puts a blue bead in $A_2$ with the other, this bi-univocal correspondence ensuring equality without having to count). Next, the experimenter offers the child a glass, B, which is narrower and taller than A or a glass C which is wider and shorter. The child is told to pour $A_1$ into B or C and is asked whether the quantities are the same in $A_2$ and in B or C. This is repeated with four little cylindrical glasses, and again the child is asked whether together they equal $A_2$.

The results obtained have already been considered from the point of view of images in Chapter 23. From the point of view of operations, they are completely similar to those for conservation of substance in the case of balls of clay. The only difference is that the notion of conservation is acquired approximately a year

## Intellectual Operations and their Development

earlier. During the first stage, there is no conservation of quantities. There follows a transitional stage during which the child achieves the notion of conservation in some instances of transfer, but not in others. In the third stage, conservation is generalized. It is seen to apply to all transfers and considered logically necessary by the subject. Here are the results obtained by Vinh-Bang-Inhelder with 83 and 90 subjects:[1]

TABLE 4

Percentage success in tests on the conservation of liquids and beads

| Age | Transfer of liquids (83 subjects) | | | Transfer of beads (90 subjects) | | |
|---|---|---|---|---|---|---|
| | Non-conservation | Transitional | Conservation | Non-conservation | Transitional | Conservation |
| 5 | 85 | 11 | 4 | 38 | 40 | 22 |
| 6 | 40 | 42 | 18 | 6 | 40 | 54 |
| 7 | 4 | 22 | 74 | 0 | 4 | 96 |

The notion of the conservation of beads is acquired slightly earlier than that of liquids, probably because it concerns solids that do not lose their shape and because their collective equivalence is measured by bi-univocal correspondence. But such correspondence is not enough to ensure the conservation of equivalence at the age of 5 or 6, as we shall again see in Section 3 when we come to consider numerical equivalences.

Let us also note that the arguments advanced by the subjects in support of conservation are identical to those which we mentioned concerning the balls of clay: 1) simple reversibility: it is possible to pour back from B to A and return to the original state; 2) reversibility through compensation of relations, for instance, the water rises higher in B but B is narrower; 3) identity in a positive form ('It's the same water', etc.) or a negative form ('nothing has been taken away or added', or 'it was simply a matter of pouring', implying that the quantity was not modified).

[1] These were not the same subjects. In addition to the technique previously indicated, a control experiment was introduced, three little glasses of a different shape (i.e. not cylindrical) being used for the transfers.

The uniformity of the arguments advanced bears witness, we feel, to the existence of a common operational process, linked to the construction of invariants.

## 6   The problem of integrated structures

Can one go a step further and assume that with the construction of invariants, operations are necessarily co-ordinated into an integrated structure (which, to our way of thinking, characterizes the very notion of operation)? Everything points to this, since if the subject spontaneously introduces reversibility, there is already an organized system including among other things the direct operation (transformation), its inverse (reversal) and the identical operation (null transformation). In other words, we have here the beginnings of a 'group' or 'grouping' (see Section 3). But let us beware on principle of logical analysis and let us try to say no more than is warranted by the facts.

It so happens that one consequence of the hypothesis advanced in the preceding paragraph can be directly verified. If the construction of invariant equivalences is due to an operational elaboration, this must entail, in the subject's eyes, certain deductive consequences such as transitivity. Thus, if a quantity A (substance, weight, etc.) is equal to quantity B and if B is equal to C, it must follow that $A = C$. Our hypothesis has therefore always been that as transitivity does not assert itself at pre-operational levels (a fact that can easily be verified in every sphere) it must develop hand in hand with notions of conservation since these involve a certain amount of transitivity and since, in return, transitivity of the type '$A = B$, $B = C$, therefore $A = C$' implies an invariant leading from A to C. A Norwegian psychologist, J. Smedslund, set out to test this hypothesis by 1) a direct study of possible correlations between a form of conservation (he chose that of weight) and the transitivity of corresponding equalities; 2) a study of the learning processes relating to both these kinds of reality. Smedslund (1959) carried out his study with 57 children ranging in age from 6·5 to 7·6 (all considered advanced by comparison with Genevan children on the basis of their performance at school). The first study revealed a 'highly significant' correlation ($\chi^2 = 31\cdot15$ significant at ·001) between 'at least an operational explanation' of the conservation of weight and the transitivity

*Intellectual Operations and their Development*

of equalities and inequalities (the latter were brought about by taking away a small portion of one of the three objects under comparison). Smedslund concluded that 'transitivity and conservation are at this stage only two different aspects of one and the same grouping'. In the course of his second study, Smedslund easily succeeded in making children learn about the conservation of weight by asking them to check on a balance that weights remained equal after the first few transformations: this leads to immediate generalization of the physical aspect of the problem. On the other hand, when the same technique was used to verify the transitivity of equalities or inequalities it did not lead to a grasp of transitivity. Thus, the logical aspect of conservation is dissociated from the physical aspect.

## 3 'Groupings' of classes and of relations and the construction of number

The psychological reality of operations thus appears verified by the spontaneous acquisition of the notions of conservation and by the justifications offered by the subjects. We must now examine the most general forms of these operations and the integrated structures which they constitute. From the end of the sensori-motor period and especially from the time of the appearance of the symbolic function (one and a half to two years of age), one can observe forms of behaviour which will lead to the constitution of these more general operations, i.e. putting objects together in piles, etc., according to their similarities, as a prelude to the addition of classes, or ordering them according to their differences (for instance superposing building blocks in order of decreasing size), as a prelude to setting up chains of asymmetrical transitive relations (seriation).

### 1 Classifications

Classification behaviour can be studied experimentally with a view to determining both the hierarchy of spontaneously elaborated structures and the level of development of the child in relation to this hierarchy. The experimenter will for example give the child a number of small everyday objects, or a set of cards cut into geometrical forms and differing in shape, size and colour. The instructions vary according to the aim of the experiment, ranging from the most indeterminate ('arrange nicely', 'sort out', 'put together what goes together') to the most restrictive ('put all the same ones together', 'put together the ones that are most alike', etc.) Indeterminate instructions enable the experimenter to observe the most spontaneous tendencies while restrictive instructions can be used to determine the maximum performance attained in classification proper.

These simple techniques serve to reveal the existence of a law of evolution which in itself throws light on the psychological nature of classification structures:

*a*) At the elementary level we find what we have termed 'figural (or 'graphic') collections'. The child may do one of two things. He may put together elements not because of similarity alone but because they 'go together' for various reasons including similarity (for instance, nails and hammer, or a triangle above a square to make a house and roof). Alternatively, he may be concerned chiefly with similarities, adjusting first similar and later dissimilar elements to make a figure in space (squares lined up in a row or put together to form a large rectangle, etc.). These figural collections make an interesting transition between sensori-motor schemata (practical concepts, as it were, transposing from one situation to another that which can be generalized in an action) and the representative classes. Figural collections are like sensori-motor schemata in that they reflect an ability to assimilate objects to one another according to their uses and similarities and also in that they likewise fail to evoke the extension of these objects (since the schema has extension only in the eyes of the observer while for the subjects it proceeds 'step by step'. There is no awareness of the objects to which it applies as a whole, hence of its extension). But, since a graphic collection is already a representative unit, it must have extension. The subject overcomes this by using the mode of extension proper to perceptual wholes which is spatial, not numerical, and figural, not abstract as will later be the case.

*b*) Subsequent classifications break free from these figural extensions. Thus, objects that are alike are simply put together in little piles. Moreover, once the pile is made (for instance a pile of

## Intellectual Operations and their Development

squares) the subjects succeed in subdividing it into sub-collections (large and small or red and blue) or in joining it to others (for instance putting the pile of squares next to the pile of rectangles so as to oppose the rectilinear and the curvilinear figures). Such behaviour is already clearly classificatory, since there is a beginning of class inclusion. We shall, however, speak only of 'non-figural (or 'non-graphic') collections' and not yet of 'classes' in the sense in which the term is used in *c*). There are two reasons for this. The first is that the subject proceeds by a method that is either descending (starting with large collections and then subdividing them) or ascending (progressively amalgamating small collections) but does not succeed in combining them with mobility. The second reason, which follows from the first, is that the subject does not yet know how to compare quantitatively the extension of a collection B with that of a sub-collection A, in the form $B > A$. This, as we shall see, is one of the criteria of the operational level.

*c*) Subjects who have reached this final level immediately establish hierarchical classifications with mobile combination of the ascending and descending processes. They are finally capable of quantifying inclusion i.e. $A < B$ (their quantification is intensive and naturally not numerical). We shall see examples of it in the experiments we are about to describe.

## 2 'All' and 'some'

Everyone admits that language contains classifications and it is easy to observe that their structure rests on a carefully regulated use of 'all' and 'some'. It is by recognizing that 'all' cats are animals but that all animals are not cats (only 'some' animals are) that the subject can, by the use of language, arrive at the inclusion of the sub-class of cats into that of animals and that he can, on the basis of this single intensive quantification (that is, without comparing the number of cats to non-cat animals), conclude that there are necessarily more animals than cats. More than forty years ago, when one of us (Piaget, 1921) was studying in Paris a test by Cyril Burt concerning these problems, he became aware of the remarkable difficulty encountered by children up to the age of nine or ten in trying to distinguish between the two expressions 'all my flowers are yellow' and 'some of (or a number of) my flowers are yellow' as if they both amounted to saying 'all my

## Jean Piaget and Bärbel Inhelder

some flowers', etc. The question that we must ask is whether this difficulty in handling inclusion is due only to its verbal expression or to deeper causes.

On the verbal plane, the experimenter shows the subject a number of mixed squares and circles in a row. There are five blue circles, two red squares and two blue squares (the colours are equally mixed). The four following questions are asked:

Cb = are all the circles blue?
bC = are all the blue ones circles?
Sr = are all the squares red?
rS = are all the red ones squares?

The correct responses that we obtained (with 10 or 12 subjects per age group) are given below as a percentage:

TABLE 5

Percentage of correct responses relating to the use of 'all'.

| Age (and number of subjects) | 5(12) | 6(10) | 7(10) | 8(10) | 9(10) |
|---|---|---|---|---|---|
| Cb + Sr (mean) | 66 | 85 | 95 | 95 | 95 |
| bC + rS (mean) | 66 | 67 | 75 | 90 | 92 |
| Cb + rS (together) | 42 | 45 | 70 | 80 | 80 |
| bC + Sr (together) | 58 | 70 | 70 | 85 | 90 |
| Cb + rS + bC + Sr* | 8 | 20 | 50 | 70 | 80 |

\* Success in all four at once, whereas the mean values Cb + Sr etc. are calculated $(Cb + Sr)/2$. It should also be noted that responses have been evaluated in terms of success, partial success and failure.

It can be seen that questions Cb + rS, which are cast in the pattern 'are all A's B's (if A is included in B)?' and bC + Sr, which have as their pattern 'are all B's A's (if A is included in B)?' are solved together only towards the age of eight or nine.

## 3 Quantification of inclusion

We shall now try to pass beyond the plane of verbal expression to see what can be understood about inclusion from the simple manipulation of objects. It is not enough to observe that when the child has constructed a collection B, he subdivides it into A and A'. In so doing, he could merely be comparing A to A' and

## Intellectual Operations and their Development

not to B—or else he could be thinking alternately of the whole B without its parts or of the parts A and A' and neglecting the whole. Thus, he would fail to attain inclusion as a link between A and B. In order to ascertain whether the child really understands inclusion, we must have recourse to an experiment involving a direct relation between A and B. The least verbal of these is the quantitative (intensive) relation $A < B$, 'are there more A's or B's?' This relation appears so immediate that one might think that perceptual inspection was sufficient to establish it. Yet, although the collection is left before the child, one finds that in fact it is not resolved earlier than the other relations (Table 5) and is, indeed, only another presentation of them (if all A's are B's but not all B's are A's, then $A < B$).

The question is as follows. I: The child is given ten wooden beads (and is asked to verify that they are *all* made of wood). Of the ten, two are red and eight are yellow. The child is asked:

*a*) 'Are there in this (open) box more wooden beads or more yellow beads?';

*b*) 'Two little girls (giving their names) would like to make a necklace with the beads. The first one (name) takes all the yellow beads. Then she undoes her necklace and puts all the beads back in the box. The second (name) takes all the wooden beads. Which of them can make a longer necklace?';

*c*) 'If you give me all the wooden beads, will there be any beads left in the box?';

*d*) Question *a*) is asked again.

II: Ten artificial flowers are used, made up of two red roses and eight yellow daisies. Same questions *a*) to *d*), substituting bunches of flowers for necklaces. The results were as follows:

TABLE 6

Total successes (as % of number of subjects) in quantification of inclusion*

| Ages | 5 | 6 | 7 | 8 | 9 |
|---|---|---|---|---|---|
| Beads | 7 | 13 | 40 | 60 | 70 |
| Flowers | 10 | 23 | 43 | 60 | 73 |
| Both | 3 | 13 | 30 | 50 | 67 |

* 30 subjects per age group.

Three English psychologists, K. Lovell, D. Healey and A. D. Rowland,* repeated this experiment and asked the same questions, with ten subjects in each age group. They found:

TABLE 7

Results of Lovell, Healey and Rowland* using the same questions as in Table 6%

| Ages | 5 | 6 | 7 | 8 | 9–11 |
|---|---|---|---|---|---|
| Beads | 0 | 30 | 40 | 30 | 100 |
| Flowers | 0 | 20 | 20 | 30 | 90 |

* Translator's Note: The reference as given is incorrect. The correct reference is Lovell, Mitchell and Everett (1962).

It should be noted concerning Tables 5 and 6 that in all standardizations of research bearing on the qualitative logic of the subjects, there is a lower rate of success for all questions *taken together* than for the most difficult questions taken separately. There are two reasons for this. One is that at the level of concrete operations logical forms are not yet independent of their content. They are a structurization of the particular content and there is no necessary generalization (cf. the stages observed in conservation, where there is no generalization at first when the contents are different even though the structures are identical). The other is that in wishing to standardize one impoverishes the substance of free clinical questioning, hence the role of factors of verbal expression, attention, interest, etc., which the clinical method neutralizes but with the result that statistics are altogether excluded for want of sufficient homogeneity between individual questionings. It also happens that a standardized question may give rise to an appearance of comprehension in cases where more subtle clinical questioning would reveal the presence of intermediate reactions.

## 4 Seriation

In classification objects are grouped according to their equivalences and, correspondingly, in seriation they are grouped according to their ordered differences. Already in Chapter 23 (Mental Images), we broached the question of the seriation of

## Intellectual Operations and their Development

sticks of varying lengths. We have already indicated part of the technique[1] (making a 'staircase' by first placing the shortest stick at one end, then going on to longer and longer sticks until finally the longest of all is placed at the other end). We have also indicated the three qualitative stages that were found: no seriation, followed by empirical seriation (trial and error) and finally systematic or operational seriation (finding the smallest, then the next smallest of those that are left, and so on). This method therefore implies that an element E is understood to be at once bigger than those already put down ($E > D, C$, etc.) and smaller than those following ($E < F, G$, etc.). To check that the child understands this double relation $>$ and $<$ (and thus the reversibility of order), the technique can be taken a step further by giving the child one by one, after the series has been constructed, a few intermediate elements to be inserted near the half-way point. Subjects at stage II (empirical seriation) prefer to begin all over again, while those at stage III succeed in interpolating each stick correctly, making their comparisons only from one end of the series, knowing full well that the result would be identical were they to start at the other end. We give below the result of these two techniques combined, standardized by Vinh-Bang and B. Inhelder on 134 subjects.

TABLE 8

Reactions to seriation (as % of number of subjects)

| Age (and number of subjects) | 4(15) | 5(34) | 6(32) | 7(32) | 8(21) |
|---|---|---|---|---|---|
| *Construction of the series* | | | | | |
| O No attempt at seriation | 53 | 18 | 7 | 0 | 0 |
| I Small unco-ordinated series | 47 | 61 | 34 | 22 | 0 |
| II Trial and error | 0 | 12 | 25 | 15 | 5 |
| III Systematic method | 0 | 9 | 34 | 63 | 95 |
| *Interpolations* | | | | | |
| O No attempt | 60 | 43 | 6 | 0 | 0 |
| I Unsuccessful attempts | 20 | 16 | 12 | 0 | 0 |
| II Partial success | 20 | 32 | 54 | 37 | 5 |
| III Successful interpolation | 0 | 9 | 28 | 63 | 95 |

[1] See in particular the sizes of the sticks used: Chapter 23 Section 7, 2.

## Jean Piaget and Bärbel Inhelder

One can see that there is a fairly regular relation between the construction of the series and subsequent interpolations. One also sees how from the age of 6–7 there is a higher degree of success with seriation than with the two tests of class inclusion (Tables 5 and 6). Seriation produces a structure which is at once a little simpler from the operational point of view and much easier to symbolize by imaged representation (see Chapter 23).

### 5 'Grouping' structures

This necessarily brings us to comment on operational structures. In our attempt to decide whether the notion of operation was psychologically justified or arose from pre-existing logical notions, we first of all observed (in Section 2) that it corresponded to constant functional reactions observed in the construction of the concepts of conservation (simple reversibility, reversibility through compensation or through identity). We are now led to observe that the formation of operations also corresponds to the constitution of integrated operational structures. We have just seen two examples of these: simple classification (as against multiplicative matrices) and seriation. But do these structures really arise out of the child's own actions or are they a product of the logic of the psychologist who observes them, particularly if he knows something of theoretical logic? There are two arguments which we believe to be decisive.

The first is that these structures can be observed in a spontaneous state. Children engage of their own accord in seriations and classifications, and there is no need of instructions imposing a model which would necessarily be artificial.

The second is that the general aspect of these early structures has in point of fact escaped logicians. One of us (Piaget) having initially observed these structures as a psychologist tried to formulate them in the language of logic and in so doing naturally aroused the resistance of professional logicians. This general aspect, which we have termed a 'grouping', corresponds in reality to a level so elementary that these structures can only be of very limited interest in logic.[1] Their common character is, in-

---

[1] Nevertheless, purely descriptive sciences, such as systematic zoology and botany, use these structures exclusively in establishing classifications and relations.

## Intellectual Operations and their Development

deed, that they can only proceed 'step by step' and not according to any combination. This is precisely what distinguishes 'concrete operations' characteristic of children between the ages of seven and twelve from the formal combinatorial systems of later years. For example, one can bring together snails and slugs to form a natural class but one cannot bring together snails and camels in the same way whereas one *can* combine any number with any other.

It ensues that a 'grouping' is a system with the following properties: 1) by means of a given operation it engenders 'step by step' new elements which take their place in the system; for instance, it brings together two classes or two relations to form a third which comprises them both; 2) the operation can be inversed; 3) the product of the operation and of its inverse is the identical operation (uniting, then dissociating, amounts to not changing anything); 4) the fact of applying the operation to the same object a second time adds nothing to the first application (this is not so in the case of number where $1 + 1 = 2$ as against $+ A + A = + A$; 5) this last property restricts the mobility of the system (incomplete 'associativity').[1]

### 6 Multiplicative 'groupings'

Classifications and seriations are the two most important 'groupings' constituted at the age of about 7 or 8. It is at this stage that we observe the beginning of what are known as 'concrete' operations, so called because they bear directly on objects and not on verbally stated propositions or hypotheses. Both rest on additive operations affecting classes or relations. But at the same level other 'groupings' are constituted which might be called multiplicative, in that they bear on several classifications or several seriations at once. It is interesting to mention them, first to show that they too appear in a highly spontaneous manner and second to warn against the interferences that may occur between the figurative and the operative aspects of thought when one is devising tests patterned on these spontaneous structures (cf. Raven's 'matrices').

The simplest of the multiplicative structures arising out of

[1] In logic, 'associativity' is the property symbolized by the equivalence $(a+b) + c = a+(b+c)$. Example $(2+3)+4 = 2+(3+4)$ since $5+4 = 2+7$.

seriation is serial correspondence. One of us (Piaget) formerly used the following test with A. Szeminska. It consisted in presenting out of order dolls of differing heights and sticks that could likewise be seriated according to length, then asking which stick corresponds to which doll or vice versa. At the level of operational seriation the child finds it no more difficult to construct a double series than a single series[1] and he uses this procedure of his own accord to find the required correspondence (similarly with three seriations, when there are also rucksacks that can be ordered in size).

As to multiplicative classifications, it often happens that the child constructs of his own accord tables of double entry (or matrices) as in the following example. A girl of six and a half is asked to classify squares and circles, which may be either red or blue. She forms two collections beginning with shapes (squares and circles), then subdivides each according to colour (red or blue). She then notices that it is possible to put together reds and blues independently of shape and of her own accord puts the pile of red circles beneath that of red squares and likewise the pile of blue circles beneath that of blue squares, thus making a table of double entry. She then stretches out her hand and points with her thumb at one pile and with her little finger at the other and says quite spontaneously: 'Here are the circles and the squares (along the horizontal) and there are the reds and the blues (down the vertical).'

Raven used this structure to construct his famous intelligence test, known as *Progressive matrices*: he gave the subjects tables in which three cells out of four were already occupied. The fourth had to be filled by selecting the appropriate element among several. It is easy to see that the child is thus free to use two quite distinct methods. One is figural and based on perceptual symmetries, the other is operational, it rests on a double classification and draws on genuine inferences. To dissociate the two methods, it is enough to ask the subject to justify his choice and in particular to ask him whether or not the elements he has not chosen (among the 6–8 elements put before him) are excluded and why. We give below the results obtained when children of different ages were presented a) with a matrix relating to two

---

[1] Except of course when the two series are in inverse order as in the temporal seriation in Table 12 (Section 4).

## Intellectual Operations and their Development

objects (a daisy and an apple) and two colours (yellow and red) and b) with another relating to two fishes and two birds of two different colours and two 'orientations' (i.e. facing different ways).

TABLE 9

Example of matrices with two criteria
(objects and colours) or three criteria (objects, colours and orientations)

| Ages (and number of subjects) | Two criteria | | | | |
|---|---|---|---|---|---|
| | 4(13) | 5(29) | 6(14) | 7(13) | 8(15) |
| Figural solutions | 35 | 29 | 28 | 12 | 0 |
| Operational solutions | 0 | 12 | 57 | 62 | 88 |

| Ages (and number of subjects) | Three criteria | | | | |
|---|---|---|---|---|---|
| | 4(13) | 5(29) | 6(14) | 7(13) | 8(15) |
| Figural solutions | 25 | 18 | 28 | 0 | 0 |
| Operational solutions | 12 | 12 | 14 | 37 | 22 |

It can be seen that this matrix technique cannot be used as an operational test without proper caution.

## 7 Construction of the whole number

The construction of operational groupings of classes and of relations leads to that of the series of whole numbers. On this point as on so many others, we must first of all beware of verbal appearances. No one disputes that the child is helped in acquiring numbers by verbal numeration. It is often assumed, however, that this verbal learning suffices to engender the notion of number yet this is clearly false. There is for example a stage when the child will admit the equality of two rows of five counters when the rows are parallel and correspond optically term-for-term. Yet he will refuse to admit equality as soon as one of the rows is altered by moving the last two elements 1–2 cm. further along. He refuses to do so even if he counts '5 and 5'. Thus, a child of four may say 'that makes 1, 2, 3, 4, 5 here and 1, 2, 3 . . . 4, 5 there, but even so that makes more there'. In this example the numbers 1 to 5 are names which serve to individualize the elements but which do not lead to the conclusion that the whole is equal to the sum of the parts and so do not lead to the conservation of the whole. It is clear that in the absence of additivity and conservation number cannot be said to exist.

In taking these two fundamental properties as criteria of number, we are once again not guided by logic but simply by what the child spontaneously recognizes on reaching the operational stage at the age of 7 or 8. At this stage he even succeeds in recognizing the equivalence of sets which he cannot count but which he sees to be equal on the basis of term-for-term correspondence. We must therefore try to discover how number is constructed since language alone is not sufficient to transmit it ready made. Without going beyond what was said in 1) to 6), we find that three hypotheses suggest themselves: a) the first is that number is independent of elementary logical structures; b) the second is that it derives directly from them (cardinal numbers arising out of classes and ordinal numbers out of seriation); c) the third is that it constitutes a new and original synthesis; all the elements of this synthesis are borrowed from 'grouping' structures but the total structure results from a new mode of composition.

## 8  So-called intuition of number and numerical correspondences

The first solution amounts to considering number as the product of a primitive and independent 'intuition'. This is the view upheld in mathematics by the 'intuitionists' (from Poincaré to Brouwer) with arguments appropriate to their discipline. From the psychological point of view, the two main difficulties which stand in the way of this solution are that, as we have seen, elementary intuitions of number are not immediately numerical but only 'prenumerical' for want of additivity and particularly of conservation. Also the transition from these preoperational structures to the operational concept of number proceeds according to stages that are surprisingly parallel (with approximate term-for-term synchronization) to those which we indicated in the construction of groupings of classes and of relations.

These two affirmations (initial non-conservation of numerical sets and parallel succession of stages) can be controlled by a very simple experiment. This has been repeated by several researchers (Churchill, Laurendeau and Pinard, etc.). It was devised by one of us (Piaget) in 1919-1920, to distinguish between normal children and young epileptics in the Voisin Division of *La Salpêtrière* (in fact normal children reacted in exactly the same way between the ages of 4 and 6, as was later observed with A. Szeminska!)[1] The child is first shown a series of 6-7 blue counters with a small space between them and then given a box of red counters. He is asked to put on the table as many red counters as there are blue. Four stages can be observed. During the first, the child merely constructs with the red counters a row of the same length as the row of blue counters. He judges quantity by the space that is filled. During the second stage, the subject establishes a term-for-term but optical correspondence (each red opposite a blue). When this optical configuration is destroyed by spacing out one of the rows, the child thinks that there is no longer equivalence either in quantity or in number. During the third stage, the child proceeds in the same way but when one of the rows has been spaced out, he admits that he will find the same number if he counts yet continues to think that the total quantity has changed (see Gréco, 1961). Finally at the operational level, correspondence, once established, is seen to involve the conservation of equivalences (including that of quantity thereafter conceived as measurable by number) despite changes in configuration.

Egg cups and eggs can also be used to reinforce the correspondence by a relation between container and content. A variant of this (used in our first experiments) takes the form of a shopping game. A coin is exchanged for an object (nine times in succession), then the experimenter hides one of the sets (coins or objects) and asks the child whether the visible set and the hidden set are equal or not. In this case a control is indispensable: the exchange is again performed, in reverse, up to a given number (six for instance) and the child is asked whether the remainder (the child's three coins and the partner's three objects which are kept hidden) are also equal in number or not. The Vinh-Bang–Inhelder standardizations have yielded the results shown in Table 10 overleaf.

It can be seen that the degree of success in both tests together

[1] See Piaget and Szeminska, 1952; P. Gréco, 1961.

is, once again, lower than for each separately. This is due to the two reasons indicated in Section 2.

TABLE 10

Complete success in tests of numerical correspondence
(as % of 25 subjects per age group)

| Tests | Shopping game | Egg Cups | Shopping game + Egg Cups + |
|---|---|---|---|
| Age 4 | 4 | 8 | 4 |
| ,, 5 | 46 | 50 | 35 |
| ,, 6 | 64 | 75 | 50 |
| ,, 7 | 88 | 80 | 80 |

| Tests | Shopping game − Egg Cups + | Shopping game + Egg Cups − | Shopping game − Egg Cups − |
|---|---|---|---|
| Age 4 | 4 | 6 | 82 |
| ,, 5 | 15 | 12 | 38 |
| ,, 6 | 32 | 14 | 4 |
| ,, 7 | 0 | 8 | 12 |

## 9  Operational nature of number

From these and many similar facts we can conclude that number does not correspond to a primitive or independent intuition but is constructed operationally, growing out of an initial level of non-conservation in the same way and at the same ages as the groupings of classes and relations. Must we therefore conclude, in agreement with Whitehead and Bertrand Russell, that cardinal numbers result simply from a correspondence between classes (as the preceding experiments seem to indicate) and ordinal numbers from a serial correspondence? This conclusion is incorrect for the following reasons. First, a simple correspondence between classes would make it possible to acquire any given number independently of the others, for example five before four (like O. Köhler's birds, trained to discern a collection of five elements yet unable to discern collections of four or three!) In actual fact, the child learns numbers in the order of their series and it is this

## Intellectual Operations and their Development

series which constitutes the natural operational structure[1] from the psychological point of view, and not isolated numbers which properly belong to logical atomism. Secondly, and above all, the term-for-term correspondence which enters into the preceding experiments ceases to be an operation concerned with groupings of classes and of relations. This is because it abstracts the qualities of objects in counting each as one (arithmetical unit). In this, it differs from the correspondences found in multiplicative matrices of classes or of relations which rest on qualitative equivalences. Number therefore supposes a new synthesis despite the fact that all its elements are borrowed from 'groupings'. It retains the structure of inclusion characteristic of classes (1 included in 2; 2 in 3; etc.) but just as it disregards qualities in transforming objects into units, so it introduces a serial order as the only means of distinguishing one unit from the next: 1 then 1, then 1, etc. (spatial or temporal order, or simply order of enumeration). Number is therefore a combination of the serial order of units and of the progressive inclusion of the sets which result from bringing the units together (1 included in $1 + 1$; $1 + 1$ included in $1 + 1 + 1$, etc.). It is a new and original synthesis, yet one which borrows all its elements from the simpler structures of logical groupings.

### 4 Spatio-temporal operations and chance

The above-mentioned operations all refer to sets of discontinuous objects and do not take into account (or have ceased to take into account) the spatio-temporal proximities or non-proximities between the elements. In the case of a single continuous object, however, problems can only be solved by operations dealing with the relations between the parts and the whole (cf. inclusions) or with those between the parts themselves (cf. asymmetrical or symmetrical relations). At the same time, spatial and temporal proximities have to be taken into account. What will happen

---

[1] In this it is comparable to 'groupings': there are no isolated classes but only classifications and no isolated asymmetrical relations but only seriations. Similarly, number does not exist in isolation but in relation to the series of numbers.

when the child has to deal with such problems? As we watch him, we are immediately struck by the admirable spontaneity of his operations (particularly when we recall that in most countries geometry is not taught until some years after arithmetic) for we find that he uses the same operations and their same groupings or syntheses, albeit on a lower plane which we shall therefore call 'infralogical' (not to be confused with prelogical).[1] The only distinguishing feature of these infralogical operations is that they take into account proximities *within* figures or continuous objects. Moreover, they begin to take shape at the same ages as, and in a closely parallel fashion to, the operations already mentioned (logico-numerical operations).

## 1  Spontaneous measurement

A striking instance of this parallelism can be seen in the elaboration of spontaneous spatial measurements. It has unfortunately not been possible to standardize the experiment in question as it would have lost all its immediate freshness had this been done.

The child is shown a tower made of blocks of unequal sizes and he is asked to build a similar tower some distance away on a lower table with blocks that are also unequal. He is naturally offered everything that he needs for measuring: strings, rods, etc. During the earliest stage, the child merely copies the model by eye without considering the level of the base, and when he is asked how he knows that it is right, he merely says: 'I have good eyes.' During the next stage, the child no longer relies purely on this visual transfer and demands a manual transfer. Having made his copy, he wants to bring it close to the model. On reaching the third stage, the child begins to understand the need for a middle term but at first he uses only his own body for this purpose. He places one hand on top of his tower and the other at the base and he tries to carry across this height as an empty interval in space. Alternatively, he stands next to his tower and places a finger where the top of the tower touches his shoulder and another

---

[1] We use the term 'infralogical' in view of the fact that logical operations deal with sets of discrete objects, disregarding what is within the object, whereas infralogical operations are concerned with links within the object (whatever its size, even if it is the spatial universe itself in its entirety—the point being that it is then conceived as a unique continuum, hence as a continuous object).

## Intellectual Operations and their Development

where the base of the tower touches his leg. He then carries across these two reference points to apply them to the model tower. It then occurs to him to use an external object. He builds a third tower and carries it from his copy to the model or else uses a stick which is of exactly the same length as his tower is high. Let us note that the use of this middle term M to judge whether towers A and B are equal indicates that an operational mechanism is beginning to function in the form of transitivity: $A = M$, $M = B$, therefore $A = B$. This cannot yet be called measurement, however. The child comes closer to it during the fifth stage when he first thinks of using a stick which is longer than his tower is high and marking off on it with his finger the point corresponding to the top of the tower. True measurement is finally achieved during the sixth stage as soon as the subject discovers that it is possible to use a stick smaller than the tower by holding it up a number of times against the copy-tower and against the model tower (this happens on an average at the age of seven or eight).

What does spontaneous measurement consist in? The answer is that there are three operations: 1) dividing the continuum into a number of parts and realizing that it is possible to nest the parts within one another and within the whole. Hence this operation of 'sub-division' corresponds to inclusion, the only difference being that it is based on proximities and not on similarities; 2) ordering the positions of the parts in a spatial sequence. This corresponds to serial ordering; 3) lastly, and above all, establishing a unit by choosing a part and holding it successively against the others. This constitutes a synthesis of sub-division and of displacement (the latter then being an ordered change of positions). Measurement is thus a synthesis of sub-division and of displacement just as number is a synthesis of inclusion and of serial order. The two constructions are thus isomorphic apart from the part played by proximities. Moreover, they are practically synchronous, with just a slight time-lag (about six months) in the case of measurement. This is because the unit has to be constructed by dividing the continuum instead of being 'given' by the presence of discontinuous objects once the abstraction of qualities has taken place.

*Jean Piaget and Bärbel Inhelder*

## 2 Other spatial operations

We have taken operations of measurement first in order to show the parallelism that exists between them and those discussed in the previous section. We must not imagine that in so doing we have exhausted the subject of operational space.

It we examine the chronological order of development of scientific geometries, we find that it has proceeded from Euclidean metrics to projective space and thence to topological structures. When we observe the child, however, we find that the order of construction of spatial operations is much closer to the theoretical order of construction of geometries as based on hierarchical 'groups' of transformations (this, incidentally, is a further argument in support of the 'natural' character of operations). We thus find that topological operations come first ('enclosure' and order, etc.) followed simultaneously by Euclidean operations (leading to metrics and to the system of natural co-ordinates) and projective operations (leading to the co-ordination of viewpoints).

We have room to quote only a few experiments in this chapter and are unable to give a sample of each variety of operational spatial structure. We could otherwise have examined each in turn: topological operations as revealed in experiments on the constitution of order and on conservation of proximities;[1] Euclidean structures as seen in such operational constructions as conservation of lengths, surfaces and volumes, and the elaboration of systems of reference (horizontal and vertical); projective structures as seen in the perspective transformations of a single object or of a system of several objects with co-ordination of viewpoints. Let us, however, confine ourselves to a single instance of projective operations and so that we need not discuss the respective part played by perception and by operations in the process of structurization, let us choose the transformation of shadows, which is in fact similar in all respects to perspective transformations.

A light source (candle) and a vertical white screen are presented to the child. He is first shown how an object placed between them and held by tweezers projects a shadow onto the screen and how the shape of the shadow changes according to the position of the object. Then the candle is put out and a rigid rod is placed

[1] B. Inhelder and M. Bovet, in preparation.

between it and the screen. The subject is asked 1) to make drawings anticipating the progressive shortening of the rod as it is rotated from the vertical into the horizontal position on the plane defined by the rod and the child's eye; 2) to anticipate that the shadow will be reduced to a point when the rod is horizontal and thus seen end on by the subject; 3) to anticipate the progressive transformation of the shadow cast by a ring. This shadow is first of all circular, then elliptical, becoming progressively flatter as the object is rotated; 4) to foresee that when the ring is viewed horizontally the shadow will be reduced to a straight line.

Here are the results standardized by Vinh-Bang–Inhelder on thirty children per age group:

TABLE 11

Anticipation of the shape of shadows
(as % of number of subjects)

| Ages | 7 | 8 | 9 | 10 |
|---|---|---|---|---|
| Correct anticipation of all four transformations | 3 | 6 | 13 | 70 |
| ,, ,, of rotation of rod | 3 | 16 | 30 | 86 |
| ,, ,, of point | 33 | 53 | 70 | 96 |
| ,, ,, of rotation of ring | 23 | 40 | 46 | 90 |
| ,, ,, of straight line | 13 | 23 | 26 | 80 |

This experiment can also take the form of asking the subjects to choose between ready made drawings. In this case, correct answers are given from a slightly earlier age.[1]

## 3 Temporal operations

In addition to perceptual time and intuitive or pre-operational time, there are temporal operations: 1) ordering operations, first of all, which consist in seriating events according to their order of succession; 2) operations of sub-division and inclusion, which

[1] K. Lovell, D. Healey and A. D. Rowland (1962, *Child Development* No. 33) repeated twelve of our experiments on space with normal and educationally subnormal children. They found good correlations between the various stages of spatial operations and mental development in general. Thus 'it is found that 14- to 15-year-old E.S.N. children have the operational mobility of about an average $7\frac{1}{2}$-year-old'.

consist in marking off the intervals of time between the ordered points and in 'fitting' the small ones within the larger ones, etc.; 3) metrical operations which consist in choosing an interval of time as a unit and using it as a standard for the measurement of all others (cf. musical notation). Like spatial measurements they are the outcome of a synthesis of sub-division and displacement. These three kinds of operations develop spontaneously in the child and can be illustrated by a very simple experiment.

The child is shown two jars, one vertically above the other. The liquid in the first jar drains into the second in stages regulated by a tap. A series of nine line drawings is also presented to the child, showing the outline of the two jars (the top one spherical and the bottom one cylindrical) and the liquid levels in the jars during each stage of the experiment. The child is asked, by way of introduction, to check the correspondence between the drawings and the real water levels. Following this, the tests begin: 1) The drawings are shuffled and the child is asked to seriate them according to the order of events: 'Where was the water at the beginning? Where was it after that? And after that?' etc.; 2) When the seriation is complete, the six drawings are each cut into half and the twelve pieces shuffled. The child is then shown a particular level in the top or bottom jar and asked to find the corresponding level in the other jar. This necessitates double seriation in inverse order for the top and the bottom. 3) The experimenter can vary his approach by drawing a line in ink on the jars to indicate levels or presenting the prepared drawings and asking whether more or less time is required for the level to be displaced from $I_2$ to $I_5$ (levels in the top jar) or from $II_2$ to $II_4$ (levels in the bottom jar, the two jars being of different shapes to avoid a simple spatial reading), etc. 4) Finally, since the bottom jar is cylindrical, it is possible by using equidistant levels to introduce the child to a measurement of time.

In Table 12, according to Vinh-Bang–Inhelder's standardization, are the results for ordering operations.

It can be seen that double seriation with inversion (falling levels above and rising levels below) is not acquired by 75 per cent of the subjects until a year after single seriation. It should at the same time be pointed out that in the case of moving objects succession and simultaneity are easy to establish only when the objects are moving at equal speeds. Young children

## Intellectual Operations and their Development

cannot cope with unequal speeds. As an experiment two dolls can be made to run together along parallel courses. Their starting point is the same and they stop together. They may do so at the same point (equal speeds, in which case the fact that they stop simultaneously presents no difficulty), or at different points (unequal speeds, in which case the simultaneity of times of arrival is denied until about the age of six and the equal duration of synchronous journeys is denied until about seven or eight).

TABLE 12

Temporal seriation
(as % of 25 subjects per age group)

| Ages | 5 | 6 | 7 | 8 | 9 |
|---|---|---|---|---|---|
| Single seriation (with spontaneous corrections) | 28 | 56 | 76 | 92 | 96 |
| Double seriation with inversion | 8 | 8 | 56 | 88 | 92 |

Alternatively, a liquid can be allowed to drain through a Y-tube into two containers. These may be identical (in which case neither simultaneities nor synchronisms present any difficulty) or they may be different so that the level of liquid rises more quickly in one than in the other (in which case neither the simultaneity of the stoppages nor the equal duration of flow are recognized until the same ages). In short, as soon as there are unequal speeds, subjects have difficulty in making judgments of succession. This applies both to simultaneity (of stoppages) and to actual duration (was the time taken equal, or longer or shorter?). The difficulty arises because it is necessary to co-ordinate the (spatially measurable) times relative to each of the movements. In this respect, time can be conceived as a co-ordination of speeds in the same way as space rests on a co-ordination of displacements (including positions but disregarding speeds).

## 4 Speed

We need only briefly mention operations relating to speed since we gave in the preceding chapter (Chapter 23, Section 6, 7) a table of anticipations concerning overtaking, catching up and partial catching up. It will be enough to point out that cinematic operations are of two kinds. Some are ordinal and concerned only with a direct comparison of the speeds of two moving objects in certain privileged situations. Others are metrical and can concentrate on a single moving object whose speed is then determined by the relation $v = d : t$. The first of these operations rest on the intuition of overtaking, which provides a univocal criterion of higher speed. But at the pre-operational level the child does not take into account the trajectory itself (except when the perception of speed, as distinct from notional judgment, is imposed on him). Essentially, he considers only the points of arrival. It is only at about the age of seven or eight, as we have seen (Chapter 23, Tables 10 and 11), that the trajectories of the two moving objects with one overtaking the other are correctly reproduced and their subsequent course anticipated. It is therefore from this level onwards that it is possible to speak of an ordinal operation referring to overtaking. The operation can be said to be fully generalized when the subject has learned to anticipate the subsequent course of itineraries visibly leading only to catching up or partial catching up. As we have seen (Chapter 23, Table 11), these anticipations are achieved only towards the age of nine or ten since they involve not only the order of positions but also a (hyperordinal) consideration of the diminution and increase of intervals. It is only when this generalization has been achieved that the metrical operation by means of which the distance covered is related to the duration of the movement can be performed. This operation, which the child becomes capable of only at eleven or twelve, naturally appears at first in a form of logical or qualitative multiplication such as we find in Aristotle's *Physica*: same space (or greater) × less time = faster, etc. (the only indeterminate multiplications, out of nine combinations, being 'further × more time =?' and 'less far × less time =?'). In order to pass from this concrete multiplication of relations to actual measurement, however, it is necessary to introduce proportions (for example, if $2d : 1t = 4d : 2t$, then the speed is the same). Proportions however, as we shall see in Section 5, necessitate the use of formal operations.

## 5 Chance

Chance is another operational notion and we should like to indicate how it comes to be formed at the level of concrete operations. In our scale of observation, we can define chance, with Cournot, as the interference of two independent causal series, thus as a product of the 'mixing' of such series. Now, mixing is the prototype of irreversible phenomena, in the sense that if one mixes a number of objects (thus interfering with the natural course of events) the probability of returning to the original order becomes less and less. It was therefore of interest, in order to check our hypotheses on the reversible nature of operational structures, to examine the notion of chance and how it is acquired. Is the discovery of chance bound up with the evolution of operations (so that at the level where operations permit deduction, chance would be seen as that which resists deduction)? Alternatively, is the notion of fortuity accessible at all levels and particularly at the level where the child conceives transformations only in an irreversible manner? (See Section 2 concerning levels of non-conservation).

The result of the experiments carried out in this connection (Piaget and Inhelder, 1953) proved very decisive. There is no comprehension of chance at pre-operational levels and the idea of irreversible 'mixing' can be assimilated only with reference to reversible operational composition. It is worth quoting one of our experiments even though we have only qualitative results to offer.

The subject is shown a rectangular box. It is tilted towards one of the short sides which is partitioned so that it is possible to line up eight white beads next to eight red beads. The subject is told that the box is going to be tilted the other way. The beads will run into the non-partitioned area and then each return to a compartment. He is asked how they will be distributed (will they be mixed or will the eight white beads still be on one side and the eight red beads on the other?) The child gives his answer, then the tilting takes place and he is asked what will happen next.

One finds that the youngest subjects anticipate a return to the initial state. When they see that the beads are mixed, they sometimes say that if one goes on there will be 'unmixing'. They often expect in particular that all the white beads will finally go to the side of the reds and *vice versa*, with a further *chassé-croisé* providing one has the patience to go on long enough. In short, children at a level of non-conservation and of irreversibility seem for once to admit the existence of a reversible process. The truth is that they do so in appearance only. This is because a reversible process is a transition from a state A to an equally significant state B, with the possibility of return from B to A according to the same transformation as that from A to B, but in the opposite direction. In this particular instance, however, there is a privileged state, which is the original order. It is followed by a state of disorder which is purely accidental (as Aristotle said of $\tau\upsilon\chi\hat{\eta}$ and of $\ddot{\upsilon}\beta\rho\iota\varsigma$). Finally there is a return to order because order, through a kind of pseudo-conservation or persistence, has not ceased in fact to exert an influence. Asking the child to draw trajectories produces very illuminating results: there is no collision between the beads. Instead there are systematic trajectories leading from one side to the other or even simple 'return journeys to and from the starting point'. From the age of eight or nine, however, the child recognizes that the beads will be increasingly mixed and regards a return to the initial state as impossible or 'just possible' provided one goes on for a very long time.

## 6 Chance (*continued*) and the game of heads or tails

A game of 'heads or tails' (with counters that have a cross on one side and a circle on the other) can be used to show that at the age of five or six nearly half the children believe that it is possible to forecast the results of tossing a number of single counters and then a handful. To go beyond verbal reactions the original counters are replaced, unbeknown to the child, by a bag of faked counters with crosses on both sides and a handful of these are tossed: before the age of seven or eight more than half the subjects accept this as natural but from the age of eight they either think that 'it's not normal' or they discover the trick (see Table 13).

We thus find that the notion of chance develops at the level of concrete operations and could be defined as that which 'resists' operations. These, however, gradually begin to take their revenge by assimilating statistical situations in the form of probability. This is a further indication of the spontaneous character of operations. We live in a society where questions of probability

*Intellectual Operations and their Development*

TABLE 13*

Reactions to the tossing of counters (chance)
(as % of 182 subjects)

| Ages | 5–6 | 7 | 8 | 9 | 10 | 11 | 12 |
|---|---|---|---|---|---|---|---|
| *Anticipation* | | | | | | | |
| Possible | 47 | 27 | 12 | 20 | 17 | 0 | 3 |
| Uncertain | 34 | 12 | 0 | 0 | 0 | 0 | 0 |
| Impossible | 19 | 61 | 88 | 80 | 83 | 100 | 97 |
| *Faked counters* | | | | | | | |
| 'Not normal' | 23 | 47 | 58 | 88 | 68 | 64 | 68 |
| Discovery of the trick | 16 | 27 | 34 | 42 | 58 | 71 | 88 |

\* Vinh-Bang–Inhelder standardization.

are more and more becoming a preoccupation of the élite, but they are not studied in school and it is not until the *baccalauréat* that pupils are given the rudiments of the combinatorial system. Yet, in spite of this, adolescents succeed in discovering for themselves the practical application (though naturally without the theory). Here first is an example of elementary quantification of probabilities:

The experimenter presents a bag containing thirty counters of four different colours (fifteen yellow, eight red, five blue and two green). A model set of identical counters is laid on the table next to the child and he is asked to forecast what pair is most likely to 'come up' if two counters are taken at random from the bag. The counters that are taken out are not put back and the child is asked to forecast the next eight draws.

The results were as follows with 138 subjects between the ages of 9 and 12 (Vinh-Bang and Inhelder):

TABLE 14

Chance drawing of pairs

| Age (and number of subjects) | 9(30) | 10(40) | 11(38) | 12(30) |
|---|---|---|---|---|
| Quantification at each draw | 23 | 42·5 | 87 | 97 |
| Beginning of quantification | 67 | 42·5 | 13 | 3 |
| Absence of quantification | 10 | 15 | 0 | 0 |

One sees that the problem is solved only towards the age of eleven, that is to say the time when formal operations begin. The reason is that this kind of solution necessitates a combinational system and, as we shall see, this system is one of the two main characteristics of higher operations.

## 5 Propositional or formal operations

The final phase in the construction of the operations peculiar to childhood and adolescence begins towards the age of eleven or twelve and a provisional state of equilibrium is reached at fourteen or fifteen. The most noticeable character of this final phase is that the subject's reasoning is no longer directly confined to concrete objects or manipulations of these (operations concerning classes, relations and numbers, and spatio-temporal operations). He can now make operational deductions on the basis of hypotheses stated verbally (propositional logic). As a result, the form of these new operational structures becomes dissociated from the content, hence the possibility of hypothetico-deductive or formal reasoning.

These new operations, however, do not arise *ex nihilo* and the fact that they appear at different ages in different environments prevents us from attributing them to maturation alone. It is therefore important to understand how they grow out of earlier operations. It is possible to do this since the two main characteristics of formal operations, that is the combinatorial system and the INRC group (or group of the two reversibilities) are both grafted on to concrete operations with their 'groupings'. At the same time, they transcend and integrate them. This is a fine example of integration of earlier structures into later ones in the psycho-biological sense of these various terms.

### 1 The combinatorial system

The combinatorial system is first found in two complementary forms from the age of twelve: combining objects and combining judgments. In the case of objects, one can for instance give the child counters of 2, 3, 4, 5 etc., different colours and ask him to

## Intellectual Operations and their Development

combine them two by two in every possible way as if they were people going out for a walk in pairs and choosing a different companion each time. One finds that a child at the level of concrete operations can achieve only a few combinations, proceeding by trial and error, while from the age of eleven, he proceeds in a systematic fashion: 1-2, 1-3, 1-4, etc., 2-3, 2-4, 3-4, etc. He is naturally not asked to find the formula, i.e. to reflect on the combinations, but simply to find an exhaustive method, i.e. to realize them all.

Another example, studied with G. Noelting,[1] consisted in giving the subjects four containers filled with colourless and odourless liquids and a burette (liquids 1, 3 and 5 together give a yellow colour, 4 is a bleaching agent and 2 is simply distilled water). The child is shown (separately) the colour that can be obtained and he is asked to reproduce it for himself. At the level of concrete operations, the child generally proceeds by incomplete pairs (1-2, 2-3, 3-4 and 4-5) or by mixing them all. At the age of fourteen or fifteen, he succeeds in realizing all the combinations and in determining that 1-3-5 give the colour, 4 bleaches and 2 is neutral. The quantitative results are as follows:

TABLE 15

Complete success (with proof) in the combination of liquids as % of subjects (number of subjects given in brackets)

| Ages | 12 | 13 | 14 | 15 | 16 |
|---|---|---|---|---|---|
| Elementary school | 7·1 (42) | 8·2 (49) | 11·6 (43) | 50 (12) | — |
| Secondary school | 10 (10) | 12·5 (8) | 18·8 (16) | 42·1 (19) | 66·6 (9) |

## 2 Propositional logic

It therefore seems that the combinatorial system as applied to objects becomes generalized during this period. It is very interesting to note that propositional operations appearing at the same level of development, such as implication ($p$ implies $q$), disjunction (either $p$, or $q$, or both), incompatibility (either $p$, or $q$, or neither), etc., do in fact derive directly from a combinatorial

[1] See Inhelder-Piaget, 1958.

system. In this they differ from the operations concerning classes and relations found at the preceding level. 'Groupings' of these consisted only in hierarchical inclusions or logical sequences along one or more dimensions but without a combinatorial system. It goes without saying that in order to check the combinatorial character of emerging propositional operations, we shall not rest content with a logical analysis since this would prove nothing as to their psychological functioning. We shall on the contrary consider them from the functionalist standpoint, which gave one of us (Piaget) the inspiration for a series of experiments on the induction of physical laws.[1] We shall ask ourselves how the adolescent reasons concerning these by comparison with a child who is still at the level of concrete operations. We shall then, in the functional context of responses to given stimuli, see the pre-adolescent and the adolescent combining their ideas, hypotheses or judgments as they combine the objects or causal factors involved. In so doing they are unwittingly using the combinatorial system which essentially characterizes what may be termed their propositional operations.

In one of our experiments, the child is given all the necessary experimental material and asked to determine what causes variations in the frequency of oscillation of a pendulum. (The subject can vary the weights that are suspended, the length of the string, the amplitude of the oscillation and the initial impetus.) Alternatively, he can be asked to determine what causes variations in the flexibility of rods attached in a horizontal position. (In this case the subject can vary the length of the rods, their substance, their thickness or the form of their cross-sections, etc.) Two important differences are found between the reactions of the adolescent and that of the child. The child immediately goes into action and gropes without any system until he has found a hypothesis: he then verifies it by means of classifications, seriations and above all correspondences, in short all the concrete operations. The adolescent also makes a few attempts but then he pauses for thought and tries to draw up a list of possible hypotheses and only then does he proceed with verification. The second difference lies in the verification itself. In the child it consists in global correspondences, without dissociation of factors. In the adolescent it assumes a new character which is all the more impressive

[1] See Inhelder and Piaget, 1958. For confirmations, see K. Lovell, 1961.

## Intellectual Operations and their Development

in that nothing of the kind is learnt in school. He tries to dissociate factors in order to vary them one by one, suppressing or neutralizing the others according to the rule 'all other things being equal'. For instance, in order to show that the length of the rods affects their flexibility, a child of nine compares a long thin rod with a short thick rod. His reply to our immediate objection is that 'Like that, you can really see the difference.' At fourteen to fifteen however, the subject carefully dissociates these two factors and explicitly states that unless this precaution is taken 'it proves nothing'.

Dissociating factors and particularly interpreting facts according to the multiple relations between them supposes a combinatorial system since concrete operations are not sufficient. The problem is the same in all cases, whether it is a question, as in the pendulum experiment, of discovering that the length of the string alone plays a part and that the weights and the amplitude of the oscillation etc. are not significant, or of establishing, as in the flexibility experiment, that all the factors operate cumulatively. Let $p$ be the affirmation of an action and $\sim p$ its negation and let $q$ be the affirmation of another action and $\sim q$ its negation, etc. It is not enough to use a multiplicative matrix $p \cdot q$, $p \cdot \sim q$, $\sim p \cdot q$, $\sim p \cdot \sim q$. One must use the sixteen possible combinations resulting from these four base associations: for example if $p$ and $q$ are always true together, or $q$ without $p$, or neither $p$ nor $q$, but $p$ is never true without $q$, then $p$ implies $q$; etc. The remarkable fact is that the subject, in his spontaneous language and naturally without any reference to logic, uses all these combinations and makes them play an essential part in his reasoning. It is in this sense that at the level of formal operations one can watch the beginning of a combinatorial system applied to ideas and judgments as well as to objects or factors.

The combinatorial approach, however, does not appear suddenly *ex abrupto*. The way is prepared for it by the multiplicative matrices that are found from the time of concrete 'groupings'. It results, also, from a generalization of the operations of classification since it is only a classification of all the classifications that are possible with $n$ elements (in the same way as the permutations that are achieved a little later constitute a seriation of all the seriations that are possible with $n$ elements). The combinatorial system therefore constitutes a generalization of

## 3 The group of the two reversibilities

The same is true of the second characteristic new feature of formal operational structures: the INRC group or group of the two reversibilities (inversion N and reciprocity R; I being the null or 'identical' transformation and C the correlative or dual transformation, i.e. the inverse of the reciprocal). Here again, it is not from logic that we draw our inspiration since the curious fact is that logicians had not noticed the existence of this group of four transformations in propositional logic until we ourselves[1] came to infer it from the generalization of 'groupings', that is, from an analysis of the operational structures of real thought in its psychological development. It turned out that this generalization of groupings in fact corresponds to what can be observed between the ages of twelve and fifteen, in the following way. There are some concrete 'groupings' (those of class) in which reversibility takes the form of inversion. This, composed with the direct operation gives the null operation: $+ A - A = 0$ (adding a class then taking it away amounts to doing nothing). In other concrete 'groupings' (those of relation), the form of reversibility is reciprocity. This, composed with the direct operation leads to the suppression, not of an object or a class, but of a difference, so that it leads to equivalence: if $a$ is the difference between A and B in the relation $A < B$, then $+ a - a = 0$, that is $A = A$. But no 'grouping' composes inversions with reciprocities. The two systems remain heterogeneous at the level of concrete operations. On the other hand, propositional operations arising from the combinatorial system always comprise an inverse N and a reciprocal R. In this way, the implication $p \supset q$ has as its inverse $p . \sim q$ (for example, when the adolescent observes in the experiment quoted above that a heavier suspended object $p$ does not modify the frequency of oscillation of the pendulum $q$, he concludes that it is false that weight is responsible for the modification and he therefore rejects the implication $p \supset q$). But the implication $p \supset q$ has as its reciprocal $q \supset p$ and if $p \supset q$ and

---

[1] Piaget, 1950 and 1952.

*Intellectual Operations and their Development*

$q \supset p$ are both true then $p = q$. Moreover, the inverse of $q \supset p$ is $\sim p \cdot q$, which is the correlative of $p \supset q$ and the reciprocal of $p \cdot \sim q$. In short, we have NR = C, NC = R, RC = N and NRC = I, that is a group of four transformations (Klein's *Vierergruppe*) applied to propositional operations. One can see how as a result a general system of this kind constitutes the final synthesis of the partial systems or 'groupings' constructed during the stage of concrete operations. It does so because it brings together in a single total organization the inversions and reciprocities that were until then separated.

The INRC group, which the adolescent naturally never formulates, nonetheless plays a constant part in his reasoning (just as the Greeks continually handled the syllogism before Aristotle had attempted to codify it). This is the case in all situations calling for the mutual co-ordination of inverses and reciprocals. Children of seven to eleven are at a loss in these situations. We find this, for instance, in problems of double systems of reference. Thus, when a snail moves about on a small board its movement in one direction[1] will be I and in the other N; but if one moves the board in an opposite direction from I movement I will be cancelled (in relation to a point of reference on the table) not by N but by a reciprocal movement R inherent to the board. The inverse of R is C, correlative of I (and cumulating with it). A child at the concrete level reasons correctly concerning either I and N or R and C, but does not succeed in co-ordinating the four transformations. From the age of 11 or 12 however, anticipatory understanding is easy.

## 4 *Action and reaction; proportions*

Another example[2] is that of hydrostatic equilibrium (see Fig. 2). In a U-shaped tube half filled with a liquid of varying density (water, alcohol, or glycerine), a piston is placed on one of the arms and loaded with variable weights. The subject is asked to anticipate the rise of the liquid in the other arm. Small children do not understand action and reaction. Thus, they think that the weight of the liquid acts in the same direction as that of the piston. At the

[1] We are using the symbol I to represent the direct operation: it is an abbreviation for I$x$ = direct operation $x$ remaining identical.
[2] These experiments (see Inhelder and Piaget 1958) have unfortunately not yet been standardized by us but they have been standardized by Lovell, 1961.

level of propositional operations, however, the adolescent clearly distinguishes and correctly co-ordinates the action of the weights I or its inverse N (removing the weights), the reaction of the liquid R (as a function of its specific weight) which acts in the opposite direction from I and its inverse C (diminution of the weight, which acts in the same direction as I).

This understanding of equilibrium goes hand in hand with that of proportions. On a lever balance, one can balance a weight either by putting the same weight at the same distance from the fulcrum, or by putting a smaller weight at a proportionally greater distance. By manipulating this apparatus, subjects succeed from the age of twelve or thirteen in understanding this proportionality, first in a qualitative way ('it comes to the same whether you increase the weight or the distance') then in simple metrical forms. The qualitative reasoning of the subject proceeds directly from the INRC group, as $I/R = C/N$ or $IN = RC$ (e.g. increasing a weight is to decreasing a distance as increasing the distance is to decreasing the weight).

In short, the action of the INRC group is shown by the development of a series of operational schemata. At first sight, one does not perceive the relationship between them for one sees nothing in common, without the analysis of inferential mechanisms, between a double system of geometrical references, a physical principle of action and reaction and the general notion of proportions. One also fails to see why they all develop at approximately the same time. Together with the schemata arising directly out of the combinatorial system, they constitute a remarkably rich and coherent pattern which characterizes the logic of the pre-adolescent and particularly of the adolescent compared with that of children between the ages of 7 or 8 and 11 or 12. Above all, it shows how this logic manifests itself through general systems and not simply through particular modes of reasoning.

## 6 General Interpretation

We hope that we have succeeded in showing both the functionally natural character and fundamental genetic significance of operational structures. By way of conclusion, we must briefly

## Intellectual Operations and their Development

indicate in what directions we can hope to find the explanation of these structures. Genetic explanations classically have recourse to three kinds of factors. In this connection we should simply like to point out—as is appropriate in a work of this nature—how far we are as yet from being able to grasp these factors at the level of positive verification. We believe that it is necessary, both neurologically and psychologically, to introduce a fourth factor and indeed this is increasingly being done.

### 1 Maturation

The maturation of the nervous system, first of all, very probably plays a part in the sequence of operational constructions. McCulloch and Pitts have shown the existence of a certain isomorphism between the 16 binary propositional operations of bivalent logic (those indicated in Section 5) and the interneuronal links which are governed by the same combinatorial pattern. But $a$) this does not mean that operational structures are all preformed within the nervous system. The latter merely opens up possibilities but the way in which they are actualized is not predetermined and depends partly on experience and the social environment. The great variation in the ages at which the various stages appear depending on environment (pronounced average backwardness in Martinique and Haiti among schoolchildren, according to Canadian research now in progress) shows that maturation is not the only factor; $b$) neurologists have not as yet succeeded in supplying any stable indication of maturation corresponding to our crucial ages of 7 to 8 and of 11 to 12. Although Grey Walter has been able to affirm the existence of some kind of relationship between the evolution of E.E.Gs and that of our structures,[1] this relation remains very global; $c$) the brain does not contain only hereditary connections but also a considerable and increasing number of acquired connections that do not depend on maturation alone.

### 2 Acquired experience

Secondly, it is possible to invoke acquired experience, which naturally plays a considerable part in the formation of operations.

[1] In Tanner–Inhelder, vol II, 1956, p. 149.

But the question is to discover how experience acts and what types of experiences play a part.

*a*) With reference to the first point, one can think in terms of a learning mechanism but the experiments by Gréco, Morf, Smedslund, Wohlwill and Matalon (1959) have shown that logical structures can be successfully learned only if there is a sound basis of other, earlier structures and that any kind of learning itself supposes a basis of logic. P. Gréco discusses this problem in Chapter 25 of this work. In a general way, interpretation and utilization of experience are not based on an interplay of associations which copy the relations between objects. The fact is that they rest essentially on an assimilation by which schemata are constructed. These schemata are the starting point for further structures (we shall have an example of this in a moment in connection with the schema of the permanent object);

*b*) We believe that there are various types of experiences, despite the empiricist bias which reduces them to a single type, that of physical experience, and maintains that abstraction springs from objects. Now, since a number of logico-mathematical notions are drawn from experience (as is undoubtedly the case at pre-operational levels), we find as a result a non-physical, specifically logico-mathematical form of experience: it also consists in acting on objects, but the new knowledge to which it leads is abstracted not from the object itself, but from the actions of the subject as applied to the object. This happens, for instance, when a child of 5 to 6 discovers through experience that if he counts from left to right ten stones arranged in a line, he obtains the same sum as when he counts them from right to left or in cyclic order. He thus learns that the sum is independent of order (which is the general form of commutativity). But what he thus discovers is a property of his own actions of ordering and summing, and not a property of the stones, for these were without order or sum before the child placed them in a line or a circle and then proceeded to count them;

*c*) The outcome of this is that the origin of intellectual operations is to be sought in the subject's actions and in the experiences and lessons arising out of them. These experiences serve to show that such actions, in their most general co-ordinations, are always applicable to the object. To return to the example of the

## Intellectual Operations and their Development

notion of order (principle of seriations, etc.), it is clear that however far one goes back (even to reflex organization) actions present an order of succession which is apparent in their most elementary co-ordinations. It follows that even in cases where the subject discovers an already established order in a collection of objects, as when a baby notices the alignment of the bars of his cot, he has to touch them one by one or look at them in turn to make sure of it. In other words, he uses the order of his actions of exploration to establish the order of the objects. This is why D. Berlyne (1960), when studying the acquisition of the notion of order from the standpoint of behaviour theory, reached the conclusion that it implies a 'counter'. We ourselves would prefer to call it 'ordinating activity' (such activity being the source of future operations of order).

*d*) We must therefore go back as far as sensori-motor activities to find the source of operations. What is remarkable is that one observes in infants from the age of 9–10 months to 16–18 months an early form of the notions both of conservation and of reversibility. On the one hand, the infant does not innately possess the schema of the permanent object (initially there is complete absence of any attempt to find objects outside the perceptual field) and he is obliged to construct it step by step according to a number of stages.[1] The permanent object is the first of the structures of conservation and it appears 6 or 7 years before the others precisely because there is no change of shape (except perceptually), but only of position. On the other hand, and because of these changes of position, the construction of the schema of the permanent object goes hand in hand with an organization of displacements and positions according to a 'group' structure, with reversibility (returning to the point of departure) and 'associativity' (detours). The only difference between this schema and operational structures is that naturally it does not yet include any overall representation of trajectories, but only a sequence of successive actions co-ordinated from one to the next on the basis of perceptual cues. These two examples nevertheless show quite clearly how probable it is that operations are sensori-motor in

---

[1] These stages have been described by one of us (Piaget) in connection with his own three children. They were also observed (and found to occur in the same order) by T. Gouin-Decarie when she administered standardized tests to 90 subjects (see Gouin–Decarie, 1962).

origin. Thus, the assimilatory and schematic character of co-ordinations of actions heralds that of operational structures.

## 3  Language and social transmission

A third important factor which is traditionally put forward in explaining development is the notion of social factors and particularly of language. There is no doubt that these factors are necessary to the attainment of operational structures, especially at the level of propositional or formal operations. Nevertheless, they cannot be regarded as the fountain-head of operations, for the following reasons:

*a*) First one finds, where language is concerned, that the usual operational structures (classification, seriation, etc.) are present in deaf-mutes, although they develop more slowly (Oléron, Vincent, etc.). It is probable that these subjects possess the symbolic function and a sign language leading to often quite advanced social collaboration. However the absence of an articulate and imposed language clearly shows that operations are not transmitted from outside through education alone. Second, when one studies speech disorders in children, as one of us (Inhelder) is at present doing with J. de Ajuriaguerra, one finds no clear-cut correlation between these disorders and the development of operations. In some cases, these are well ahead of linguistic attainment, in other cases it is the reverse.

*b*) In order to understand a logical structure expressed by language (of which an example can be found in Section 3, *2*, dealing with 'all' and 'some'), the subject requires an instrument of assimilation which takes in the essential aspects of the structure, failing which he cannot assimilate it. It is striking to observe that until propositional operations appear (at the age of 11 or 12), operational development is ahead of its verbal expression. The whole stage of 'concrete' operations is a proof of this and shows that operational structures are more closely linked with co-ordinations of actions than with their own verbalization.

*c*) Social exchange is nonetheless necessary for the elaboration of operational structures, but in the form of co-operation rather than imposed transmission. In analysing the mechanisms of social exchange, one finds a system of operations: reciprocities, unions, intersections, negations, etc. In this respect exchange is in a literal sense a system of co-operations. This means that operations are in origin neither social nor individual in the exclusive sense of these terms. Rather do they express the most general co-ordinations of actions, whether these are carried out in common or in the course of individual adaptations.

## 4 Equilibration

These few remarks help to show that in trying to account for the development of operations, one is obliged to bring in a fourth factor implied by each of the others yet having an originality of its own. This fourth factor is equilibration.

*a*) Let us begin by noting that although operations are derived from actions and from their co-ordinations (see 2, *b* − *d*), one cannot conclude from this that they are pre-formed or fully developed from the beginning. They are subject to continual elaboration because abstraction from actions is not the same as abstraction from objects. The latter tries to reach a datum and to dissociate it from all other perceived characteristics. The former, on the other hand, is 'reflective', in both senses of the term, because in order to attain a link that is unconsciously contained in an action, it must be projected (or reflected in the physical sense) on to a new plane, that of representation or consciousness (with reflection in the mental sense). Reflective abstraction is thus necessarily constructive in that it reconstructs and at the same time broadens and enriches the elementary structure given in the action. An example of this is the difficulty experienced by small children in picturing the journey from home to school or *vice versa*, although they make the journey by themselves every day (reconstruction of a practical 'group' of displacement into a representational 'group').

*b*) Reflective abstractions and constructions of this kind do not have a speculative function, however, and nothing could be further from the truth than an intellectualist interpretation of the development of operations. Their true character lies in transforming situations and objects, and thus in acting on the world. Such transformations arise, in effect, only in the presence of problems, gaps, conflicts, i.e. states of disequilibrium. The operational solution consists in reacting to restore equilibrium. This has been observed by many authors writing in various languages and when Wallon, for example, stressed the part played by crises in development, and the dialectics required to overcome them (in the sphere mainly of affectivity and of the development of personality), he was expressing the same idea and emphasizing the necessary role of states of disequilibrium and of equilibration.

*c*) In the sphere of intellectual operations, the notion of equilibrium is particularly enlightening, since it is characterized by compensation: the equilibrium of intelligence is not a state of rest but a 'mobile equilibrium'. This means that a subject faced with external disturbances tends to compensate these by transformations oriented in the opposite direction. There are two consequences of this. The first is that equilibration leads functionally to reversibility which is the fundamental property of operational structures. The second is that seen in this light operations constitute the higher forms of the regulations found at all stages. The term 'higher' merely means that operations attain complete reversibility whereas the regulations found at earlier levels are content with approximate compensations.

*d*) Translating the development of operations into terms of equilibration is not merely of functionalist interest. It is probably the best introduction to their interpretation from the neurological and mechanico-physiological standpoints. To explain the origin of adaptive behaviours, W. R. Ashby (1960) suggests that the brain should be conceived as functioning like a homeostat. This is not merely a verbal comparison for the distinctive feature of the mechanical models that have been constructed (such as the famous homeostat to which Ashby himself gave his name) is precisely that they comprise operational structures, combined with a system of probabilities of connections. These early models do not include intermediate stages of equilibrium (thus when the solution has not been found, the machine begins again at zero). However, S. Papert (1963) has evolved mathematically a model closer to genetic data, the 'genetron'. It is closer in that equilibration is achieved in stages so that a particular level of equilibrium must be reached at each stage before it can proceed to the new operational combinations of the next.

# Bibliography

ASHBY, W. R., *Design for a Brain*, London, Chapman and Hall, 1960
BERLYNE. D. E., 'Les équivalences psychologiques et les notions quantitatives', in *Théorie du comportement et opérations*, E.E.G.,* vol. XII, Paris, P.U.F., 1960, 1-76
BINET, A., *The Psychology of Reasoning*, London, Kegan Paul, 1899
— *L'étude expérimentale de l'intelligence*, Paris, Schleicher, 1903
BRAINE, M. D. S., 'The Ontogeny of certain Logical Operations: Piaget's Formulation examined by Nonverbal Methods', *Psychol. Monogr.*, 1959, **73**, no. 5, 43
BRUNER, J., GOODNOW, J. J., AUSTIN, G. A., *A Study of Thinking*, New York, Wiley, 1956
BUHLER, K., *Die geistige Entwicklung der Kinder*, Leipzig, Hirzel, 1931
CLAPARÈDE, E., 'La genèse de l'hypothèse', *Arch. Psychol.*, 1933, XXIV, 1-155
DUNCKER, K., *Zür Psychologie des produktiven Denkens*, Berlin, Springer, 1935
ELKIND, D., 'Children's Discovery of the Conservation of Mass, Weight and Volume: Piaget Replication Study II', *J. genet. Psychol.*, 1961, **98**, 219-28
GOUIN-DECARIE, T., *Intelligence et affectivité chez le jeune enfant*, Neuchâtel et Paris, Delachaux and Niestlé, 1962
GRÉCO, P., 'L'apprentissage dans une situation opératoire concrète', in *Apprentissage et connaissance*, E.E.G., vol. VII, Paris P.U.F., 1959, 68-182
— *Structures numériques élémentaires*, E.E.G., vol. XIII, Paris, P.U.F., 1961
INHELDER, B., *Le diagnostic du raisonnement chez les débiles mentaux*, Neuchâtel and Paris, Delachaux and Niestlé, 1943
INHELDER, B., PIAGET, J., *The Growth of Logical Thinking from Childhood to Adolescence*, London, Routledge and Kegan Paul, 1958
— — *The Early Growth of Logic in the Child*, London, Routledge and Kegan Paul, 1964
KÖHLER, W., *The Mentality of Apes*, London, Kegan Paul, 1927
LAURENDEAU, M., PINARD, A., *Causal Thinking in the Child*, New York, International Universities Press, 1962
— — Work in preparation on the child's conception of number and quantities (continuation of the above)
LOVELL, K., 'A Follow-up Study of some Aspects of the Work of Piaget

* E.E.G. refers to *Etudes d'Epistémologie génétique*.

and Inhelder into the Child's Conception of Space', *Brit. J. educ. Psychol.*, 1959, **29**, 104–17
— *The Growth of Basic Mathematical and Scientific Concepts in Children*, Univ. of London Press, 1961. (Preface B. INHELDER)
LOVELL, K., HEALEY, D., ROWLAND, A. D., 'Growth of some Geometrical Concepts', *Child Developm.*, 1962, **33**, 751–67
LOVELL, K., MITCHELL, B., EVERETT, I. R., 'An Experimental Study of the Growth of some Logical Structures', *Brit. J. Psychol.*, 1962, **53**, 175–88
— 'A Follow-up Study of Inhelder and Piaget's "The Growth of Logical Thinking" ', *Brit. J. Psychol.*, 1961, **52**, 143–54
LOVELL, K., OGILVIE, E., 'A Study of the Conservation of Substance in the Junior School Child', *Brit. J. educ. Psychol.*, 1960, **30**, 109–18
— — 'A Study of the Conservation of Weight in the Junior School Child', *Brit. J. educ. Psychol.*, 1961, **31**, 138–44
— — 'The Growth of the Concept of Volume in Junior School Children', *J. Child Psychol. Psychiat.*, 1961, **2**, 118–26
LUNZER, E. A., 'Some points of Piagetian Theory in the Light of Experimental Criticism', *J. Child Psychol. Psychiat.*, 1960, **1**, 191–202
MATALON, B., 'Apprentissage en situations aléatoires et systématiques', in *La logique des apprentissages*, E.E.G., vol. X, Paris, P.U.F., 1959, 61–91
MEILI, R., 'Experimentelle Untersuchungen über das Ordnen von Gegenständen', *Psychol. Forsch.*, 1926, **7**, 155–93
MORF, A., 'Apprentissage d'une structure logique concrète (inclusion)', in *L'apprentissage des structures logiques*, E.E.G., vol. IX, Paris, P.U.F., 1959, 15–83
PAPERT, S., 'Étude comparée de l'intelligence chez l'enfant et chez le robot', in *La filiation des structures*, E.E.G., vol. XV, Paris, P.U.F., 1963, 131–94
PIAGET, J., 'Essai sur quelques aspects du développement de la notion de partie chez l'enfant', *J. Psychol.*, 1921, **17**, 449–80
— *The Origin of Intelligence in the Child*, London, Routledge and Kegan Paul, 1953
— 'Principal Factors Determining Intellectual Evolution from Childhood to Adult Life', in *Harvard Tercentenary Publications*, 1937 (17 p.)
— *Les notions de mouvement et de vitesse chez l'enfant*, Paris, P.U.F., 1946 (*a*)
— *Le développement de la notion du temps chez l'enfant*, Paris, P.U.F., 1946 (*b*)
— *Traité de logique*, Paris, Colin, 1950
— *Essai sur les transformations des opérations logiques*, Paris, P.U.F., 1952

— *Logic and Psychology*, Manchester Univ. Press, 1953
PIAGET, J., INHELDER, B., *Le développement des quantités physiques chez l'enfant*, Neuchâtel and Paris, Delachaux and Niestlé, 2nd ed., 1962 (1st ed., 1941)
— — *The Child's Conception of Space*, London, Routledge and Kegan Paul, 1956
— — *La genèse de l'idée de hasard chez l'enfant*, Paris, P.U.F., 1953
PIAGET, J., INHELDER, B., SZEMINSKA, A., *The Child's Conception of Geometry*, London, Routledge and Kegan Paul, 1960
PIAGET, J., SZEMINSKA, A., *The Child's Conception of Number*, London, Routledge and Kegan Paul, 1952 (original French edition, 1941)
SELZ, O., *Ueber die Gesetze des geordneten Denkverlaufs*, 2 vol., Stuttgart, 1913, Bonn, 1922
— *Die Gesetze der produktiven und reproduktiven Geistestätigkeit*, Bonn, 1924
SMEDSLUND, J., 'Apprentissage des notions de la conservation et de la transitivité du poids', in *L'apprentissage des structures logiques, E.E.G.*, vol. IX, Paris, P.U.F., 1959, 85-124
SPEARMAN, C., *The Nature of Intelligence*, London, Macmillan, 1923
TANNER, J. M., INHELDER B., (Ed.) *Discussions on Child Development*, vols. II to IV, Tavistock Publications, London, 1956, 1958, 1960
VINH-BANG, 'Évolution des conduites et apprentissage', in *L'apprentissage des structures logiques, E.E.G.*, vol. IX, Paris, P.U.F., 1959, 3-13
VINH-BANG, INHELDER, B., Work in preparation on the standardisation of operational tests
WERTHEIMER, M., *Productive Thinking*, New York, Harper, 1945
WOHLWILL, J. F., 'Un essai d'apprentissage dans le domaine de la conservation du nombre', in *L'apprentissage des structures logiques, E.E.G.*, vol. IX, Paris, P.U.F., 1959, 125-35

# Chapter 25

# Learning and Intellectual Structures

## Pierre Gréco

## 1 Introduction

This chapter, which follows several others expressly devoted to learning (Volume 4) and to intellectual activities or structures (Chapters 22 and 24 above), is not intended merely as an exhaustive account of the various findings in each of these fields, nor yet as a statement of where they agree and where they differ. There are two reasons at least against proceeding on those lines. The first is that the literature on the subject appears either overabundant and disparate or else singularly restricted, depending on whether the problem is defined in a broad or a systematic fashion. The second reason, which probably explains the first, is that the questions which can be asked concerning the relations between intellectual structures and learning are possibly less a matter of experimental decision than of viewpoint and formulation. Indeed, we shall continually come across problems of psychological conceptualization (and not only of criteriology) which sixty years of experimental research have not yet finally elucidated.

When authors of technical dictionaries and general works on psychology attempt to give generally acceptable definitions of terms such as 'learning', 'thinking', 'intelligence', they promptly add a warning that such definitions are neither operationally nor conceptually adequate since they make use of terms that have not been defined. They also point out that the difficulties are due less to semantics than to the fact that there are various underlying theories (cf. Hilgard, 1956, pp. 3 and 6; Estes *et alia*, 1954, p. xiii). The big American handbooks which are not the work of one man and which aim at being eclectic, give in to usage by calling one chapter *Learning* and another *Thinking*. At the same time, they apologize to the reader for this distribution of subject matter, which does not rest on any theoretical basis or any precise operational criterion. And it is definitely to the theories rather than to the experimental facts that they refer us. This is true of Woodworth's handbook and of the handbook on methodology edited by T. G. Andrews, both of which are widely available in translation in France.

Moreover, the wording of a question, while conveying a general meaning, may in fact denote very different lines of investigation in which the same words may not have the same connotations or significance. For instance the question may be one of determining whether there is continuity in the scale of behaviour between the higher adaptations which are commonly termed intelligent and the progressive adjustments which are arrived at by way of conditioning and trial and error. This is the question raised by Pavlovianism, Anglo-Saxon behaviourism and the comparative psychology of Henri Piéron. Unfortunately, their common negative answer in no way implies any profound agreement between them. Alternatively, the question may consist in asking whether the fundamental organization of intelligent behaviours ranging from the mere apprehension of relations to the abstract reasoning of verbal thought differs, by a peculiar structure, from the organization of learning in general or of perception. This question, which is not to be confused with the first, was raised by the *Gestalttheorie*. Or again, there is the question, raised by the functionalists, which seeks to determine whether solving so-called 'thinking' problems proceeds according to different laws and along different lines from learning a path through a maze or a regular sequence of events. Yet another question, raised by J. Piaget, consists in asking whether the formation of the successive structures of intelligence in the course of the child's development, is to be explained by the recognized laws of learning in the strict sense (i.e. associative learning).

The very diversity of these questions shows how naïve it would be to ask at the outset whether intellectual structures can be reduced to the mechanisms of learning (or of behaviour in general, in view of the fact that in American twentieth-century literature learning and behaviour have become practically synonymous). It would be equally naïve to ask whether they are formed through the action of such mechanisms or whether they are in fact radically opposed in both origin and development. Even authors who have subscribed to one or the other of these extreme views have done so less by virtue of experimental evidence than of theoretical elaborations and models which are in fact largely conjectural. The data so far gathered in the laboratory are more often heterogeneous than contradictory. Thus, they are continually being reinterpreted after having been selected or obtained from predetermined standpoints. 'Standpoint' does not mean doctrinal prejudice or philosophical bias but the fact remains that we must first of all consider the way in which an author views the problem and his method before assessing his results in relation to them.

It is for this reason that despite academic usage we shall take care not to put forward at the beginning of this study any fixed definitions of the concepts under discussion. Were we to adopt definitions that were too vague, we should gain nothing as it would immediately be necessary to make them more specific and to call them in question. On the other hand, if we made them too strict, this would tend to prejudice our answers. There is no doubt that in defining intelligence as 'the capacity to reason according to the laws of logic' (Marbe, 1901) or as the faculty of 'sudden comprehension' as opposed to groping (K. Bühler, 1922), or again as the capacity for '(mental) adaptation to new situations' (Stern and Claparède) one has *ipso facto* if not solved the problem in advance at least strongly oriented the search for a solution. The giving of unambiguous definitions should therefore be regarded as a goal to be reached after studying the data and not as the necessary starting point of our enquiry.

2 'Intuition' and groping

It was long thought—and the conviction survives to this day among authors who profess to deny it—that the observable phenomenon of *insight* provided an adequate criterion for distinguishing between learning in the narrow sense (that is, the acquisition of new forms of behaviour by a series of trials involving the progressive elimination of errors) and intelligence (consequently considered as the ability to resolve a problem immediately through a sudden and original reorganization or *structurization* of situations or responses). It would be unjust to attribute to W. Köhler, despite his evident responsibility in the matter, so categorical a view and so terse a formulation. The concept of insight can only be understood within the general framework of the theory of Form, which is a theory of behaviour structures and not an intellectualist theory in the generally accepted sense. A brief historical survey will serve to show in what context of problems the debate on insight and 'groping' (the name we shall give to learning by trial and error) was originally opened.

## 1 Learning through 'trial and error' and learning through 'ideas'

When in 1894 C. Lloyd Morgan put forward his now famous observations on his fox-terrier and other animals, his intention was to show how animal behaviour can be explained by very simple mechanisms: progressive elimination of errors and consolidation of correct responses by the effect of repetition alone. There was no need to presuppose in animals any faculty of judgment or reasoning. But, at the beginning of the century, Hobhouse devised situations that have since become classic: the animal had to obtain an inaccessible bait by pulling a string, or choose within a given lapse of time between three strings of which one had been tied to a piece of meat before his very eyes, etc. His observations, which were admittedly not very systematic, led him to conclude that animals (dogs in this instance) were capable of 'observing' and of 'understanding' immediately, without preliminary groping, certain causal sequences of events involving simple relations of means to end (Hobhouse, 1901). Hobhouse therefore thought that it was necessary to recognize in animals, in addition to learning processes, a true intelligence, made up of 'practical ideas', themselves defined as 'a combination of efforts to effect a definite change in the perceived object'. The techniques and also the expression of the results of this now forgotten precursor foreshadow, as we can see, the work of Köhler.

*Pierre Gréco*

E. Thorndike later sided with Lloyd Morgan against Hobhouse. Thorndike had been studying associative learning in animals since 1898. In order to show the generality of this process throughout behaviour, he began to study problem-solving in connection with puzzle boxes. The subjects (dogs mostly, but also cats, monkeys and even fish) were shut inside a box fitted with an appropriate mechanism and had for instance to press a button to escape or to obtain food. Thorndike later noted his conclusions in a monograph. Those that interest us here[1] are that animals are not capable of higher processes such as reasoning. The great majority of observed subjects did not 'discover' the solution to the problem. All that happens is that the time taken to release the mechanism decreases from one trial to the next and the number of unnecessary movements and gestures diminishes slowly and irregularly. According to the picturesque vocabulary of the period, animal intelligence is unable to solve the problem by 'catching on'. It is subject to the mechanisms of *stamping in* (establishment of correct responses) and *stamping out* (elimination of errors) (Thorndike, 1911). These are clearly anti-intellectualist conclusions but they can be interpreted in two ways. For instance, Thorndike's results could be taken to mean that animals are incapable of intelligence, in the usual and exalted sense of the term, and that the only type of behaviour open to them as a means of problem-solving is learning through groping. Alternatively, it could be, as Thorndike himself was to stress, especially after 1930, and as many learning theorists have always maintained, that these results suggest that groping is the characteristic and fundamental process in problem-solving and that so-called 'intellectual' activities, while situated on a higher plane, do not proceed any differently (cf. Thorndike, 1932, 1940, 1949).

## 2 The notion of 'insight' and Gestalt views

W. Köhler in his studies disputed the validity of both these interpretations. The reaction of intellectualist psychology, however, had been to accept the first interpretation and to recognize

[1] We need not consider here Thorndike's conclusions concerning the *laws* of learning (laws of exercise, effect, etc.) which he set out particularly in the second volume of his *Educational Psychology* (*The Psychology of Learning*, New York: Teachers College, 1913) and which are reported in Chapter 12 of this work (Volume 4).

## Learning and Intellectual Structures

a discontinuity between learning and intelligence or, more exactly, between animal and human intelligence. While W. S. Small was at the turn of the century studying progressive learning in rats and J. B. Watson was towards 1911 repeating Thorndike's experiments on which he was later to found behaviourism, the American psychologist A. J. Kinnaman was studying learning curves in Macaco rhesus monkeys. He noted at times swift and sudden progress and supposed without as yet being able to put forward any facts to support his hypothesis[1] that human learning is fundamentally distinct from animal learning by virtue of the sudden discovery of the solution (Kinnaman, 1902); this insight (although it was not yet called by that name) was for Kinnaman the sign of intelligence. The generic term of 'learning' thus came to embrace two very distinct types or levels of behaviour: groping and intuition. Similar views can be found in Karl Bühler. He believed that the *Aha-Erlebnis* of the higher apes was the operational criterion of intelligence which he regarded as a *sui generis* level of behaviour and adaptation, distinct from habit and instinct (cf. Bühler, 1922). Claparède and A. Binet upheld similar views. The discussion then centred on groping which is normally the first stage in problem-solving. Is it an integral part of the intellectual act (in which case inductive hypotheses constitute the highest form of intelligent groping) or does it merely precede and prepare the intuitive appearance of the *Aha*? In either case there is a marked gap between habit (or learning) and intelligence, even though it no longer coincides with the distinction between man and animals. Let us recall, however, the contribution made by Boutan in 1914. He confirmed this distinction through his genetic and comparative study of chimpanzees and young children and attributed to language the original intellectual progress of which the child shows himself capable from the third year onwards.

The *Gestalt* conception dismisses these problems as fictitious. The fundamental experiments of Köhler are well known and are referred to in other chapters.[2] Let us for the moment see what

---

[1] Kinnaman used a lock device, which could only be unlocked by a fixed sequence of movements. He found that the solution was suddenly discovered by adults after one or two exploratory attempts. Monkeys on the other hand learned the order of movements only after a succession of attempts during which unnecessary gestures were gradually eliminated.

[2] Cf. Chapter 12 (Volume 4) and above, Chapter 22, p. 10.

they contribute from the conceptual angle. 1) *Einsicht* or *Insight*, of which the operational criterion is the sudden discovery of the solution (or the sudden drop to zero of curves of error in learning situations) is probably the sign of an activity that could well be called intelligent. But 2) this activity is nothing more than the restructurization into a 'good form' (as defined by its laws of equilibrium) of the field data which are at first apprehended in part or in isolation. In this sense, intellectual structurization continues, and goes beyond,[1] the structurization which operates at the level of perception or elementary motor activity. (According to Köhler the laws of the Gestalt are isomorphous with the laws of equilibrium applying to fields of physical forces and structure is therefore a completely general concept). It follows that 3) learning can be considered as a set of successive restructurizations. The limit is set not by limitations in the structuring ability of the organism, but by the limits of the field itself.[2] Learning and understanding do not correspond to two processes of different levels or nature. They both follow the same laws of structural organization. The *Gestalttheorie* is monistic in nature.

Thus, in Köhler's eyes—if not in those of all his Berlin disciples or in particular of all his American disciples—the structurization betokened by insight is not finally the mark of true 'thinking' nor even the exclusive privilege of higher organisms. Its behavioural significance is thus very different, in this respect, from the *Aha* of Karl Bühler in spite of only too apparent analogies. Groping according to Köhler is the characteristic procedure of an organism which explores the data within a field that is originally ill structured and if the regularly decreasing curves of trial and error really do indicate learning it is only where the problem to be solved exceeds, temporarily or finally, the structural capacities of the organism.[3] To construct an associationist theory of be-

[1] In the same way that a single integrating system can continue, and go beyond, multi-systems (except that Köhler's conception, while 'physicalist' in a precise sense, was never probabilistic).

[2] We must admit that we do not ourselves fully understand this subtle distinction which has nevertheless always been upheld by orthodox Gestaltists.

[3] To speak here of 'structuring' capacities would not be true to the spirit of the classical *Gestalttheorie*. Structures are present in behaviour as in the object, but it is not the subject's activity which imposes them on the data. They are objective: their discovery is due to observation or at most to assimilation and it is only in this sense that they are related to the subject.

## Learning and Intellectual Structures

haviour on the basis of associative learning is to take as a model of behaviour a particular case of acquisition-habituation or even a laboratory artifact (Köhler, 1925, *Intr.*; 1941; cf. also Koffka, 1935).

It is a remarkable fact that in a fairly recent work on the *Gestalttheorie*—a work that is admittedly highly schematic but at the same time systematic and orthodox—the term *insight* is used only in a non-technical descriptive sense. It is not given in the index as a separate notion and thus seems relegated to the metalanguage of the theory (Katz, 1950). The fundamental concepts of the theory of Form refer to structures as types of organization and not as signs or products of intelligence. The experimental fact which plays a vital role in this system is really that of transposition. Since the time of von Ehrenfels it has been the basic criterion of the existence of perceptual 'forms'. We shall have occasion to return to it in detail a little later.[1]

The fact remains that Gestalt findings and interpretations can be pulled and twisted in two different directions. One can for instance find in them essentially a condemnation of associationist empiricism; one will accordingly regard structurization as an essentially cognitive element and try to bring out in various learning situations the existence and role of these cognitive structures as against mere *stamping in* and *stamping out*. Alternatively, one can adhere to the idea of a total continuity, *at once functional and structural*, between the lower and the higher levels of adaptation. Thereafter, the possibility of reducing elementary behaviours to the operation of simpler and more 'objectifiable' mechanisms than the *Gestalt* concept, and in particular to mechanisms of conditioning and association may seem to imply the complete reducibility of intelligence to these mechanisms. There has been no lack of psychologists ready to follow one or the other of these two paths.

### 3 Cognitive structures in animal learning

The fact that the *Gestalttheorie* goes beyond the old debate between intelligence and habit does not mean that the problem of learning and of intellectual structures is thus disposed of. On the contrary it seems that the divorce between them became more

[1] See below, p. 222.

spectacular for a time. Anglo-Saxon associationism—undoubtedly stimulated by Pavlovian physiology of conditioning (however badly interpreted it may have been as it spread in the United States after a time-lag due to delays in translation)—progressed and became increasingly rigorous. Guthrie's contiguity theory carried on Thorndike's 'connectionism' by rejecting the law of effect and adhering particularly to the first type of learning recognized by Thorndike, learning through 'shifting' of responses. Skinner, on the other hand, laid stress on the second type, instrumental learning or operant conditioning. Hull's systematic behaviourism is openly and rigorously 'mechanistic'. We do not propose to give an account of this era of great theories, as such an account can be found elsewhere,[1] but simply to note their common orientation. The problem as they see it no longer consists in deciding between learning and intelligence for example. The aim of the behaviourists is to elaborate a general theory of behaviour, of how it is produced and to what diachronic or synchronic changes it is subject. Learning situations are, operationally speaking, the simplest to realize and to manipulate rigorously. The task is the same as in every sound positive science: to assemble the facts, measure them as accurately as possible, establish laws, construct theories based on these laws, and validate the theory by confirming the predictions that it warrants and by showing that it is possible *to derive from the theory an explanation of those more complex types of behaviour* which cannot be studied directly in any rigorous fashion. All the authors concerned have clearly stated this intention,[2] which from the epistemological standpoint might well justify preliminary discussion.[3]

At the same time, other authors who have since somewhat cursorily been lumped together under the disparaging label of 'mentalists' tried, successfully as they thought, to find in animal learning not only the existence of structures irreducible to the play of associations but also evidence of a truly intellectual activity or at least an activity that could be directly assimilated to behaviour normally considered as intellectual. The monograph by N. R. F. Maier published in 1929 in *Comparative Psychology*

[1] Chapter 12 (Volume 4).
[2] See for example, Hilgard, 1956, pp. 1–6, and his classification of problems, *ibid.*, pp. 8–13.
[3] A number of possible themes for criticism have been suggested apropos of genetic problems in a note on 'Learning and Development' (P. Gréco, 1959 *c*).

is unhesitatingly entitled 'Reasoning in white rats' and the article by Krechevsky which appeared three years later in the *Psychological Review* is called ' "Hypotheses"—in inverted commas this time—in rats' (Krechevsky, 1932). Before pausing to discuss a few significant examples, let us bring out the various aspects of this trend of interpretation.

Three themes, variously exploited by their authors and not implying one another, can be distinguished: 1) acquired behaviours, provided that the tasks which are set are not too simple, make up configurations or structures of behaviour, directly transposable to new situations and not reducible to a sum (even an ordered sum) of successive responses. This is merely another manifestation, more or less systematic, of Gestalt notions. We shall not return to them directly except to discuss them in section 5, 2) acquisition is itself relative to pre-existing behaviour structures. This idea is probably a little too general. It cannot be an embarrassment to anyone, as these pre-existing structures can be considered as the product of previous learning; 3) finally we have what is probably the most central and the most debatable idea, which is that learned structures, as well as the instruments of acquisition, are cognitive in nature.

It is true that formulated in this way the third idea does not commit one any more than the second, since it is always possible to take 'cognition' in a wide enough sense to include the most elementary forms of adaptation. However, a controversy has indeed developed around the 'habits—cognition' dilemma. The following example will show the true significance that this operationally-not-very-clear distinction can have when applied to facts.

## 4 *'Inferential expectation'*: *The experiment by Tolman and Honzik*

Tolman and Honzik reported in 1930 an experiment which has remained a classic despite the many reservations or objections that have since been made by various experimenters and theorists. This experiment tends to demonstrate, in opposition to Hull, the part played in learning by 'cognitive structures' represented in this instance by a certain form of spatial organization. Learning the correct way through a maze does not involve merely principles of reinforcement. What is learned is not only a sequence of hierarchised responses but a cognitive map which enables the animal to make immediate inferences when confronted with new situations. The experiment by Tolman and Honzik shows that it is possible for rats, after ordinary learning, to reorganize spontaneously (i.e. without relearning) their maze-running behaviour in a situation where they choose a solution which does not depend on the probability of previously learned behaviour. That is why it is often quoted as a test of *insight* and reasoning. Analytical behaviourism confines itself, as we shall later see, to the terms 'assembly of behaviour segments'. Tolman, for his part, spoke of 'inferential expectation'.

The apparatus consists in an elevated maze (i.e. one in which the runways are formed by little strips of wood laid edgewise[1]). Figure 1 (left-hand drawing) shows the plan view. It can be seen that three paths of unequal length, numbered 1, 2 and 3 in order of increasing length, lead from the starting-point to the food-goal. Paths 1 and 2 have a common final section, which is not common to path 3. Fifteen rats were used as subjects.

During the preliminary training period, it was first observed that when all the paths were left open, the rats quickly adopted path 1, the most direct and the shortest. This path was then blocked at A. The subjects went as far as the block, retraced to the intersection $x$ and followed path 2 right to the goal! (In actual fact, they began by choosing either 2 or 3 but very quickly learned to prefer path 2 which was shorter.) Finally, they were made to learn 3. This was done by simultaneously blocking 1 (at A) and 2 (at C). This preliminary training served a double purpose. It allowed the rats to explore the whole of the maze and to establish a preferential order of choice between the three paths: $1 > 2 > 3$ according to the classical laws of reinforcement.

The next stage was the test situation in which the blocks at A and C were removed and a new block was placed at B. The rats were placed in the starting position and began by following path 1. They came up against B and went back to $x$, whereupon fourteen of them (out of fifteen) immediately chose path 3, which was the right one and not path 2 despite the fact that it was 'preferred' to 3 in the course of the preliminary training. It is as if during the training the rats had learned that paths 1 and 2

[1] Translator's Note: The runways are in fact 30 inches above the floor.

had a common section and as if they immediately 'understood', during the test situation, that B blocks this common section and that it is *therefore* useless to try path 2. One sees how it is possible to speak of reasoning or inferential expectation (the obstruction of 1 by B, on the section that is common to 1 and 2, 'implies' the obstruction of 2) and also of insight.

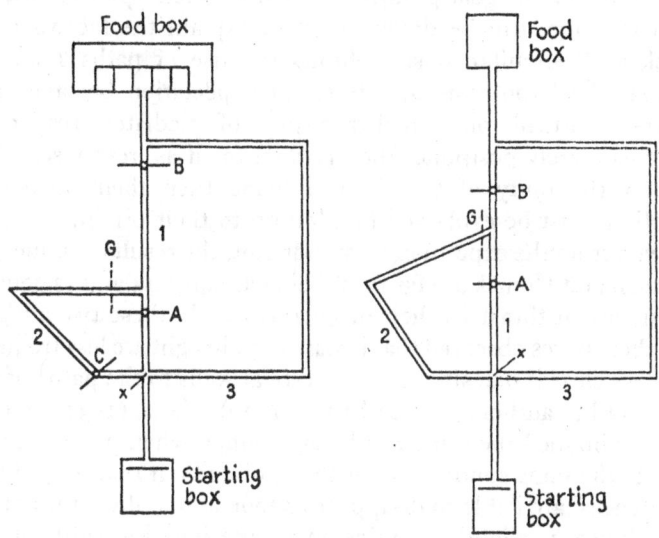

Fig. 1   MAZES USED TO STUDY INSIGHT IN RATS
*Left*: Maze used by Tolman and Honzik (1930); *right*: maze adapted by Dove and Thompson (1943), in which instances of insight are less frequent and more open to question. In both figures there is a starting box and a food box which is of course the goal; 1, 2, 3 designate the various paths; A and B are the blocks used to bar the paths; G = gate; *x*: choice point.

## 5   Control experiments and discussions

This experiment which at first sight appears so conclusive in fact reveals itself as somewhat insubstantial. From the theoretical standpoint first of all (to which we shall come back later, in connection with Maier's experiments as reinterpreted by Hull),[1] it is clear that one could go on indefinitely discussing precisely *what* is learned and reinforced during preliminary training and

[1] See below, p. 219.

later inhibited when the animal comes up against the block at B. Tolman assumes that learning reinforcements globally affect the use of paths 1, 2 and 3 whereas one can probably analyse the corresponding chains of behaviour and assign the reinforcements in various ways to the elements of these chains, for instance to partial responses such as 'turn left', 'turn right', etc. The principle of goal gradient, which is often open to flexible interpretation, can be drawn upon to explain the fact that the block at B simultaneously inhibits the use of paths 1 and 2, so that the hypothesis of inferential expectation becomes unnecessary. Finally one can always speak of 'mediatory responses' but this merely postpones the problem for if as 'responses' they respect the unity of the S—R schema then their mediatory function must be explained in addition to their origin.

Even from the experimental standpoint, the results obtained by Tolman and Honzik are far from being as constant and as general as one might think. In their original research, these two authors had themselves observed that instances of insight are less frequent and less clear if one simply adds vertical walls to the paths of the maze. Other authors such as Evans (1936), Harsh (1937) or Kuo (1937) obtained the same results as Tolman when proceeding in exactly the same conditions but they pointed out that insight and 'inferences' are liable to disappear as soon as one alters the apparatus, however slightly (for instance, altering the width of the pathways). It therefore seems that the cognitive structures (if indeed they are still worthy of the name) remain closely tied to the objective properties of the particular stimuli.

An experiment designed to control that of Tolman and Honzik was made by Dove and Thompson with decisive results. They blocked the paths with transparent celluloid doors which were hinged at the top so that they could be locked or unlocked at will (by the experimenter). In these conditions, they found that insight is no longer the general rule. Animals which have just learned the three paths cannot know at the time of the test situations whether the door is locked and thus whether path 1 is practicable or not. On the first run, only two subjects out of eleven spontaneously chose path 3 when path 1 was blocked; nine succeeded only on the second run, thus after having once tried path 2. On the third run, however, all subjects were successful. Not convinced by this result, Dove and Thompson altered

*Learning and Intellectual Structures*

the plan of the maze (see Fig. I, diagram on the right). Path 2 no longer enters path 1 at a right angle and the block at B is nearer the intersection of 2 and 1. Out of the twenty-six rats studied, not one chose path 3 on the first run in the test situation and only ten succeeded in doing so on the third run. Finally, when they used as obstacles blocks on which were painted parallel black lines, clearly visible from the choice point, they no longer found any insight in favour of path 3 during the three successive trials of the test (Dove and Thompson, 1943). The interpretation that they put forward stresses that the choices made by the animals are not the product of 'inferences', which should be more general in character, but of the evocation or inhibition of partial anticipatory responses, such as turning to the left or to the right, without reference to an overall 'map' of the maze.

## 6 *'Cognitive' and behaviourist formulations*

The facts presented by Dove and Thompson attack 'cognitive' interpretations on their own experimental ground. But in a more general way so-called 'inferential' behaviour in animals can be interpreted in strict behaviourist fashion within the framework of an S–R theory for example. Hull (1935) demonstrated this in a subtle way in his discussion of an explanatory diagram by N. R. F. Maier. Maier published many experiments on learning (Maier, 1929; 1931) in which one sees white rats assembling separately acquired behaviour segments into an 'intelligent' organization which Maier interpreted as true 'reasoning'. The example chosen and diagrammatically represented by Hull in his critique is shown below (Fig. 2).

The apparatus consists of four boxes or platforms, linked by paths, and quite distinct in shape and in the texture of the floor (in view of the rat's tactile sensibility). S, the starting box has for instance a rubber floor; $D_1$, where the rats find water, has a metal floor that is cold and rough; F, where he finds food, is covered with floss silk and $D_2$, where he finds drink as in $D_1$, has a polished and warm metal floor.

Preliminary training consists in blocking each time the unnecessary paths[1] so that the animals may learn successively path

[1] It is important that each behaviour segment should be acquired in an unambiguous fashion and without any question of preferential choice.

## Pierre Gréco

(or sequence) I (from S to F to find food), II (from D1 to F for the same reward), III (from S to D1 to find drink) and IV (from S to D2 for the same reward). To make the test situation valid,

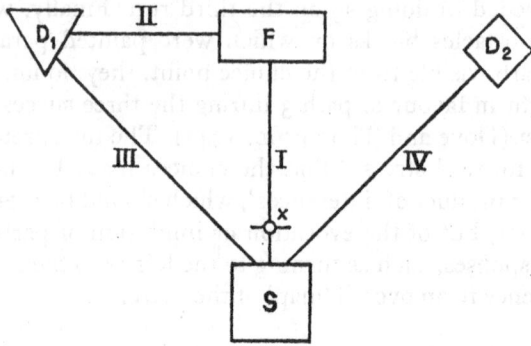

Fig. 2  DIAGRAMMATIC REPRESENTATION OF
MAIER'S EXPERIMENT AS RE-INTERPRETED BY HULL
(After Hull, 1935)

S: Starting box; D1 and D2 enclosed boxes containing drink; F enclosed box containing food.
I, II, III, IV: paths that are successively or simultaneously open. $x$ shows the position of the barrier during the final test situation.

it is necessary at this point that sequences III and IV which both lead to drink should be reinforced in identical fashion or more precisely, as Hull himself expressed it, that the force of the habit sHr corresponding to sequence III should be equal to that which corresponds to sequence IV. This can be checked by placing a thirsty rat in S and verifying that he goes with equal probability towards either D1 or D2, when I is blocked. Let us now place a hungry animal in S barring only path I which leads directly to the food. Maier observed in this case and in many other similar cases a marked preference (though not a systematic one),[1] for sequence III which alone leads to F via D1. There would thus be an assembly of sequences III and II in a spon-

---

[1] It would be pleasing to suppose that a hungry animal looks for food and a thirsty animal for drink. Things are not so simple, however. Heron (1949) showed by means of a very simple T-shaped apparatus, offering only one choice, that animals that were both thirsty and hungry chose food in 100 per cent of all cases and that animals that had previously been sated with food and drink chose drink in 92 per cent of all cases.

*Learning and Intellectual Structures*

taneous detour behaviour, a cognitive co-ordination of means to end in Tolman's terminology, which Maier himself interpreted as true reasoning: everything happens as if, he writes, the rat 'said to himself' that he has never been to F from D2 but that he has on the other hand reached F from D1 and that he must therefore go first to D1 ... etc. Naturally, even as Maier sees it, this inference is only *implicit* in behaviour.

Hull (1935) went on to show that one can dispense with all higher processes, with all descriptions in terms of 'as if'. When a hungry animal learns sequence II, a part r' of the total $r_G$ (goal-response) is conditioned by traces of the D1 stimuli, then short-circuited. When a thirsty animal learns sequence III, the D1 stimuli elicit the fractional anticipatory goal response r' and the drink provides a reinforcement[1] of r', a habit already acquired. The short-circuit mechanism explains, as before, how it is possible for r' to be elicited by stimuli from S. The two goal reactions concerning drink and corresponding to sequences III and IV are of equal strength and can be indifferently evoked, one or the other, by stimuli from S. On the other hand, if a hungry animal is in S and I is blocked, the internal stimuli linked to hunger will evoke r', which amounts to an auto-stimulation associated with sequence III and not with sequence IV. It is therefore III which will be preferentially chosen. In support of this interpretation, Hull derives from the quantitative laws of learning contained in his theory a number of consequences which Maier's findings confirm particularly in the matter of speeds of locomotion.

Hull's 'demonstration' does, however, call forth two kinds of remarks. First, one can see that the order in which separate behaviour segments are learned in the preliminary training period is not a matter of indifference. The final choice of sequence III indeed presupposes, according to the explanation by means of successive short-circuits, that sequence II was learned before sequences III and IV. If on the other hand the animal had learned III and IV before learning II, it seems that food-reactions in the direction of D1 and D2 would have been equiprobable. It is curious to note that no one has ever thought of experimentally

---

[1] The theory of need reduction, as found in Hull, does not require that the reduction be adequate to the need. Drink can therefore act as a reinforcement for a food-response.

checking this consequence of Hull's schema.[1] Secondly, it is possible from a more theoretical standpoint to consider that this retranslation into SR language brings in quite a number of 'intervening variables'. These probably have the effect of 'shifting' the problem to which Maier had given a somewhat metaphorical answer. Hull in effect puts forward a 'dementalized' explanation and dispenses with an analogical definition of behavioural inference but no matter how associative his model is, it does not dispense with the notion of structure. It is in the last analysis the principle of short-circuiting which acts as the basis for, and operationally explains, the transitivity expressed by 'III leads to D1 which leads to F', in which Maier had seen the proof of a genuine inference. All things considered, Maier's mistake was possibly simply that he confused a behaviour structure and an inference structure or more precisely that he assimilated without more ado a sensori-motor implication to a notional or at least a representative implication.

## 7 Transposition and generalization of learning: Spence's models

A more serious indictment not only of naïve mentalism but of the fundamental structuralism of the Gestalt psychologists is to be found in the theoretical generalizations advanced by Spence on the basis of experimental facts established with minute care. One of the essential arguments of structuralism had long consisted in pointing to facts of immediate transposition. Such transposition was considered by some as a purely structural transfer and by others as the sign of an intellectual process of the type known as 'eduction of correlates'. In Köhler's view however, immediate transposition following discrimination learning for instance, showed two things: the structural character of even the most elementary apprehension of stimuli, and continuity between perception and intelligence which he explained by their isomorphism. Thus, we have the well-known experiment in

---

[1] At the same time, one is free to doubt whether the experimental control which could be applied would be as crucial as Osgood, for instance, hopes. It is in any case difficult to ensure rigorous control of the different variables. It seems to us that if in an experiment of this kind the choice of III was more probable than the choice of IV, one could not automatically conclude that rats 'reason' as Maier believed. An additional mediatory response would suffice, or so we believe, to integrate the fact in Hull's schema.

which chicks, trained first of all to peck grains on a board B which was darker than another board A, then confronted with board B and a new board C, darker than B, chose C which they had never seen before and not B to which the response had been associated (Köhler, 1918). This was proof, according to Köhler, that this relatively lowly creature does not react to the absolute physical properties of a stimulus (here, the colour-stimulus B) but to an organized configuration of stimulations, to the relation 'B darker than A'. When confronted with the configuration 'C darker than B', it is the relation which is transposed. In the present context it does not matter whether we say that the animal 'perceives' or 'learns' relations. Köhler is interested only in the transposition itself, the learning phase being negligible in his eyes as if it had no other purpose than to teach the bird that it must make a choice. The chicken is trained to choose one of two boards, but no attempt is made to discover how it learns to do this. The ultimate transposition is considered sufficient to show *what* has been learned, or if one prefers 'understood'. Nor is the 'intelligent' behaviour of the chimpanzee interpreted any differently (Köhler, 1918, *ibid.*).

Spence, however, on the basis of various experimental studies devoted to discrimination learning and to generalization gradients of excitation and inhibition, showed that the facts adduced by Köhler (1917, 1918) or by Krechevsky (1932) and explained by each of them in terms of 'hypotheses' or '(structural) transposition' could be better and more simply explained in terms of associative learning. Spence's criticism, which he revised several times, deserves to be carefully considered. First of all, in his reply to Krechevsky he showed that the apparent discontinuity of insight behaviours in no way contradicted a *continuity* theory of progressive learning (Spence, 1936). Then he criticized the very notion of relation or relativity of stimuli described by Köhler and showed that a response to a relation can be explained with reference purely to the *absolute* properties of stimuli and to mechanisms of generalization (Spence, 1937). He then went on to elaborate his arguments in various publications. There was his reply to a study by Razran on stimulus generalization in conditioning (Spence, 1939), followed by his critical review of Köhler's book *Dynamics in Psychology* (Spence, 1941). A particularly clear statement of his views is given in two publications, one

*Pierre Gréco*

theoretical and the other experimental, on discrimination learning (Spence, 1940; 1945). There are also two summarized accounts of his work (Spence, 1950; 1951).

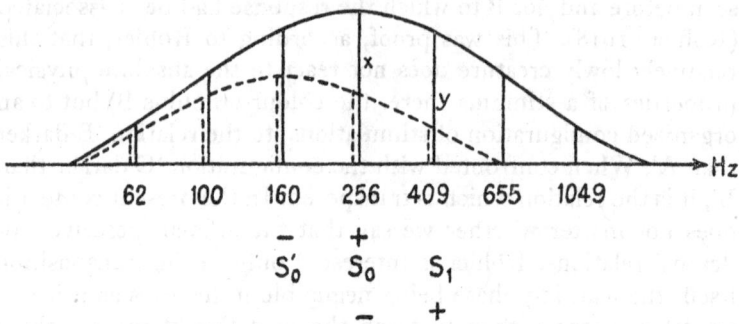

Fig. 3 Diagrammatic Representation of a 'Continuous' Interpretation of Discrimination Learning and of 'Transposition'
(After Spence)

As abscissa, the intensity of the stimulus (sound) in hertz; as ordinate, the intensity of the excitation (upper curve) or of the inhibition (lower curve). Conditioned at first to respond positively to So and negatively to S'o, the animal is then presented with So and S1. It then reacts positively to S1 and not to So, the excitatory strength $y$ of S1 (the distance between the ordinates of the two curves) being greater than the excitatory strength $x$ of So.

Let us consider a classic situation of conditioning a response R to a predetermined sound So = 256 Hz. If one then presents a sound S'o = 160 Hz, there will first of all be a generalization of R to S'o: a gradient of excitation has thus developed around So; but if one continues to present So and S'o reinforcing only So, a gradient of inhibition develops around S'o. These phenomena are well established following the work of Konorski and Miller (1934), Konorski (1938) and Hovland (1937). Thus, when the subject has learned to discriminate between So and S'o, one finds two superposed gradients of generalization (cf. Fig. 3): a positive gradient around So (shown as a continuous curve in the diagram. and a negative gradient (of inhibition) around S'o (dotted curve) They affect a whole range of stimuli, the corresponding intensities of excitation or inhibition decreasing regularly as the value of the stimulus diverges, in one direction or the other, from So and S'o respectively. The excitatory strength of each particular stimulus is then measured by the distance between the ordinates of the two curves representing the gradients. One sees that if one presents to the animal $S'1 = S0 = 256$ Hz and $S1 = 409$ Hz, it will react to $S1$ because the excitatory strength of $S1$ is stronger, and not to $S'1$, although the sound is identical to that to which the animal was originally conditioned. Spence later attacked the problem of the transposition of relations of size in the chimpanzee and drew up a similar diagram, the variable along the abscissa being in this case the size of the stimulus in square centimetres.

## 8  Criticisms and discussion

Unfortunately, subsequent experimental studies which various authors based on Spence's hypothesis or on his schema have produced ambiguous results or shown that Spence's interpretation still called for at least some technical or conceptual adjustments. Thus, it has not been possible to reach agreement concerning the shape of the curves representing gradients (Spence, 1937; Hull, 1939, 1950).

Ehrenfreund, who finally unhesitatingly sided with continuous interpretations, simultaneously presented two contradictory experiments. He trained rats in a jumping apparatus to recognize an upright triangle A as opposed to an inverted triangle B. Forty trials established a response to A, for instance, then in the test situation one group of subjects was required to choose A and the other group to choose B. It was found that in the second of his experiments the second group was at a disadvantage during relearning—as the continuity interpretation would naturally lead one to expect—but in the first experiment relearning was equally quick in both cases (Ehrenfreund, 1948). He accounts for this paradox by comparing the experimental conditions in detail. He argues that in the first experiment the rats did not 'pay attention' to the stimulus figures because the triangles were drawn in the upper part of the stimulus cards and preliminary training was thus limited to partial stimuli of position. In the second experiment on the other hand, the jumping platforms were raised so that during preliminary training the animals jumped up against the stimulus figures which were placed in the centre of the cards and it was therefore the whole figure which effectively acted as a stimulus.

*Pierre Gréco*

Other authors, repeating similar experiments, likewise stressed the role of the 'attention' paid to the stimuli by the animal. They distinguished between 'relevant' and 'irrelevant' stimuli (or cue stimuli) and in order to explain discrimination learning they reintroduced a functional principle of selection (or assimilation) of cues (Lawrence, 1949; 1950). On the other hand, animals trained to discriminate between two clearly distinct stimuli A and B and then required to react to two other stimuli C and D, achieved transposition more quickly in the final test discrimination than animals originally trained to distinguish the two test stimuli C and D succeeded in relearning the same pair[1] (Lawrence, 1952—research on the transfer of a discrimination along a continuum). His conclusions, following theoretical elaboration of the results, suggest that while a continuity model based on the two generalization gradients, as in Spence, is not absolutely invalidated by the facts, it is nevertheless not sufficient to account for transfers in which responses have to be reversed in relation to those acquired during the original training. He stresses the fundamental fact that where original training relates to a pair of clearly distinct stimuli, the transfer takes place even when the relearning situation calls for instrumental responses (and not simply conditioned reactions) that are completely different. In thus stressing 'acquisition of distinctiveness' and the part played by it, one reintroduces, indirectly by way of functionalism, the relativity of stimuli in which Köhler had seen a structural principle (Lawrence, 1955). And, more generally, when recent studies on transfer show the existence and importance of a 'transfer of principles'[2] are we not led back to the idea that learning, far from being reducible to associations of responses, in fact, produces, and probably brings into play from the beginning, an organizing activity which should be considered as a process of schematization rather than a 'habit-family hierarchy'? Before we attempt to decide this issue, we shall pause to consider a few genetic facts.

[1] Translator's Note: This is not quite accurate as no *re*learning was involved in the case of the animals which received all their trials on the test stimuli. Lawrence's actual conclusion was that 'learning was more efficient when animals were first trained on an easy and then shifted to the test discrimination than if all the training was given directly on the latter'.
[2] Cf. Chapter 13 (Volume 4).

## 3  Thinking and learning

In continuing to confine ourselves, as we have done so far, to sensori-motor learning in animals, we would run the risk of finally denying ourselves through prejudice or method, all access to the higher forms of cognition and to intellectual structures in what could well be their most original aspect. What is more, we have on many occasions recognized or suspected a dangerous tendency towards analogy, a kind of sophistry characterized by explanations of the 'as if' type. This amounts to systematically seeking the image of higher processes in observed lower processes and in confusing isomorphism and identity. This sophistry may take one of two opposing forms. The first consists in attributing to the most elementary behaviours the properties or the form of the highest and thus leads to mentalism. The second imputes to psychological reality its own economy of technique and method and thereby leads to operational formalism and to theoretical reductionism.

### 1  Method and concepts

A simple example will serve to reveal this ambiguity in a concrete form. In studying the child's search for vanished objects (Piaget, 1953), one can observe the following behaviour from the end of the first year. First the experimenter hides, in full view of the child, an interesting object $x$ behind a 'screen' A (which may be a box, a clenched fist...). He then slips the hidden object behind a second screen B and finally takes away A leaving $x$ under B; the child first looks for $x$ under A and does not find it. Before the age of 11–12 months he will give up at this point and show his disappointment, but a little later he proceeds without hesitation to look behind screen B.[1] This can be called sensori-motor *inference* or even 'practical transitivity' applied to the relation 'placed behind'. But how can one simply assimilate this behaviour

---

[1] See, for example, J. Piaget, *The Construction of Reality in the Child*, London, Routledge and Kegan Paul, 1955. These observations were first reported in *The Origins of Intelligence in the Child*, London, Routledge and Kegan Paul, 1953. (Original French edition, 1936.)

## Pierre Gréco

structure to the operational transitivity of asymmetrical relations which does not appear on the plane of notional thought until six years later? A definition of intelligent behaviour that was too broad and *a priori* monistic would in this case do away with a problem which genetic observation clearly shows to exist. We shall come back to this point.

On the other hand, are there not equally great risks in looking straight away in the direction of adult thought, verbal or otherwise, and naturally discursive? The lines of approach and first the problems involved require careful discussion. An objective study of 'thinking' imposes particular methodological conditions on the psychologist. The most obvious of these is that one cannot study thinking except in its manifestations. At the same time, if the aim is to describe its instruments and its forms of organization, there is nothing to guarantee that a particular manifestation or the steps leading up to it, express or adequately reflect these instruments and these forms. Must one rest content, therefore, with discovering, at best, the 'structure of functioning' that is characteristic of thinking, if indeed such an expression is not amphibological? Or, without pining for the lost paradise of philosophical introspection and for the 'essence' dear to phenomenologists should we rather look for *intellectual structures* beyond the actual functioning of thought?

An operational decision can naturally—and indeed *must* if science is to go forward—put a term to these speculative scruples. But is one then entitled to elevate this decision to the plane of theory? 'Mind is behaviour . . .', postulated J. B. Watson, who presumed to add 'and nothing else' thereupon quickly passing from semiology to explanation without realizing it.[1] Alfred Binet, being more practical and probably more disillusioned, affected to define intelligence in terms of the instrument that measured it. One of the most spectacular errors in psychology, which arose shortly afterwards, was to impute to intellectual

---

[1] After giving several definitions of the word *thinking*, English and English (*A Comprehensive Dictionary of Psychological and Psychoanalytical Terms*, New York, etc.: Longmans Green and Co., 1958, p. 553) give the following behaviourist definition 'Subvocal or covert speech behaviour' but they do not conceal the fact that this meaning, though fairly common, is a *theory* about thinking that masquerades as a definition. Concerning this illegitimate elevation of operational concepts to the plane of theory, one can consult the very rigorous criticisms addressed by Sigmund Koch to Hull, in Estes *et alia* (1954).

*Learning and Intellectual Structures*

evolution the metrological peculiarities of this instrument.[1] But when Binet finally resigned himself to writing that thought was 'an unconscious activity of the mind' (Binet, 1903), was this to be interpreted as a sally intended to evade a false psychological problem, or was it an admission that his method of controlled association and experimental introspection had failed?

In examining a few facts concerning thinking and its structures, we shall need to undertake if not an inquiry into the nature of thinking which would not be within our competence, at least a constant methodological appraisal of technical set-ups and concepts, which we must consider together since they go together.

## 2 Problem-solving tests[2]

We shall use the by now classic expression *problem solving*[3] whenever we have cause to point out the ambiguity, involuntary or deliberate, that exists between the definition of a task—solving problems—and that of a type of behaviour or a mental process.[4] The methodological handbook by T. G. Andrews devotes a single chapter to 'Studying human thinking'. The author of the chapter writes that 'Thinking may then be defined as that activity, whatever its nature, by which a person solves a problem'—let it pass! She immediately adds this startling specification: 'an activity which may be more or less thoughtful as the situation is more or less problematic'. (Edna Heidbreder, 1948) This more or less amounts to asserting that thinking is what enables one to solve problems through thinking! Other handbooks on the other hand, such as those by Woodworth, Osgood, etc., have two separate chapters, one on thinking and the other on problem solving. Osgood actually includes the word *insight* in the title of the second. It is clear at least that one can distinguish several categories

[1] We refer to the work of L. Bonnis, the methodological absurdity of which was denounced by R. Zazzo (*Intelligence et quotient d'âges*, Paris, Presses Universitaires de France, 1946).

[2] For a detailed inventory of techniques and findings see above, Chapter 22.

[3] Translator's Note: Gréco actually says that he will use this expression *in English* where he considers it necessary for the reason stated. In fact he only does so once, towards the end of the following paragraph, where the words are printed in italics. When they appear elsewhere, it is as a translation of the French expression *la résolution des problèmes*.

[4] The dictionary by English and English, quoted above, defines problem-solving as 'the *process* of selecting from a number of alternatives those that lead to a desired goal'.

or types of problems. Unfortunately their morphological classification does not in any way resolve the question of the corresponding classification of the relevant mental processes.

Let us consider for example the famous problem of the 'nine dots' (Maier, 1930), the discovery of a law of double alternation AABB ... otherwise known as the 'temporal maze' (Gellerman, 1931; Hunter and Bartlett, 1948) and a complex geometrical problem such as the Gestalt psychologists have often put forward.[1] Are they structurally comparable? In all three cases it is possible (although it may first be necessary to choose subjects of a suitable age) to observe a 'search' which proceeds by successive steps, in the form of hypotheses and controlled trial and error, followed by the sudden emergence of the solution. One can thus speak of insight and induction (the search for a deductive solution to a mathematical problem can be based on an inductive method of discovery). Yet the operations required in each of the three cases are different just as the processes are different. The difficulty presented by the problem of the nine dots is due to an attitude or set as a result of which the subject gratuitously forbids himself to go beyond the limits of the given dots. The difficulty of the third problem (apart from the formal knowledge which it requires) is probably also due to the Gestalt imposed by the figure which has to be restructured but restructurization can in this instance be expressly guided by relevant knowledge and by systematic deduction of hypotheses based on the terms of the problems. As to the second problem, it is solved almost immediately by an adult, whereas at the age of 8–10 one observes either more or less belated insights or progressive but often very irregular decreases in errors (Oléron, 1957; Matalon, 1959; Gréco, unpublished). Mathematical learning models can reduce this situation to that of random learning or partial reinforcement, without presupposing any pre-existing cognitive structure, except for an ability to react—unconsciously—to contingent probabilities (Estes, 1957).[2] Finally if one puts to a child of 8 a

---

[1] For instance: 'prove that the three altitudes of a triangle bisect the angles of the triangle formed by joining the feet of these altitudes'. This problem is analysed in P. Guillaume, *La Psychologie de la Forme*, Paris, Flammarion, 1937 (pp. 178–9).

[2] The models actually constructed are concerned with single alternation ABAB (which, unfortunately, is discovered immediately from the age of 6 at least) but they can be generalized.

question regarding conservation (for example: does a quantity B of liquid, which is seen at the beginning of the experiment to be equal to a quantity A, remain equal to it when it is poured into a narrower vessel in which the level is therefore higher?) can it be said that one is going beyond the bounds of *problem-solving* on the grounds that the subject no longer sees any problem and that equality seems to him supremely evident? In this case, evidence points to the necessary character of equality and is not this very necessity the sign of the acquisition of an intellectual *structure*?

## 3 'Mental mazes' and pre-experimental artifact

Thus, the controversy over insight and groping which may have been fruitful historically but is speculatively a little vain, assumes a pre- and not a post-experimental character when we come to the study of thinking. Since it is not possible to give an unambiguous definition of thinking, one is in danger of discovering in the course of research only what one was looking for. We have elsewhere set out a few arguments of this kind to show the initial divergence of perspective between a synchronic and a diachronic study of behaviour (P. Gréco, 1959 *c*) but a synchronic study can itself harbour dangerous artifacts.

A trivial but classic example is that of 'mental mazes'. 'In most psychological experiments on thinking,' admits Edna Heidbreder (*loc. cit.*, p. 116) 'the methods employed are adaptations of procedures first used in studying other psychological activities.' Maybe we can be permitted to deplore the fact. When Peterson, in 1920, first had the idea of using non-spatial symbolic mazes, he was trying to place the adult human subject in a situation as complex and as unusual as that of the rat confronted with unknown pathways or the cat shut in a puzzle box. However 'mental' they were, these problems were well and truly mazes that had to be learned and Woodworth, for example, did not consider them in any other light. Thus he wrote, 'A maze has a serial character; it presents a series of situations or choice points in a constant order. At each point it presents two or more alternatives. Which is right can only be discovered by exploration.' (*Experimental Psychology*, p. 153.) Unfortunately not every researcher is as cautious as Woodworth. If 'problem-solving' is *the* way of studying how thinking proceeds and if solving consists, according

*Pierre Gréco*

to the definition by English quoted above in a footnote,[1] in 'selecting from a number of alternatives . . .', one has only to set a rather complicated problem to assign a preponderant and even an exclusive role to 'exploration' at the expense of true intellectual 'structurization'.

These considerations lead us on to a fundamental point which is that a satisfactory account and explanation of intellectual structures cannot be given without recourse to a genetic enquiry. If one sets the subject a problem which it is beyond him to solve immediately, one runs the risk, already denounced by Köhler with reference to Thorndike, of assimilating *a priori* learning and intelligence and of failing to recognize intellectual structures. We shall come back to this in *4* below. If the subject is set only problems which he can solve immediately, one does get an idea of the intellectual structure, by reference to the objective structure of the problem, but one is prevented from seeing the origin and the peculiar organization of the structure thus revealed.

## 4   *'Concept formation': discussion of a classic example*

'Concept formation' is a notion at least as ambiguous as 'problem-solving'. The classic experiment on Chinese characters (Hull, 1920),[2] on which so many others have been patterned,[3] will serve to make the point clear. The first thing to be noted is that this experiment deliberately uses the technique of paired associates normally used in the study of memory. Six successive series of twelve characters, each containing a different stroke or 'element', to which a nonsense syllable is associated by way of a name, are first presented at regular five-second intervals with a tachistoscope. Then six test series of twelve characters are presented. This time the twelve elements are not represented in each of the series. Instead the same elements can occur in two or three different characters. At the beginning of the experiment ('sorting out' series) the experimenter names each of the characters and the subject looks at it for five seconds. With the second series, the subject is required to name the character presented to him and the experimenter confirms or corrects his response. The series is repeated until the subject has learned all the names.

---

[1] See p. 229, note 4.   [2] Cf. above, Chapter 12 and Chapter 22, p. 16.
[3] Cf. above, Chapter 22, p. 11.

The experimenter then turns to the next series, in which the same elements occur but in characters other than those of which the subject has learned the names. The number of presentations required, for each series, in order to attain complete recognition of the characters gives a measure of learning. The percentage of correct responses to the first presentation of each series (27 per cent for series 2, 38 per cent for series 3, then 47, 55 and 56 per cent of the responses given by the eighteen university students used as subjects) is supposed to give a measure of 'conceptualization'. It must at the same time be stressed that subjects are not forewarned regarding the structure of the material presented and that the instructions present the task as a problem of memorization and naming, without encouraging them to look for common elements. Hull stresses the fact that at the end of the experiment, the percentage of recognized characters is higher than one would expect if only methodical abstraction of common elements were involved. A control showed that learning was no better if, during the 'sorting out' series, one presented six 'naked' common elements and six others imbedded in the characters.

What does this experiment show? Does it show that the abstraction of qualities common to different objects (empiricism has never doubted that this was the true definition of conceptualization) proceeds according to learning mechanisms with reinforcements? This is apparently Hull's view for he expressly points out, at the beginning of his study, that a young child learns in this way to call a dog a dog (*art. cit.*, p. 5). But Goldstein and Scheerer (1941) dispute that calling a dog a dog is an activity which belongs on the same plane as that which consists in abstracting a meaning. Osgood (1953, p. 667) for his part suggests the term *labelling* and not *concept-formation* for the process studied by Hull.[1] In point of fact Hull's findings give us information on two points. First, they show by means of a technique of evaluation which is as precise as it is ingenious how a number of empirical schemata are formed through learning.

---

[1] Nevertheless, it is often Hull's vocabulary and conception that prevail. This is so both in animal psychology (cf. *Studies in Concept formation* by P. E. Fields on the 'development of the concept of triangularity by the white rat', *Psych. Monogr.*, 1932, 9, p. 2) and in many Anglo-Saxon studies of language ranging from Bloomfield to Roger Brown. The latter's book *Words and Things* has on the cover a drawing showing a label 'Words' attached by a highly symbolic piece of string to 'Things'.

They include schemata of perceptual recognition and verbal schemata or schemata of naming. Secondly, they show us that university students have an undoubted capacity for abstracting Chinese strokes from the abominably complicated material that is presented to them, and this without any encouragement to look for what remains the same beneath the apparent diversity. But should the intellectual structure which determines the concept be sought in the functional process through which a *particular* concept is realized—or is it not already present in this aptitude for conceptualizing? A child of four to five, asked to classify counters of different shapes and colours by putting 'all those that are the same together' cannot achieve a subdivision of the set (into disjoined and exhaustive sub-sets), although he is quite capable of recognizing the red squares, the blue squares, the blue circles, etc. (Piaget and Inhelder, 1964) and although learning through reinforcement to distribute counters into four piles presents no difficulty.[1] There is probably more to be learned about the structures involved in 'conceptualization' from such failure to achieve spontaneous classification than from successful learning of an empirical classification. At this level, the quantification of class inclusions is undoubtedly a more reliable structural index than mere categorization according to a common criterion.

Thus, the experimental learning of a task which the experimenter has made sufficiently complex, or has defined sufficiently mysteriously, to give rise to learning, may well give no information as to the intellectual structures brought into play, and even give false ideas as to the formation of these structures. This is because their actual genesis and diachronic development are not isomorphic simply because the experimenter has postulated the fact by way of metaphor or for the sake of convenience.[2]

## 5 Specificity of intellectual structures: Gestalttheorie and Denkpsychologie

The opposite method, as it were, consists in looking for structures in tasks solved without trial and error, or in the part which is free

---

[1] At least at the age of six, according to an investigation which we carried out in 1957 with 12 subjects, in order to perfect a test on the learning of logical structures which we in fact abandoned because it proved too easy.

[2] See below, paragraph 6, and Section 4.

from trial and error, and this, too, is fraught with dangers. The Gestalt psychologists, concerned mainly with structures, were prone to neglect structurizations. Köhler (1918), delighted to find in the chicken or the chimpanzee an immediate transposition of relations, did not concern himself with the 20 to 30 per cent of subjects which did not transpose nor, as we have seen,[1] with the preliminary learning period. Research of the same kind was later undertaken with guinea pigs in Cambridge and revealed the existence of Gestaltist subjects and (less gifted) associationist subjects (Bartlett, 1932)! Likewise, when Wertheimer spoke of a 'realization of internal structures', the vicissitudes of the realization, whether in adult life or in the course of the child's development, held his attention less than the presence of insight and its suddenness. The wonderful but improbable child who at the age of five and a half called for scissors in order to find the area of a parallelogram (Wertheimer, 1945) must have had, besides precocious notions of conservation, a fairly substantial experience of cutting out—and probably did no more than cut out! When Gauss, at his primary school, 'structured' the series $1 + 2 + 3 \ldots + 8$ into four symmetrical sums each making 9, according to the anecdote related by Guillaume, he was of course Gauss and as such had a sure operational intuition of numerical iteration, unless he simply found a 'trick', a fortuitously operational *Gestalt*! In writing that 'the order which expresses itself in physical laws *resembles* that found in human intelligence' Guillaume (1937) gives to Köhler's 'isomorphism' an expression which comes very close to the neo-empiricism of Hull, Spence or Skinner. It is, of course, the nature of the *order* in question which constitutes the difference, but it is in any case outside intelligence that the order of intelligence must be sought.

Some psychologists went even further than this. The German *Denkpsychologie* from Marbe (1901) to the Würzburg School (cf. Burloud, 1927) and even to Duncker (1935), used experimental introspection and verbal associations commented on by the subject or pre-oriented by the experimenter, in an effort to arrive at the structural factors of intelligence through the actual functioning of ideation and especially of reasoning. While they agreed that one finds something other than mere images and associations, they believed that this irreducible 'remainder' was a kind of

[1] Cf. p. 223.

eidetic and transcendental consciousness. This conception is related to the ideas of Brentano and Husserl even if it is rechristened in terms that may be psychological (*Bewusstheit*), scholastic (*intentio*) operational (effects of instructions) or functional (*Ergänzung*). In short, this method which set out to show the specificity of intellectual structures and which has now fallen into utter desuetude, leads us back to logical *a priorism*. This does not satisfy any psychologist of behaviour, particularly a developmental psychologist. We refer the reader to Piaget's definitive critique of this kind of logicism, whether avowed or not (cf. Piaget, 1950, pp. 25-50).

## 6 Reductionism or unification: two recent models

The 'reductions' which we have so far discussed consist mainly in operational reductions. Concern for objectivity demands that intellectual structures should first be studied by experimental investigation of the activities through which they express themselves. What we have at times disputed is whether these activities have always been well chosen. Reductionism and unification can also proceed by another road, that of conceptual deduction and reconstruction. The elaboration, and often also the axiomatization of the great theories of behaviour has progressed sufficiently (see for instance Hull *et alia*, 1940; Estes *et alia*, 1954) for such reconstruction to be both possible and desirable. The interest which the behaviourists have explicitly shown, especially during the last ten years, in the problem of thinking (see for instance Maltzman, 1955), calls for some reference to what has been done in this direction even though this takes us out of the realm of established fact.

### (A) APOSTEL'S REDUCTION AND ALGEBRAS

One of the most systematic attempts at reduction was made by the Belgian logician L. Apostel. He tried to show that 'the laws of learning are such that, regardless of what tasks are set, provided that they are sufficiently numerous and complex, one necessarily learns behaviours which correspond to classification, establishment of relations and judgment,' and thus to logical structures of classes, relations and propositional inferences (Apostel, 1959). In outline Apostel's method is as follows: 1) he begins by rigorously defining behaviours corresponding to logical notions of class, relation, proposition, inference, etc.; 2) he elaborates on the axiomatic plane a 'general theory' of learning. In his view, the theories of Hull, Tolman and Guthrie could be considered as particular cases of this general theory and they appear to contain even the theory of learning which underlies Piaget's work on the development of sensori-motor intelligence; 3) he shows that this general theory can account for the behaviours previously defined and finally 4) he evolves the structure of an 'algebra of learning operators'. His work is therefore of great importance to psychologists, despite the fact that it is purely speculative, since he offers at once an axiomatization, a demonstration and a model.

Without having the presumption to discuss in a few lines so rich and so subtle a memoir, we would like to make a few remarks concerning the points mentioned. Taking 4) first, it should be pointed out that an algebra of operators of reinforcement and of extinction (Apostel proposed two versions of unequal complexity, B and H) is only a model and not a theory. Apostel himself carefully distinguishes the problem of the algebraic structure of operators, and that of the structure of the reactions produced by the operators, which has still to be studied through fresh experimental investigations. But, on the other hand, what are these algebras psychologically, but structures of behaviour and physiological substructures? Piaget (1959 a, pp. 51–67) sees in them a sign that a 'logic' (in the sense in which he himself understands the term, namely 'general form of the co-ordination of actions') pre-exists learning and is already present in the hereditary reflex organization, so that it does not derive from it: if one goes back from a piece of learning to the one before, one does not finally arrive at an 'empty organism'. Taking 2) next, the reduction of the theories of Hull, Guthrie, Tolman and Piaget to a common schema probably has the effect of eliminating from these theories their theoretical particularities. These, however, are not mere speculative luxuries, since they direct the choice of facts and experiments (Gréco, 1959 c) and the facts thus obtained are not yet sufficient to decide between the theories or to reconcile them. Finally 1) and 3), psychologists are left with the formidable problem mentioned at the beginning of this section which Apostel himself dispenses with or deliberately eludes. Even if

*Pierre Gréco*

there is isomorphism between a particular piece of sensori-motor behaviour 'corresponding to' the logical notion of class or inference, and the operational structures of classes or inferences as manipulated by a child of 7 or 14, this in no way justifies a possible reduction, since the chronological time-lag would still require explanation. Depending on the standpoint that one adopts, the partial isomorphism between the generalization of the Pavlovian reflex, for instance, and the inferential generalization of deductive thought appears either as a fact or as a mystery. As psychologists, it is of no great interest to us to know that Spinoza, Pavlov and Köhler agree that man is part of nature. Even if they did not, we should postulate the fact. The prefiguration of intellectual structures in elementary behaviour, however, does not imply that they are already present in it nor that they are directly derived from it.

(B) D. E. BERLYNE'S ADAPTATION OF HULL'S IDEAS

Another noteworthy attempt in this direction was made by D. E. Berlyne. His work on 'curiosity' (i.e. orientation–exploration behaviour), conflict and learning in animals is known and acknowledged even in the U.S.S.R. After spending a year working in close collaboration with J. Piaget's team in Geneva, Berlyne proposed a solution to (or a dialectical advance on) the so-called Hull–Piaget dilemma. His belief is that by adopting a broader S–R schema, group structures can be shown to develop out of the notion of habit-family hierarchy (Berlyne, 1960). He professes to be continuing, and extending to the problem of the structures of relations, the work which Apostel carried out on the structures of classes. His construction is more closely related to the concepts of psychologists. It starts from a general schema of behaviour, into which he introduces the notion of transmitted information (though finally he makes but little use of communications theory) and within which he situates intelligence and 'thinking' in relation to the most elementary adaptations. He goes on to give a mathematical expression, in terms of graphs and groups, to Hull's structure of habit families and examines such problems as notions of conservation and numerical or algebraic equivalences, etc., in the light of novel views on the stimulus-response connection, the various mechanisms of generalization and the equivalences

## Learning and Intellectual Structures

acquired through learning. We shall here consider only two remarkable points in Berlyne's monograph and note that 1) in putting the accent on stimulus-response generalizations (which Hull discovered although he actually made very little use of them) Berlyne interpreted the stimulus-response connection as an active process of schematizing assimilation instead of as a mere association through similarity or proximity; 2) in order to explain conservations, for instance, he was not content with the copy-responses (i.e. responses to stimuli which are made up of what Piaget would call 'states') which are alone recognized by strict empiricism. He introduced a second category, that of 'transformational responses' which Piaget would be quite prepared to accept. Unfortunately, Berlyne sometimes allows a doubt to subsist as to the distinction between 'transformational responses' and 'representations of transformations'. The fact is that correct representation of a transformation is probably not a sufficient condition of the operation itself, as shown by some of the results of Inhelder and Piaget.[1] At all events Berlyne admits that hierarchical families do not necessarily require preliminary learning in the strict sense. Thus the co-ordination of actions can be achieved according to internal laws of structurization or, as Piaget says, of equilibration.

(C) FINAL REMARKS

It is not for us to draw a lesson from attempts of this kind, which still require a considerable amount of experimental proof and probably also of conceptual refinement. In analysing the work of Apostel and Berlyne, Piaget (1959 a; 1960) indicated the points of disagreement between them but also and especially the convergence between these two elaborations (despite their difference of origin and intention) and a general theory of equilibrium which he himself had begun to form at a time when his ideas had as yet found expression only in a philosophical novel (*Recherche*, Lausanne, La Concorde, 1918). This theory which he has since continually developed and of which the latest embodiment is the recent probabilistic model (Piaget, 1957),[2] has now reached a stage where it requires to be given a more precise mathematical

---
[1] These are reported above, Chapter 23.
[2] See also above, p. 201 and concerning learning itself, Chapter 12.

expression. All these investigations allow us to hope that we shall soon see if not doctrinal unity at least the suppression of some controversies arising from mutual incomprehension.[1] They show besides, so we believe, that this whole problem cannot be solved simply by theoretical structures or by the Hunt of Pan[2] of experimenters but only by a close interchange between facts and ideas.

## 4 Logical structures, learning and development

The problem of the relations between learning and intelligence can probably be most categorically formulated in psychogenetic terms. Is the child's acquisition of knowledge to be explained in terms of experience? Does the process of intellectual development amount to a set of learning mechanisms? Thus put, the question invites experimental controls—and we shall now give an account of those that have been undertaken and show what they can teach us. At the same time, it brings us back to an old epistomological debate: that of empiricism as opposed to rationalism or nativism. This is a debate that cannot altogether be eluded, even in a study such as this which is concerned mainly with techniques and facts.

A few remarks must be made at the outset. First, it is clear that a considerable amount of 'knowledge' including specialized skills such as reading and writing, and areas of knowledge such as familiarity with physical laws or the properties of objects, etc.— are direct products of experience and of learning. Indeed, it is possible without risk and without additional proof to postulate that experience and learning are necessary conditions for the acquisition of all knowledge: before a baby can use a support as a means of reaching a desired object or before a child of 6–7 can recognize that two sticks equal to a third are equal to one another, there is need for groping and empirical inspection. The

[1] 'Köhler,' writes Osgood (p. 625), 'would have just about as much difficulty in really understanding Hull's *Principles of Behaviour* as Hull would have really understanding Köhler's recent discussions of the figural after-effect.'

[2] Translator's Note: This expression was used by Francis Bacon. It refers to the procedures used in the investigation of nature before scientific induction was adopted.

problem therefore is not to show that learning plays a part, and a necessary one, in intellectual development but to determine whether the processes and the laws of learning are sufficient to account for this development and in particular for the form it takes, by which we mean the general structures of thinking characterizing the successive stages in the development of intelligence in the individual.

Secondly, it would be futile for similar reasons to reopen now a debate on maturation. Unless one is actually prepared to accept Watson's enthusiasm which led him to declare (on the strength of a few spectacular results of conditioning and deconditioning in children) that it is possible to teach anyone anything at any time, one has no need to be reminded that physiological maturation imposes strict limiting conditions on the acquisition of skills and knowledge. At the same time, the fact that a child of three cannot be taught the combinatorial system or transitivity, or even the use of a bicycle without stabilizers, in no way endangers the laws and theories of learning. The problem which remains, however, is to discover whether the combinatorial system is acquired by the same process as the use of a bicycle or, to take a less crude example, whether a child learns to recognize the conservant and non-conservant transformations of a ball of clay in the same way as he learns to recognize colours, or the particular function of each of the switches in a complex electrical apparatus.

We shall endeavour to defend the opposite view and to advance if not a complete proof and justification at least a number of likely hypotheses and a fairly general explanation which will serve as our conclusion. We shall take as our first example the notions of conservation or 'operational invariants' normally acquired by the child from the age of seven. The way in which they are formed empirically or through teaching was studied at the C.I.E.G.[1] in 1957–1958. The question is: Is it possible, through suitable training, to make a subject who does not yet possess these notions, discover, understand and recognize them in a way that is lasting and even capable of generalization? Assuming that it is possible, what is this synchronic acquisition worth and what are the mechanisms underlying its genesis? These questions will lead us to work out more precisely how far

[1] *Centre International d'Epistémologie Génétique*, directed at Geneva by Professor J. Piaget (Rockefeller Foundation).

experiments can assist learning and to distinguish between operational activities arising from the situations and the empirical observation of data. We shall then have to define the specific nature of the process of structurization and compare it to learning processes in general.

## 1 Notions of conservation, transitivity and learning

(A) EXPERIMENT ON WEIGHT INVARIANTS

Jan Smedslund, of Oslo, studied on a population of English speaking children in Geneva the possibility of acquiring notions of conservation and transitivity of weight (Smedslund, 1959). If two balls of clay A and B are originally recognized to be of the same weight ($a = b$) or of different weight (e.g. $a > b$), is it certain that $a = b'$ (in the first case) or $a > b'$ (in the second) after B has been transformed into B' by being flattened, drawn out or split into fragments, etc? Likewise, if after noting the equality or inequality in weight of two objects A and B one then notes the equality or inequality in weight of B and C, can one directly infer the equality or inequality of A and C? According to earlier work by Piaget and Inhelder (1941, 1962), and Piaget's interpretation, conservation and transitivity are both based on the same operational 'grouping' structure, such a structure being a fundamental characteristic of what is known as the level of 'concrete operations'. It should be noticed, however, that in their 'concrete' form these operations do not immediately apply to any content. In particular we find that notions of conservation and transitivity are acquired later in the case of weight than in that of length, substance and numerable quantities. The same time-lag between notions of weight and those of substance[1] for instance, would appear to exist in the case of conservation and transitivity alike. Smedslund planned to check three things: 1) whether in the case of a subject who has acquired these notions without experimental intervention conservation and transitivity of weight mutually imply one another; 2) whether a subject who

[1] The notion of *quantity* (of substance) is operationally defined by judgments in terms of 'more ....', 'less ....', 'the same (or "as much")...'. Let us point out, in passing, that transitivity-schemata have not yet been studied directly and systematically but have been shown to exist by the results of experiments on seriation for instance (transitivity of asymmetrical relations).

## Learning and Intellectual Structures

does not yet possess these notions can learn one or the other after a relatively short series of verifications using a balance; 3) whether learning one of these notions, assuming that it can be learned, immediately leads to the acquisition of the other.

As a pre-test Smedslund presented two balls of clay of the same weight after which he transformed one of them into a cup, then a ring and then a cross. Another experimental situation consists in removing a small piece of clay from A and transforming B into a sausage. To test transitivity, the experimenter uses three balls of clay of the same size and of identical or different weight (achieved by means of an invisible metal core), or three dolls of different sizes of which the biggest is the lightest. The situations present various relations of weight between the three elements: $a = b$ and $b = c$ or $a < b < c$ or $a = b$ and $b > c$ etc. Out of 57 subjects between the ages of $5\frac{1}{2}$ and $7\frac{1}{2}$, 20 (35 per cent) passed the conservation test[1] but only 3 passed all the tests on transitivity although 21 made a correct response supported by logical argument to one at least of the transitivity tests. Smedslund took into account that the transitivity test brought in a great number and an even greater variety of relations, that it presented greater visual contradictions and finally that it required, according to him, more complex verbal formulations. He therefore used various criteria of success and concluded that there was a close association between the two notions.

The subjects who had failed the pre-test questions were then used for an experiment on conservation learning and afterwards (three weeks later) underwent a post-test on transitivity. Fifteen subjects were used as a control group C which received no training, eight subjects were put into an experimental group A whose training consisted in various deformations of the ball of clay (17 situations were presented during the first session and 13 of them again presented two days later). The remaining eight subjects were put in an experimental group B in which training included both situations in which shape was changed and others

---

[1] This percentage appears very high, compared with those obtained after the standardizations of Vinh-Bang on Genevan schoolchildren (12 per cent successful at age 6–7, 24 per cent at 7–8, 52 per cent at 8–9) and with those which we ourselves observed on a population of Parisian children of mediocre socio-economic status (15 per cent at most at age 6–7). The tests were not exactly the same, but the main point is that Smedslund's subjects belonged to a high socio-cultural milieu and were without question educationally 'advanced' children.

## Pierre Gréco

in which the experimenter added or took away clay from one of the balls (same conditions as for B). In these training sessions the original situation is one in which there are either two balls of the same size and of the same weight or two balls of the same size but of different weights (3 situations). The changes of shape are produced by drawing out ('short sausage', 'long sausage', 'snake'), flattening ('cake', 'pancake') or dividing (ball divided into 2, 4, 6 or 8 fragments) but not by crumbling. Each time, the child is made to verify, on a Roberval balance, that the original equality (or inequality) of weight has persisted (or, in the case of group B, that adding and taking away substance have modified it). Smedslund took into account not only the accuracy of responses but also the quality of the arguments put forward. He established that 1) there is very definite evidence of learning in groups A and B; 2) group A makes more progress than group B if one considers the number of correct responses but not if one considers the number of 'operational' explanations ('because they weighed the same at the beginning', 'because you've only changed the shape', 'you've not taken anything away' . . .); 3) the acquisition of conservation leads in the case of about half the subjects to correct judgments of transitivity in some post-test questions but never in all of them. The table below gives some of the results obtained by Smedslund.

| | Pretest | | After training | | |
|---|---|---|---|---|---|
| | | | Conservation | | Transitivity |
| | C.R | O.E | C.R | O.E | |
| Group A (N = 8) | 3 | 0 | 27 | 16 | — |
| Group B (N = 8) | 9 | 1 | 21 | 16 | 9* |
| Group C (N = 15) (no training) | 3 | 2 | 3 | 1 | 2† |

*Acquisition of conservation of weight* (J. Smedslund)

C.R. = total number of correct responses, calculated over all the items of each test.

O.E. = total number of operational explanations supporting the correct responses, calculated in the same way.

\* This number refers to the subjects who gave *at least one* O.E. during the final transitivity test.

† The same applies in this case. The number was calculated on the basis of the 15 subjects who had not been trained, of whom 5 only were able to undergo the post-test on conservation.

## (B) ACQUISITION OF TRANSITIVITY OF WEIGHTS

In the experiment on acquisition of transitivity, 13 children who did not spontaneously have this notion were divided into a control group C of five subjects and an experimental group E of eight subjects. Subjects in group E had a learning session on three consecutive days. This consisted in the presentation of four different situations (thus, twelve different situations in all for each subject). A few days later, all the subjects underwent the same post-test on transitivity as the subjects in the experiment already described (4 situations $a = b = c$, $a > b > c$, $a = b > c$, $a < b < c$). In each of the training situations the experimenter presented three objects differing in weight ($a > b > c$), size, shape and colour. The original relations were also presented in different orders: $a > b$, then $b > c$ or else $b > c$ then $a > b$. For instance:

*2nd session, 4th situation*

a) the children were made to note that a blue 'cake', of medium size, was heavier than a large yellow ring;

b) they were made to note that the large yellow ring was heavier than a small brown square;

c) they were asked whether the blue 'cake' was more or less heavy than the brown square and this was followed by verification on the balance.

*3rd session, 2nd situation*

a) noting that a large yellow cup is heavier than a small green 'cake';

b) noting that a blue snake of medium size is heavier than the yellow cup;

c) question on the relative weight of the snake and the 'cake', followed by verification.

To avoid 'perserverative' responses ('it's always the same thing . . . .'), learning was confined to asymmetrical relations and to avoid cue associations which could have led to purely discriminative pseudo-learning, care was taken to use various combinations of weights, sizes (eliminating combinations such as those where the order of sizes corresponds to that of weights), shapes and colours. The results of this experiment were decisively negative, as shown in the following talbe:

|  | Before training | | After training | |
|---|---|---|---|---|
|  | C.R | O.E | C.R | O.E |
| Experimental group (E) (N = 8) | 16 | 1 | 12 | 0 |
| Control group (C) (N = 5) | 17 | 1 | 8 | 3 |

*Acquisition of transitivity of weight relations* (J. Smedslund)

Same notation as in the previous table. Naturally, subjects in the control group were given no training and the results in the 'after training' column are those of the post-test, administered to both groups after the same interval. The fact that there are some correct responses at the beginning and at the end of the experiment can be attributed to chance or to recourse to irrelevant visual cues which nevertheless coincide in certain cases with the relative value of the weights.

Individual results do not show any greater evidence of progress, during or following the training period, according to the various criteria applied by the author (some of which are far from exacting). Smedslund explains both the occurrence of occasional correct responses and the absence of learning in this test by the fact that 'perceptual strategies' (judgments based on perceptual cues) lead to correct responses in some of the situations chosen. Thus they are not systematically 'penalized' by the record on the scales as they were in the experiment on the acquisition of conservation.

(C) DISCUSSION

We have deliberately reported this experiment in some detail, because it can suggest a number of tests of the same kind and also the findings call for several important comments. First, although a negative result is not sufficient to prove non-existence, it is remarkable that transitivity, which is a truly operational structure, cannot be acquired in conditions where it is however possible for conservation to be 'learned' by some subjects. But what is the conservation of weight and what do we mean by 'learning' that weight remains invariant throughout the deformations of the ball of clay? If, by definition, concrete operations do not allow a separation of structure and content, we must ask

## Learning and Intellectual Structures

ourselves whether learning based on repeated verification simply gives the subject information concerning the content of the proposed situations or allows him also to construct new operational forms. In considering notions of conservation, it is necessary from the epistemological standpoint to distinguish between the notion itself (something is conserved)—which we can consider with Piaget as the invariant of a group or grouping of transformations—and the content of the notion (that which is conserved) which the child, like the physicist, can establish only by means of empirical observations. In the course of 'natural' development, that is in the absence of systematic training, it is remarkable to find that the conservation which appears first is in fact that of 'quantity of matter', which Piaget termed 'substance'. It is a quantity which the child, on reaching the age of 6 or 7, declares to be invariant although he still believes that the weight and the volume vary! Everything is as if, contrary to empiricist suppositions, intelligence began by constructing a conceptual frame in the shape of 'abstract' notions of invariance, before learning to interpret experience and thus to determine the physical nature of the invariants. Once this is realized the exact significance of the acquisition of notions of conservation in Smedslund's experiments becomes clear. Although his subjects were at most $7\frac{1}{2}$ years old they were fairly advanced as we have already pointed out (p. 243, note 1). It might have been a good idea to check whether some of them had not already acquired the notion of conservation of quantities of matter and if so whether these were not the very children who were able to learn the conservation of weight. It is apparent that this learning is neither constant in all subjects nor total. Consequently, within the limits of the experiment, the most that training can do is to cause subjects to pass from a level of non-conservation to one of partial conservation (when the visual cues, for instance, do not too obviously contradict the identity of weights) but in these circumstances conservation is only provisional. The results published by Smedslund are unfortunately not detailed enough to enable us to pronounce definitely on this point but he has subsequently undertaken further research in Oslo on the same subject.[1] Conditions of

---

[1] Translator's Note: This has now been published in *Scand. J. Psychol.*, 1961, 2 and 1962, 3 in a series of seven articles under the general heading of *The acquisition of conservation of substance and weight in children*.

*Pierre Gréco*

training have been varied (longer practice sessions and greater number of empirical controls than in the Geneva experiments, training in transitivity by exercises in which the child is asked to seriate three or four objects of clearly differing weight by using either a balance or simply his sense of weight, etc.). Similarly variations have been introduced in the tests used to control possible acquisitions (introduction of faked situations, see below). The results obtained, despite the fact that numerical details are not yet available,[1] confirm those found in Geneva. They bear out what we have said and led Smedslund himself to more categorical conclusions than those of 1957–58. It appears that transitivity of weight is practically never acquired (although there were a few exceptions in the case of subjects who were given four weights to manipulate and to seriate without a balance). As to conservation acquired by training, the faked control experiment on extinction of conservation carried out by Smedslund shows how precarious it is. The experimenter alters the shape of one of the balls of clay and removes a little of the clay unbeknown to the subject. The subject predicts equality but the balance invalidates his prediction. While children who have attained conservation of weight in a 'normal' way before the experiment are surprised at this result and often suspect trickery, those who have acquired conservation through training (given in a form close to that used with group A in the earlier experiment) are not surprised at all and have no difficulty in explaining this result by arguments referring to the perceptual appearance of the objects and thus belonging to the pre-operational level: 'it's heavier because it's longer, or wider, or rounder . . .' etc.

It therefore appears that the effectiveness of learning based on external reinforcements, or at least on empirical verification (since many learning theorists would dispute the equivalence of verification and reinforcement), is limited to the content of notions and does not extend to the structures themselves. It could be said that it substitutes for true notions (i.e. operationally constructed concepts) pseudo-notions which are in fact only contingent and provisional. It will be seen later that these conclusions need to be qualified. What does seem clear is that experimental results of

[1] Translator's Note: These details can now be found in the articles mentioned in the previous note. At the time when this chapter was written, however, Smedslund had produced only an unpublished report.

## Learning and Intellectual Structures

this kind go against the classical empiricism of the philosophers and of the early behaviourists and against those of the S–R type of learning theory which, explicitly or covertly, are bound up with this kind of empiricism.[1] Objective events and external sequences are not the sole source of intelligence. So wrote Smedslund at the end of his unpublished report. 'Cognitive development,' he concluded, 'is a function of internal conflict and of reorganization (even) in the absence of external reinforcement.' The basic concepts serving to explain the evolution of intelligence are, he believes, those of 'assimilation and equilibration'. These affirmations are all the more significant that Smedslund had at first shown some reservations in the face of these notions dear to Piaget.

(D) OTHER RESULTS

We shall quote the findings of three more of Smedslund's experiments. The first of these, in which an attempt was made to induce notional learning without external reinforcement, directly confirms his previous conclusions. The notion chosen was that of quantity of substance, which does not admit of any empirical control since it could only be verified indirectly through the conservation of volume or weight. The situation devised by Smedslund consists in inducing a 'cognitive conflict' in the child. Thus, given two identical balls of clay A and B, which the child recognizes to be equal, the experimenter proceeds to remove a little clay from B and then alters the shape of B so that it appears to be 'bigger' than A. After a series of exercises of this kind, Smedslund found 4 subjects, out of 13 children aged 5–7, who succeeded in affirming conservation and in justifying it by 'operational' arguments ('nothing added, nothing taken away'). This result may appear low but it is distinctly superior to that obtained in a set of other tests in which external reinforcement

---

[1] One can note, with S. Papert, that although the followers of Hull have frequently denied that their empiricism was so schematic and as they would say so 'outmoded', the stimuli S of which Hull speaks in his theory were thought by him to correspond, term for term as it were, to the variables $s$ of objective events. Besides, this kind of empiricism rises periodically from its ashes and is reincarnated in the ideas of various educationists (Anglo-Saxons especially or Russians who are more Pavlovian than Pavlov himself) or psychologists who see in it a means of exorcizing mentalism and 'philosophy'.

was used (2 cases of learning among 103 subjects). Smedslund sees in this a sign of 'purely internal equilibration', since there can be no direct measure of equalities.

The second of Smedslund's results is a negative one but it does at least serve to show that not only is repeated empirical verification insufficient to lead to the formation of structures but that it is meaningless to the subject unless he can assimilate it within a previously established frame of reference. Smedslund (1963) discovered this when he repeated the experiment on horizontality of liquid level described by Piaget and Inhelder in *The Child's Conception of Space* (1956). Children of 5–7 are shown a bottle containing coloured liquid and are asked to draw the level of the liquid when the bottle is tilted in various ways. Those who do not predict horizontality are told to observe the liquid level carefully while the bottle is being tilted. Then they are once more asked to predict the level. Improvements are practically nil, even when the child is asked to choose between several model pictures instead of making a drawing himself. To observe the permanence of horizontality does in fact call for a 'placing into relationship' of the water level and a spatial framework of reference external to the bottle. This frame rests on a representative structure and it cannot be derived from observations as these cannot be made, or at least made with any certainty, unless a frame already exists. This experiment was worth mentioning as one might well have thought *a priori* that the task was purely a matter of observation and direct perception of external data.

A third piece of research undertaken by Smedslund raises an important question. Are denials of conservation, before the age of 7, due to the fact that subjects consider only visual cues instead of relying on 'reasoning' and do operational invariants develop only as a result of growing distrust of 'perceptual strategies' after experiments have progressively exposed their fallacious character? If that is the case, training consisting in systematically invalidating judgments based on perceptual appearances should lead to conservation. Smedslund presented children at the pre-operational level with pairs of objects in which the 'smallest' was systematically the heaviest. The effect of this training was completely nil.

Thus we find that the various results obtained by an author who was far from making such categorical hypotheses at the start

## Learning and Intellectual Structures

of his research converge in a way that must convince us that the development of intelligence, at least at the level of concrete operations, is neither simply the product of empirical learning nor simply a matter of breaking free from visual appearances. Pure empiricism and rationalist *a priorism*, which paradoxically co-existed peacefully in some genetic psychologists of the introspectionist period, such as Ribot or even the great Alfred Binet in his early works, must now be ruled out of court. The history of individual intelligence appears as a construction, and not as a succession of emergences. Repeated observation of facts is not enough to produce it but on the other hand its categories and its operations are not preformed and ready to appear as a result of a simple internal dynamism or of the inhibition, through experience, of 'false convictions' such as the 'perceptual strategies' mentioned by Smedslund. Thus it is presumably legitimate to speak of learning in so far as there is acquisition of new concepts and modification of behaviour as a result of practice ('it is only by functioning, once wrote Piaget in his preface to a work by André Rey, that intelligence becomes structured'). But what is this learning? Three series of experimental findings will help to throw light on this question.

## 2 Empirical observation and operational practice

### (A) ACQUISITION OF NUMERICAL INVARIANTS

The American psychologist Joachim F. Wohlwill (1959) studied by means of non-verbal techniques (choice according to a model as used by Kohts and Harlow) the development of notions of number and went on to examine the formation of concepts of conservation of sets. The apparatus consisted in a vertical panel with three windows each displaying a different stimulus card. A counter was hidden behind one of the windows and the instructions were to find it at once by referring to a model-card. The purpose of the card was briefly explained to the subject in the verbal presentation of the experiment and was made clear by a pretest. The stimulus cards had respectively 2, 3 or 4 points and the model-cards likewise had 2, 3 or 4 points variously arranged. The subjects were thus invited to choose according to the cardinal value of the sets of points. After six consecutive correct choices,

## Pierre Gréco

followed by various transfer tests, the main test was administered. It consisted in presenting stimulus cards with 6, 7 or 8 points and placing collections of little buttons in front of the panel instead of model-cards. The first time, the collection was set out in exactly the same pattern as on the corresponding stimulus-card. Then the model-collection was altered either by displacement of the buttons ('conservation' items) or by clearly visible addition or subtraction of an element ('addition-subtraction' items). Naturally the child was not allowed to count. The actual test consisted of:

— three conservation items, serving as a pretest;

— six learning items: there were two experimental groups. With the first of these (group C) these were once again conservation items, while with the second group (AS) they were addition-subtraction items;

— three conservation items acting as a post-test.

All subjects then underwent a verbal conservation test according to the usual techniques used by Piaget and Szeminska (1952). Fifty children aged $5\frac{1}{2}$ to $6\frac{1}{2}$ approximately were divided into three groups; group C with 15 subjects, group AS with 19 subjects and a 'supplementary' group composed of the 16 subjects who were successful from the beginning with the first three items but who were nevertheless given the same practice as those in group AS.

The results of this brief and elegant experiment were reported by Wohlwill with great subtlety of detail and interpretation. Three conclusions can be drawn:

1) The positive effects of learning as seen from the results of the non-verbal test (success in the last three items after training) are relatively few in number (9 cases out of 34, thus a little more than 25 per cent);

2) They are more numerous in group AS (37 per cent) than in group C (13 per cent);

3) Success in the non-verbal test, following training, does not always lead to correct responses to the verbal conservation questions (4 cases out of 9 show discordance). Similarly out of the 16 subjects in the supplementary group, who succeeded in the non-verbal test from the beginning and who were in addition

given practice with AS items, only 6 gave correct judgments of conservation in the verbal test.[1]

Complementary tests on transfer (stimulus cards having a different cardinal value, which supposes a capacity for abstracting cardinal value) and tests in which an ordinal-cardinal correspondence has to be established benefit from what has been learned on the plane of conservation. Taking into account the age of his subjects and some aspects of the results, Wohlwill concluded that effective learning in these conditions is probably confined 'to the few children who were already on the point of outgrowing non-conservation'. He likewise pointed out that the acquisitions lacked stability and generality. It is true that we should not be unduly pessimistic in view of the fact that the training periods were very short.

The fact remains—and this is the most important result as far as we are concerned—that however precarious the conditions of learning, recourse to operations or actions of addition and subtraction proves much more effective than the mere variation of perceptual arrangements. On the other hand, classical laws of learning, nowadays interpreted much more broadly it is true, state that effectiveness of transfer rests on similarity between situations. Subjects in group C should have been at an advantage in this respect—yet this did not prove to be the case. We can therefore, without doing violence to the author's ideas,[2] draw from his work two important conclusions. The first is that cardinal notions are certainly not acquired (or not only acquired) through an associative and generalizing mechanism of the concept-formation type, as has been supposed by many Anglo-Saxon psychologists and 'figuralist' educationists who attach paramount importance to perceptual appearances. The second is that the notion of conservation is indeed an operational notion (linked fundamentally to reversible operations of addition and

---

[1] The author, who is a convinced behaviourist at least from the technological standpoint, nevertheless recognizes that it is possible to use this as an argument against the use of non-verbal methods in the study of logical notions such as equivalence. For instance, can it be assumed that equivalence which is recognized at the level of choice-behaviour can be assimilated *ipso facto* with a recognition of notional identity? The counter argument is to say that when a subject is required to make a verbal affirmation, his response is apt to be disturbed by purely linguistic factors.

[2] Wohlwill accepted these conclusions during the discussions which followed the presentation of his work at a Symposium held in June 1958.

not to intuitions of permanence). Hence it is learned through operational practice and not through generalizations based on appearances. What must be 'reinforced' in order to achieve the acquisition of these notions is not the responses associated to an equivalent class of stimuli but genuine inferences. We can thus state more definitely what some of Smedslund's[1] results had already suggested from a different angle.

(B) QUANTIFICATION OF CLASS INCLUSION

These interpretations were confirmed by the results which Albert Morf obtained after very detailed research into children's learning of logical quantification of class inclusions or (if one prefers) learning to understand the relations between parts and the whole (Morf, 1959). The experimenter presents a collection B made up of two sub-collections $A + A'$ (with, for example, $A > A'$). (The number of elements is small enough for all of them to be simultaneously perceptible and intuitively comparable). It is ascertained that the child correctly recognizes the Bs, the As and the A's and that he understands that all As are Bs but that not all Bs are As, etc. He is asked to decide whether there are more As or Bs. Until the age of 7, the majority of children are unable to understand the question because they are unable to understand except in a verbal way the relation of inclusion and they evade the problem by comparing the disjoined sub-classes A and A'. No reminder of the semantic connotation of the terms can overcome this difficulty. Morf returned to this problem which had formerly been studied by Szeminska and Piaget and more recently by Piaget and Inhelder. He had recourse to varied material (9 plastic beakers, of which 6 were yellow; 14 little cars, of which 11 were blue, 20 beads of which 13 were red, etc.). He gave the subjects training sessions according to three groups of methods which can be formulated as follows:

I. Method based on observation of the result. B and A are first evaluated separately then compared by means of various

[1] Smedslund however did not observe, either in Geneva or in Oslo, that training using addition and subtraction helped children to acquire the notion of conservation of weight. But, as Wohlwill pointed out, this divergence may be due to the continuous or discontinuous character of the quantities concerned.

procedures appropriate to the material (counting, aligning and measuring spatial extension, etc.)[1]

II. Method consisting simply in allowing the child after a number of ineffectual observations to handle the material freely in play;

III. Method based on operational practice: *a*) a collection B' is added and C is presented as an inclusive class (C = B + B'). This logical inclusion is symbolized by means of two pieces of string. One is tied round the Cs and the other round the Bs (thus the logical inclusions are concretely represented by topological inclusions as in Euler circles); *b*) a series of varied situations is used to demonstrate overlapping classes. The children are made to realize that some objects can be characterized as belonging to two classes at once, etc.[2]

Three groups of findings emerge from Morf's very detailed observations: 1) Method I based on empirical comparisons of the quantities involved led to 'numerous and important learning effects in the realm of observation itself...'. The child 'can quite quickly learn behaviours of comparison, direct and simultaneous evaluation and prediction even'. But: 2) 'Not once does he succeed in overcoming the obstacles which prevent him from deductively stating that B > A' (*art. cit.*, pp. 51 and 77). None of the 58 4-to-7-year-old subjects trained by Method I came up to the criterion for operational comprehension of inclusion.

3) The only subjects who succeeded after practice and who then generalized immediately to analogous situations were found in the groups trained according to Methods II or III*b*. Even here success was rare. In the first case, 2 out of 43 subjects were completely successful and 7 showed marked improvement while in the second 7 were successful out of 30.

(C) INTERPRETATION

As the different groups were comparable in respect of age and original level of responses, the lack of effectiveness of empirical

[1] Morf calls this the 'cyclic method': the material is presented; the relations between the classes are ascertained; the next set of material is presented and so on. After presenting the sixth and last set of materials, the experimenter goes back to the first set, then the second, etc.

[2] The reader should refer directly to Morf's study which includes many other variants and gives detailed information concerning the formulation of instructions and the conduct of the experiment in general.

*Pierre Gréco*

observations is clearly established. A particularly curious and interesting case is that of subjects who, after a number of observations (Method I) came to acknowledge or to anticipate that $A + A' > A$ but who obstinately refused to state or to admit that $B > A$ (22 cases out of 58). One might think that since $B = A + A'$, the misunderstanding is purely verbal but detailed study of subjects' responses, arguments and resistance together with a subsequent control by Morf (he asked 13 of the 22 children concerned to compare B and $A + A'$ and found that 11 of them considered that the whole was bigger or smaller than the sum of its parts) showed that the two judgments $A + A' > A$ and $B > A$ have in fact a very different notional status. What exactly is the difficulty that this problem presents to children of 5 to 7? Clearly it does not lie in understanding that the yellow cars and the blue cars together make up the collection of cars, nor that they are all made of plastic, etc. There is no doubt about this since a preliminary check is made to ensure that the child understands these things. Nor does the difficulty lie in conceiving that if one adds the blue cars to the yellow there will be a greater number of cars, since this is quite a trivial inference. The peculiar difficulty pertains to the fact that relation of inclusion has to be envisaged as a reversible operation. It is one thing to construct the whole, B, by physically or mentally uniting the parts A and A' but it is another to construct it in accordance with a law of operational composition, of which the formal expression would be: $A + A' = B \Rightarrow B - A = A'$ ... etc. The psychological manifestation of operational composition is quite simply the conservation of the whole B after the sub-class A has been mentally or physically withdrawn in order to compare it with B. The response $A + A' > A$ does not imply conservation. The composition indicated by the sign $+$ is as yet only a concrete and irreversible composition. We are now justified in stating what to some may seem self-evident from the start, namely that observation can throw light only on what is observed and a structure is something that cannot be observed.

It is interesting to find that operational acquisition occurs in children taught according to Method III *b*. These were the children who instead of engaging in the empirical comparison of A and B, were trained to consider an element as belonging to several classes, in other words trained to handle operational

## Learning and Intellectual Structures

(multiplicative) compositions. As against this, training based on the perceptible representation of inclusions (Method III *a*) remained completely ineffective (15 subjects) and did not give the subjects any of those *Gestalten* by which Wertheimer explained syllogisms of inclusion. The divorce between perceptual and operational processes is very obvious here. As to the very rare cases of success following free manipulations (Method II), one has only to read the protocol set out in detail by Morf (*art. cit.*, pp. 56–58) to find the explanation. As the child plays with the material, he makes fortuitous or deliberate arrangements and in so doing he is really manipulating classes and sub-classes. Thus free activity amounts here to spontaneous operational practice.

A fundamental ambiguity, which we have not declared until now so as not to appear to prejudge the solutions, can now be brought to light. 'Experience' and 'learning' can denote two very different processes. If experience consists in simply 'reading' the raw data and if learning is nothing more than the stamping in of responses directly associated, by whatever mechanism, to objective sequences, then clearly the structures of intelligence do not proceed from them. But if one preserves the right to affirm that intellectual development is dependent on experience and learning, then one must assume that experience and learning are concerned with the handling of action- and operation-schemata, in connection with objective situations certainly, but in the direction of an internal co-ordination. Several concrete examples of this emerge from the facts reported above.

## 3 Learning and structurization

(A) INVERSIONS OF LINEAR ORDER THROUGH ROTATIONS OF 180°

We must therefore be careful to distinguish between empirical learning and operational learning or, more exactly, between learning in the strict sense and structurization. We believe that we have succeeded in establishing this distinction following a series of research studies in which we compared the child's acquisitions in two different conditions. The first is when the situations are morphologically similar but structurally different and the second is when various methods of presenting the data are used apropos of the same structured situation. We first chose the problem of double inversion through rotations of 180° (P. Gréco, 1959 a). Three beads A, B and C are aligned on a rigid support. The child first notes the order of the beads, then the support is concealed in a horizontal tube which is rotated once, or twice consecutively, through an angle of 180°, each time in the same direction. The child must predict the ensuing order of the beads (CBA or ABC, which we shall call 'inverse' or 'direct') when the tube is removed following the rotation(s). We know for a fact that the effect of a double rotation is deductively anticipated (and explained as inversion of inversion) towards the age of 7. Seventy-eight subjects ranging in age from $4\frac{1}{2}$ to 6 were divided into five groups:

$a$) A reference group made up of 9 subjects who were successful right away;

$b$) A control group made up of 8 subjects drawn by lot;

$c^1$) An experimental group D of 22 subjects (see below);

$c^2$) An experimental group S of 19 subjects;

$c^3$) An experimental group V of 20 subjects.

In addition, for purposes of comparison, there was:

$d$) A second reference group made up of 10 subjects above the age of 7 who were successful from the beginning.

We deliberately chose a logico-geometrical situation because the transformations involved are physical displacements, which the child can see and follow with his eyes in space. At that age, space is already differentiated if not yet structured (thus, inversion following a single rotation is immediately anticipated in the great majority of cases). On the other hand, it was not unreasonable to suppose that in cases where the effect of the double rotation was not originally understood, it could be observed as an empirical event: 'when it turns twice, we don't know at first what is going to happen and then we see that A is once again first or that everything is back as it was', etc. Thus induction would follow observation. The following methods of presentation or learning were accordingly used:

— Method D: single training session; single-rotation items until the subject fully recognizes (as evidenced by at least five consecutive correct responses) the permutation of ABC into CBA, and of CBA into ABC; double-rotation items until the subject recognizes the invariance of the order consequent upon these two rotations; mixed sequence of one-rotation and two-rotation items until the subject succeeds in discriminating between situations where 'it changes' and those where 'it stays (or comes back to) the same again'. All the subjects examined succeeded, after a varying number of items, in satisfying these learning criteria.

— Method S: several training sessions at the rate of two sessions a week, each comprising a fixed sequence of 10 + 18 items, as follows: 10 one-rotation items (dispensed with from the the second session onwards if complete success was achieved in the first), followed by 18 items made up of 4 one-rotation items (repeated each time), 10 mixed one-rotation and two-rotation items of which the sequence was too complex to be learned and 4 successive two-rotation items. The criterion of success was a correct solution to the 18 items presented at each session. All the subjects attained this after a number of sessions varying from one to eight;

— No specific method was applied to group V but attempts were made to find out whether there was a method of presentation which would lead to immediate discovery of the 'law'. The methods tried included a 'free' method in which the child can manipulate the material as he wishes, methods intended to facilitate perceptual apprehension such as using a translucent tube or putting marks on the tube to indicate the original position of A (or C), verbal teachings and explanation, and an 'analogical' method in which a disk is rotated with the effect that a black sector takes the place of a red one and vice versa, etc. These various methods produced absolutely negative results and their only interest lies in proving that the fact of perceiving events does not imply that they are understood and that the problem set before the children did genuinely involve an operational structure.

As all the subjects in groups D and S were successful after training, the next step was obviously to check the stability and generality of their acquisitions. The controls took the form of 1) an actual post-test (administration of the S series of items one to three months after the successful test; 2) generalization tests including items with 3, 4 or 5 successive rotations; 3) a test to

*Pierre Gréco*

check the possible 'transposition' of the law of double permutation to a rotating disk with 6 elements, the questions referring to the permutations of diametrically opposed elements).

| Number of subjects | Groups | % of correct responses ||||| 
|---|---|---|---|---|---|---|
| | | Pre-test | After training | Post-test | Generalization | Transposition |
| 8 | Control group (*b*) | 0 | | 0+38 | 0+0 | 0+0 |
| | *Experimental groups (c)*: | | | | | |
| 22 | Method D | 0 | 100 | 0+18 | 0+9 | 0+0 |
| 19 | Method S | 0 | 100 | 84+16 | 26+53 | 16+23 |
| 20 | Other procedures | 0 | 10 | 10+0 | 5+5 | 0+5 |
| | *Reference groups:* | | | | | |
| 9 | (*a*) (age 5–6) | 100 | | 78+22 | 66+22 | 33+45 |
| 10 | (*d*) (age 7–8) | 70 | | 70+30 | 90+10 | 40+30 |

Acquisition of double inversion of linear order (P. Gréco, 1959)

(Extract from general table of results; *art. cit.* p. 147)

Despite the small number of subjects, the results were expressed as a percentage to make them easier to read. The subjects' ages in groups *b* and *c* ranged from $4\frac{1}{2}$ to 6. The subjects in group *a* were children of 5 to 6 preselected on the grounds of spontaneous success in the test. Those in group *d* were a random sample of children of 7 and 8. The subjects trained according to methods S and D described in the text continued their training until they were fully successful. The post-test is the basic test which was administered some time after the end of the training. The control tests concerned either generalization of the law to cases involving 3 4 or 5 successive rotations, or else the transposition, following permutations, of the diametrically opposed points on a disc.

In each case, the first indicates the percentage of complete successes, and the second the percentage of partial successes, defined for each test according to criteria designed to indicate a marked improvement or a predetermined level of structurization.

It is probably true that the two forms of training S and D are comparable only from the point of view of the imposed criterion

## Learning and Intellectual Structures

of success and not, for instance, from that of the total time taken. The *dispersion* of the number of attempts required by different subjects to achieve success is similar, however. If one accepts that Method D favoured learning of an associative or discriminative type, in which external reinforcements arising from observations would serve to link appropriate responses to particular types of situations while Method S favoured an intelligent re-elaboration of the subject's inferential schemata, then the results summarized in the foregoing table constitute massive evidence: 1) All children of $4\frac{1}{2}$ to 6 are capable of learning to solve the problem, that is to anticipate the effect upon linear order of one or two rotations of 180°. They can, however, learn it in two very different ways; 2) 'Empirical' learning, oriented towards simple factual observations, leads to provisional knowledge which is quickly lost (there were more than 80 per cent complete failures at the post-test administered one to three months after the end of training). Such knowledge cannot therefore be generalized or transposed in a lasting fashion to related situations. A subsequent control that we carried out revealed that immediate transfers (directly following learning) do occur but they are precarious, unstable and limited to situations presenting a close perceptual analogy with the learning situation; 3) 'Structural' learning hypothetically resulting from the articulation of inferential schemata leads to a lasting cognitive organization (no complete failure at the post-test administered after the same interval as before). This organization is *to some extent* generalizable and transposable to the situations chosen as a control. Generalizations and transpositions remain distinctly inferior to those observed in either of the reference groups (the 5 to 6 year-olds and the 7 to 8 year-olds) which are made up of subjects who have already acquired the relevant notions without experimental training.

### (B) TWO KINDS OF LEARNING

The radical distinction between these two types of learning is clearly apparent if one analyses the evolution of performances during training and also the spontaneous or induced verbal comments of the subjects. As there are various technical reasons against comparing learning curves, we chose instead to examine response sequences. It was clear from these that 'structural' learning does not proceed by trial and error. The experimental conditions (i.e. the mixing of one-rotation and two-rotation items) were not conducive to stamping in good responses and stamping out the bad. Thus, the subject cannot 'get by' except by realizing that the invariance which follows two successive rotations is the product of a double inversion. With Method D, however, such invariance was learned as a regular, but not a 'necessary', occurrence. The children's formulations are significant in this respect. In short 'understanding' in this experiment consists in co-ordinating the schema of inversion as an involute operation, as opposed to simply linking an event (or a type of event) to a particular given situation. This view can also account for the stability of acquisitions, their generalization to any number of successive inversions and their transposition to situations that are perceptually dissimilar. It can also account for the limitations that are part of such transpositions since the schemata that are thus co-ordinated do not yet have the organization characteristic of true operational structures. We have accordingly termed them 'quasi-structures'. In this particular case, they are induced by experimental practice but we have since found many examples of them in various fields of natural cognitive development. Since 1960, thanks to the combined efforts of the logician J. B. Grize and the psychologists of the *Centre international d'Epistémologie génétique*, a formalization is in progress with a view to conferring on these quasi-structures a more precise status than they can derive from mere operational description. At the same time, it will indicate their lacunae and limitations and help to show how these 'weak structures' assist in the formation of well (or better) structured operational notions.

(c) EMPIRICAL LAWS AND 'NECESSARY' LAWS

Finally we tried to compare the acquisition of a structure such as double inversion with that of a law which was morphologically similar but arbitrary and empirical (P. Gréco, 1959 *b*). The child is shown single or double boxes (the latter consisting of two single boxes one on top of the other). The boxes have a sliding drawer and at each end there is a coloured spot which may be red or blue. The 'law' consists in discovering that the double boxes have the same colour at both ends (red–red or blue–blue) while the single boxes have opposite colours at each end (red–blue or blue–red). The experimental technique is to show the colour of one end and ask the subject to guess the other after he has been told that 'there is a trick which will give you the right answer every time if you can discover it'. A succession of items is presented in which single and double boxes, with a visible red or blue end, are mixed in the same order as the one- or two-rotation items in the preceding experiment. There were a hundred trials. It was found that out of the subjects below the age of 7, there was only one case (out of 12) in which the law was discovered whereas at age 7–8, 8–9, 9–10 and with adults, it was eventually arrived at although the number of trials required varied considerably (from 2 to 66). Intra-group variability is actually higher than that found between different age groups. The number of trials required is from 20 to 27 according to groups, the dispersion of performances is comparable except that none of the 20 adults (apart from 2 aberrant cases who were 'sophisticated' subjects) required more than 23 trials. Indeed eight of them immediately made a hypothesis in accordance with the law (on the grounds that it was 'the most plausible'). The interest of this experiment, however, does not lie in considering the genetic evolution of inductive behaviours but in comparing the processes of discovery with the learning processes examined above.

We find that the curves for the 6 to 7 year-old subjects (who, except for one, all failed to discover the law during the 100 trials) are similar to trial and error curves, with a slight tendency to drop, and with no trace of 'local' learning (i.e. none of the subjects learned, for instance, that with single boxes the colours are opposed). On the contrary, error curves plotted separately for single-box and double-box items are symmetrical so that when one rises the other falls. It is as if the child was successively trying out the hypotheses of 'opposition' or 'identity' of colour without being able to distinguish the cases where this one or that one is successful. We later verified (unpublished research into the inductive discovery of predetermined and arbitrary laws) that in a situation of this kind a planned method such as Method D in the preceding experiment leads to quicker success (but before the age of 6 the law is quickly 'forgotten').

The curves for 7 to 11 year-old subjects, reduced to a common scale whatever the total number of trials required to discover the law, are more like insight curves, in that the cessation of errors (the drop to zero) is nearly always sudden. In the stages which precede discovery, errors tend rather to increase (from 30 to 50 per cent on an average).

A more detailed analysis of response frequencies and sequences including a comparison of the performance in the two experiments of the various groups of subjects (classified in the first experiment according to the training method adopted and in the second according to the type of curve) reveals remarkable analogies and especially differences. It is clearly apparent, in particular, that the 'opposition' and 'identity' of colour anticipated by the subject do not have at all the same status as inversion or invariance of the original order had in the other experiment. In the first case, we are in the presence of response-schemata, linked to empirical situations which the subject perceives as such. In the second case we find inference-schemata—whether correctly applied or not—linked to situations of which the content is admittedly empirical but of which the form is perceived by the subject to be 'logical' (in the broad sense of the term). Factual necessity and logical necessity are not to be confused here. In the first case learning consists essentially in associating adequate responses with appropriate situations while in the second it consists mainly in co-ordinating schemata, not by fortuitous links determined solely by the objective organization of external events but by internal articulations whose general laws are identical with intelligence structures.[1] The modalities of learning—considered now as a behaviour process and not as the result of experience—accordingly vary in relation both to the operative[2] structures which the subject has at his disposal at the beginning and to the hypotheses which he forms regarding the proposed situation (or, of course, the hypotheses which can be artificially induced).[3]

---

[1] It seems clear to us that these laws cannot themselves be anything other than laws of nature, but the question belongs to metaphysics.

[2] Operational structures are only a particular instance of operative structures. For a definition of the term 'operative', see Chapter 23 above, pp. 87.

[3] We refer in particular to the learning sets described by Harlow and to all the sets that can be induced by various procedures, as in the many well known experiments on mental rigidity, etc. Cf. Chapter 22, p. 31.

(D) THE LOGIC OF LEARNING

These conclusions which are in fact somewhat banal when stated in general terms appear much more cogent when shown as above to rest on a number of categorical facts. It is remarkable that they should have been reached in very different fields by authors who, while they collaborated in a programme of research, nevertheless had rather diverse preoccupations and inspiration. Thus, they were arrived at by M. Goustard after studying children of 5 to 11 and adolescents as they solved a maze problem similar to that which he once used with cockroaches (Goustard, 1959). In particular, they were arrived at by B. Matalon in one of his studies on learning in a random situation, in which he compared such learning with the learning of regular laws (double alternation) (Matalon, 1959). He noted that in these situations the subjects 'learn more than simple response probabilities (and) link each attempt to previous events'. He was thus led to distinguish between stimuli, operationally defined by the psychologist, and 'events', grouped or otherwise, which are the stimuli as perceived, assimilated and organized by the subjects, as a function both of their individual mental structure and of the conditions affecting the apprehension of stimuli, results, reinforcements, etc. In this way, the 'determination of truly operative stimuli, would stem from a genuine 'logic of learning'. These results can be compared with all those obtained in classical learning situations, from the already distant studies showing that the initial behaviour of rats in a maze is not random but depends on previous acquisitions (Dennis, 1932; Dashiell, 1935, etc.) to recent research by J. F. Richard (1960) from which it transpires, among other results minutely analysed according to information models, that adults who are required to learn to put out various lights by discovering the appropriate switch proceed from the outset according to coherent strategies. We cannot however presume to impute to these various authors conclusions similar to those that follow.

## 4 Tentative conclusion

We must distinguish *a priori* between not only two but three varieties of learning.

1) Learning in which the subject acquires new behaviour,

## Pierre Gréco

adapted to a situation which is at first unknown to him. The consolidation of this behaviour is essentially to be explained by the sanctions which experience confers on the more or less arbitrary or random attempts and predictions of the subject. The laws of reinforcement (or conditioning) would suffice in this case to explain the process of acquisition and the very nature of the knowledge thus acquired. However, it is clear that even in this extreme case the discrimination of stimuli and the effectiveness of reinforcement are dependent on the organism's structures or on previous learning. This variety can therefore be included in the next.

2) Learning which consists in 'induction of laws' (physical laws or arbitrary regularities) in which experience and observation serve to confirm or to invalidate 'hypotheses'. The process of acquisition and the quantitative or qualitative value of what is acquired can no longer be explained merely by the volume (and mechanism) of reinforcements. They must be referred to the motor or cognitive structures which define either the subject's level of development or his state of preparedness for the experiment. The basis of learning is no longer an S-R association but an *assimilation* (in the sense in which Piaget uses the term) of reality to the subject's structures, with the distortions that are apt to result from such assimilation and also with the repercussions on the structures themselves that can sometimes occur. This leads to:

3) Structural learning or, more exactly, structurizations based on experience, in which the function of experience is to disconcert, to upset previously established schemata by showing their inadequacies and possible internal contradictions. This is what happens to a child who observes, in the double-rotation experiment, that 'it turned round and *yet* it didn't change' or who is made to note that as a ball of clay is rolled into a 'snake' it becomes extremely long (which at first leads one to think that it is getting bigger) and at the same time extremely thin (which suggests that it is getting smaller).[1]

[1] Experiments are in progress using classical tests presented *without external reinforcement* in situations where perceptual cues are exaggerated. Cases of 'learning' in the course of the tests are rare but do exist. They amount to 10 per cent at age 6, 20 per cent at 6½ and the acquisitions appear to be stable when a post-test is administered two months later. In addition, since this chapter was written, systematic research on the effects on learning of different kinds of train-

## Learning and Intellectual Structures

This structural learning, which we have shown to be original and irreducible to purely empiricist explanations, consists in a re-elaboration of schemata which are at first incomplete and disparate. This re-elaboration must have its own laws which go beyond the classical laws of conditioning and reinforcement. They probably give us the key to what may seem to a developmental psychologist at once problem number one and a paradoxical wager: accounting for the specificity of the general structures of intelligence, in relation to the synchronic acquisition of particular habits, knowledge and solutions, and yet at the same time explaining their relationship and making it clear that functioning and thus experience in a sense, is essential to their progressive genesis. It is well known that Piaget found it necessary to distinguish, in this connection, between two kinds of experience: physical experience relating to the properties of objects and the results of action and what he calls logico-mathematical experience which also refers to objects and to states but at the same time to actions and above all to their co-ordinations.[1] It is also known that the laws which govern the evolution of this second type of experience and which give it increasing co-ordination and cohesion are considered by Piaget to be laws of equilibration, more general in character than the laws of learning. He has put forward a subtle probabilistic model applicable to the laws of equilibration which will probably require further refinement and quantification (Piaget, 1957).[2] The present efforts of logicians such as J. B. Grize or S. Papert are concerned less with finding an approximate mathematization of this model than with constructing formal models of the relationship of structures. In other words, their first aim is to isolate the numerous intermediate structures whose general co-ordination into a single system, equilibrated and non-contradictory, would define the levels of intellectual development. Naturally, psychologists have for their part undertaken the experimental identification of these multi-systems and of their evolution taking as their guide (but not as their goal!) the heuristic instrument provided by the logicians concerned (cf. Apostel, Grize *et alia*, 1963).

---

ing (verbal, empirical, etc.) has been undertaken at Harvard under the direction of Jerome S. Bruner, with the assistance of experimenters trained in Geneva and directed by Bärbel Inhelder.

[1] See Chapter 24, p. 198.  [2] See also Chapter 24, p. 201.

*Pierre Gréco*

In establishing *a priori* distinctions just now between three varieties of learning we were not implying that they are discontinuous nor that they are three irreducible and incompatible psychological processes. On the contrary, the transitions which we indicated and the notions of schematism and assimilation which we introduced clearly show that we recognize a complete functional continuity between the three varieties. We do not in the least renounce a unitary explanation. Monism, however, is one thing and reductionism another. If there really is functional continuity, we must not be surprised to find the equivalent of what will later be recognized as intellectual processes at the most elementary levels and even in the biological sphere. Assimilation, generalization, etc. are terms which henceforth belong to the vocabulary of neurobiology as well as to that of the psychology of intelligence. The term 'structure' likewise, despite the fact that it is still too often used in a metaphorical or imprecise manner. The logical formalization of intellectual structures is in no way a mentalist option. Direct experimental study of these structures in preference to the study of problem-solving and concept formation etc. is not the outcome of an intellectualist bias, provided one has been careful to situate these structures in the concrete context of their evolution. The fact that certain synchronic acquisitions can be adequately explained by means of associationist models and empiricist theories does not mean that every acquisition, and in particular every diachronic acquisition, can be reduced to these by atomistic analysis or by assimilation of the higher to the lower. The genetic method is probably more apt than any other to preserve us from such a risk. This is because it forbids us on the one hand to consider the higher structures of intelligence as given *a priori* and on the other to merge without more ado sensori-motor structures with structures of thought, since there is a time lag of several lustra between the first and the second. If it is true that even where the ethology of lower or elementary behaviours is concerned, 'the era of the empty organism' is past, then it is clear that the analysis of behaviour, intellectual or motor, and of acquisitions, whether attained in adult life or in the course of the child's development, can be deliberately centred on the study of structure and structurization.

# Bibliography

ANDREWS, T. G., (Ed.), *Methods of Psychology*, London, Chapman and Hall, 1948
APOSTEL, L., 'Logique et apprentissage', in *E.E.G.*,* vol. VIII, Paris, P.U.F., 1959, pp. 1–138
APOSTEL, L., GRIZE, J. B., PAPERT, S. and PIAGET, J., *La filiation des structures*, *E.E.G.*, vol. XV, Paris, P.U.F., 1963
APOSTEL, L., JONCKHEERE, A. R. and MATALON, B., *Logique, apprentissage et probabilité*, *E.E.G.*, vol. VIII, Paris, P.U.F., 1959
APOSTEL, L., MANDELBROT, B. and PIAGET, J., *Logique et équilibre*, *E.E.G.*, vol. II, Paris, P.U.F., 1957
BARTLETT, F. C., *Remembering*, Cambridge, Cambridge Univ. Press, 1932
BERLYNE, D. E., 'Les équivalences psychologiques et les notions quantitatives', in *E.E.G.*, vol. XII, Paris, P.U.F., 1960, pp. 1–76
BÜHLER, KARL, *Handbuch der Psychologie*, Iéna, Fischer, 1922
— *Die Krise der Psychologie*, Iéna, Fischer, 1927
BURLOUD, A., *La pensée, d'après les recherches expérimentales de H. J. Watt, de Messer et de Bühler*, Alcan, 1927
DASHIELL, J. F., 'A Survey and Synthesis of Learning Theories', *Psychol. Bull.*, 1935, 32, 261–75
DOVE, C. C., THOMPSON, M. E., 'Some Studies on "Insight" in White Rats', *J. genet. Psychol.*, 1943, 63, 235–45
DUNCKER, K., *Zur Psychologie des Produktiven Denkens*, Berlin, Springer, 1935
EHRENFREUND, D., 'An Experimental Test of the Continuity Theory of Discrimination Learning with Pattern Vision', *J. comp. physiol. Psychol.*, 1948, 41, 408–22
ESTES, W. K., 'Individual Behavior in Uncertain Situations', *in* Thrall: *Decision Processes*, New York, Wiley, 1954
ESTES, W. K., KOCH, S., MCCORQUODALE, K., MEEHL, P. E., MUELLER, Jr.

---

* *E.E.G.* refers to *Etudes d'Epistémologie génétique* published since 1957 by Presses Universitaires de France in volumes each having a separate title (Bibliothèque de Philosophie Scientifique). These volumes appear in the bibliography under the name of the author who comes first in alphabetical order, which is how they are usually quoted. To assist cross-checking, the authors are as follows:

II. APOSTEL, MANDELBROT and PIAGET
VII. GRÉCO and PIAGET
VIII. APOSTEL, JONCKHEERE and MATALON
IX. VINH-BANG, MORF, SMEDSLUND and WOHLWILL
X. GOUSTARD, GRÉCO, MATALON and PIAGET
XII. BERLYNE and PIAGET
XV. APOSTEL, GRIZE, PAPERT and PIAGET

# Bibliography

C. G., SCHOENFELD, W. N., VERPLANCK, W. S., with the editorial assistance of A. T. POFFENBERGER, *Modern Learning Theory*, New York, Appleton-Century-Crofts, 1954

ESTES, W. K., 'Theory of Learning with Constant, Variable, or Contingent Probabilities of Reinforcement', *Psychometrika*, 1957, **22**, 113–32

EVANS, S., 'Flexibility of Established Habit', *J. gen. Psychol.*, 1936, **14**, 177–200

GELLERMAN, L. W., 'The Double Alternation Problem', *J. genet. Psychol.*, 1931, **39**, 50–72, 197–226, 359–92

GOLDSTEIN, K., SCHEERER, M., 'Abstract and Concrete Behavior, an Experimental Study with Special Tests', *Psychol. Monogr.*, 1941, **53**, no. 2

GOUSTARD, M., 'Étude psychogénétique de la résolution d'un problème (labyrinthe en T)', in *E.E.G.*, vol. X, Paris, P.U.F., 1959, pp. 93–112

GOUSTARD, M., GRÉCO, P., MATALON, B. and PIAGET, J., *La logique des apprentissages*, *E.E.G.*, vol. X, Paris, P.U.F., 1959

GRÉCO, P., *a*) 'L'apprentissage dans une situation à structure opératoire concrète: les inversions successives de l'ordre linéaire par des rotations de 180°', in *E.E.G.*, vol. VIII, Paris, P.U.F., 1959, pp. 68–182

— *b*) 'Induction, déduction et apprentissage', in *E.E.G.*, vol. X, Paris, P.U.F., 1959, pp. 3–59

— *c*) 'Apprentissage et développement, notes pour servir à une épistémologie critique de la psychologie', in *E.E.G.*, vol. X, Paris, P.U.F., 1959, pp. 131–58

GRÉCO, P. and PIAGET, J., *Apprentissage et connaissance*, *E.E.G.*, vol. VII, Paris, P.U.F., 1959

GRIZE, J. B., 'Des groupements à l'algèbre de Boole: essai de filiation des structures logiques', in *E.E.G.*, vol. XV, Paris, P.U.F., 1963, pp. 25–63

GUILLAUME, P., *La psychologie de la forme*, Paris, Flammarion, 1937

HARSH, C. M., 'Disturbance and "Insight" in Rats', *Univ. Calif. Publ. Psychol.*, 1937, **6**, 163–8

HERON, W. T., 'Internal Stimuli and Learning', *J. comp. physiol. Psychol.*, 1949, **42**, 486–92

HILGARD, E. R., *Theories of Learning*, 2nd ed., New York, Appleton-Century-Crofts, 1956 (1st ed. 1948)

HOBHOUSE, L. T., *Mind in Evolution*, New York, Macmillan, 1901.

HOVLAND, C. I., 'The generalization of conditioned responses: IV. The Effect of Varying Amounts of Reinforcement upon the Degree of Generalization of Conditioned Responses', *J. exp. Psychol.*, 1937, **21**, 261–76

HULL, CLARK L., 'The Concept of the Habit-Family Hierarchy and Maze Learning', *Psychol. Rev.*, 1934, **41**, 33–54 and 134–52

— 'The Mechanism of the Assembly of the Behavior Segments in

*Bibliography*

Novel Combinations Suitable for Problem Solution', *Psychol. Rev.*, 1935, **42**, 219–45
— 'The Problem of Stimulus Equivalence in Behavior Theory', *Psychol. Rev.*, 1939, **46**, 9–30
— 'Quantitative Aspects of the Evolution of Concepts', *Psychol. Monog.*, 1920, no. 123
HULL, CLARK L., HOVLAND, C. I., ROSS, R. T., HALL, M., PERKINS, D. T. and FITCH, F. G., *Mathematico-deductive Theory of Rote Learning*, New Haven, Yale Univ. Press, 1940
HUNTER, W. S., BARTLETT, S. C., 'Double Alternation Behavior in Young Children', *J. exp. Psychol.*, 1948, **38**, 558–67
KATONA, G., *Organizing and Memorizing*, New York, Columb. Univ. Press, 1940.
KATZ, D., *Gestalt Psychology, its Nature and Significance*, New York, Ronald Press, 1950
KINNAMAN, A. J., 'Mental Life of Two Macacus Rhesus Monkeys in Captivity', *Amer. J. Psychol.*, 1902, **13**, 98–148, 173–218
KOFFKA, K., *Principles of Gestalt Psychology*, New York, Harcourt Brace, 1935
KÖHLER, W., *Intelligenzprüfungen an Menschenaffen* (1917); English translation by E.Winter: *The Mentality of Apes*, New York, Harcourt Brace, 1925
— Nachweis einfacher Strukturfunktionen beim Schimpanzen und beim Haushuhn, *Abh. der. kön. preuss. Akad wiss.* (Berlin, 1918, no. 2, 1–101). There is a condensed English translation under the title: 'Simple Structural Functions in the Chimpanzee and in the Chicken' in Ellis, W. D., *A Source Book of Gestalt Psychology*, New York, Harcourt Brace, 1938, pp. 217–27
— On the Nature of Associations, *Proceed. Amer. phil. Soc.*, 1941, **84**, 489–502
— *Gestalt Psychology*, New York, Liveright, 1947 (most recent edition of a work which first appeared in 1929)
KRECHEVSKY, I., ' "Hypotheses" in Rats', *Psychol. Rev.*, 1932, **39**, 516–32
— 'A Study of the Continuity of the Problem-solving Process', *Psychol. Rev.*, 1938, **45**, 107–33
KRECHEVSKY, I. and HONZIK, C. H., 'Fixation in the Rat', *Univ. Calif. Publ. Psychol.*, 1932, **6**, 13–26
KUO, Z. Y., 'Forced movement or Insight?' *Univ. Calif. Publ. Psychol.*, 1937, **6**, 169–88
LAWRENCE, D. H., 'Acquired Distinctiveness of Cues: I. Transfer between Discriminations on the Basis of Familiarity with the Stimulus', *J. exp. Psychol.*, 1949, **39**, 770–84

*Bibliography*

— 'Acquired Distinctiveness of Cues: II. Selective Association in a Constant Stimulus Situation', *J. exp. Psychol.*, 1950, **40**, 175–88
— 'The Transfer of a Discrimination along a Continuum', *J. comp. physiol. Psychol.*, 1952, **45**, 511–16
— 'The Applicability of Generalization Gradients to the Transfer of a Discrimination', *J. gen. Psychol.*, 1955, **52**, 37–48
LAWRENCE, D. H. and MASON, W. A., 'Systematic Behavior during Discrimination Reversal and Change of Dimensions', *J. comp. physiol. Psychol.*, 1955, **48**, 1–7
LLOYD MORGAN, C., see MORGAN, C. LLOYD
MAIER, N. R. F., 'Reasoning in White Rats', *Comp. Psychol. Monog.*, 1929, **6**, no. 29
— 'Reasoning in Humans: I. On Direction', *J. comp. Psychol.*, 1930, **10**, 115–43
— 'Reasoning and Learning', *Psychol. Rev.*, 1931, **38**, 332–46
— 'The Effect of Cerebral Destruction on Reasoning and Learning in Rats', *J. Comp. Psychol.*, 1932, **12**, 181–94
MALTZMAN, I., 'Thinking: from a Behavioristic Point of View', *Psychol. Rev.*, 1955, **62**, 275–86
MARBE, K., *Experimentell-psychologische Untersuchungen über das Urteil*, Leipzig, Engelmann, 1901
MATALON, B., 'Note sur les modèles d'apprentissage', in *E.E.G.*, vol. VIII, Paris, P.U.F., 1959, pp. 173–84
— 'Apprentissages en situations aléatoires et systématiques', in *E.E.G.*, vol. X, Paris, P.U.F., 1959, pp. 61–91
MORF, A., 'Apprentissage d'une structure logique concrète (inclusion): effets et limites', in *E.E.G.*, vol. IX, 1959, pp. 15–83
MORGAN, C. LLOYD, *An Introduction to Comparative Psychology*, London, W. Scott, 1894
NEWELL, A., SHAW, J. C. and SIMON, H. A., 'Elements of a Theory of Human Problem-solving', *Psychol. Rev.*, 1958, **65**, 151–66
OLÉRON, P., *Recherches sur le développement mental des sourds-muets*, Paris, C.N.R.S., 1957
OSGOOD, C. E., *Method and Theory in Experimental Psychology*, New York, Oxford Univ. Press, 1953
PIAGET, J., *The Psychology of Intelligence*, London, Routledge and Kegan Paul, 1950
— 'Logique et équilibre dans les comportements du sujet', in *E.E.G.*, vol. II, Paris, P.U.F., 1957, pp. 27–117
— 'Apprentissage et connaissance', 1st part: in *E.E.G.*, vol. VIII, Paris, P.U.F., 1959, pp. 21–67. 2nd part: in *E.E.G.*, vol X, 1959, pp. 159–88
— 'La portée psychologique et épistémologique des essais néo-hulliens de D. Berlyne', in *E.E.G.*, vol. XI, 1960, pp. 105–23

# Bibliography

PIAGET, J. and INHELDER, B., *Le développement des quantités chez l'enfant, conservation et atomisme*, Neuchâtel and Paris, Delachaux and Niestlé, 1941. [An enlarged second edition has just appeared under the title: *Le développement des quantités physiques chez l'enfant* (1962)].
— *The Child's Conception of Space*, London, Routledge and Kegan Paul, 1956
— *The Early Growth of Logic in the Child*, London, Routledge and Kegan Paul, 1964
PIAGET, J. and SZEMINSKA, A., *The Child's Conception of Number*, London, Routledge and Kegan Paul, 1952
RICHARD, J. F., *Étude de l'utilisation de l'information dans l'apprentissage*, Monogr. franç. de Psychologie, no. VII, Paris, C.N.R.S., 1960
SIMON, H. A., 'A Comparison of Game Theory and Learning Theory', *Psychometrika*, 1956, 21, 267–72
SMALL, W. S., Various articles in *Amer. J. Psychol.*, 1899–1901. Cf.: 11, 80–100, 133–65; 12, 206–39
SMEDSLUND, J., 'Apprentissage des notions de la conservation et de la transitivité du poids', in *E.E.G.*, vol. IX, Paris, P.U.F., 1959, pp. 85–124
SPENCE, K. W., 'The Basis of Solution by Chimpanzees of the Intermediate Size Problem', *J. exp. Psychol.*, 1942, 31, 257–71
— 'Cognitive versus Stimulus-Response Theories of Learning', *Psychol. Rev.*, 1950, 57, 159–72
— 'Theoretical Interpretations of Learning', *in* STONE, C.P., (Ed.) *Comparative Psychology*, (3rd ed.), New York, Prentice Hall, 1951
— (Same title) in: STEVENS, S. S. (Ed.), *Handbook of Experimental Psychology*, New York, Wiley, 1951
THORNDIKE, E. L., 'Animal Intelligence: an Experimental Study of the Associative Processes in Animals', *Psychol. Rev., Monogr. Suppl.*, 1898, 2, no. 8
— *Animal Intelligence*, Experimental Studies, New York, Macmillan, 1911
— *The Fundamentals of Learning*, New York, Teachers College, 1932
— *Human Nature and the Social Order*, New York, Macmillan, 1940
— *Selected Writings from a Connectionnist's Psychology*, New York, Appleton-Century-Crofts, 1949
TOLMAN, E. C. and HONZIK, C. H., '"Insight" in Rats', *Univ. Calif. Publ. Psychol.*, 1930, 4, 215–32
VINH-BANG, MORF, A., SMEDSLUND, J. and WOHLWILL, J. F., *L'apprentissage des structures logiques*, E.E.G., vol. IX, Paris, P.U.F., 1959
WERTHEIMER, M., *Productive Thinking*, New York, Harper, 1945

*Bibliography*

WOHLWILL, J. F., 'Un essai d'apprentissage dans le domaine de la conservation du nombre', in *E.E.G.*, vol. IX, Paris, P.U.F., 1959, pp. 125-35

WOODWORTH, R. S., *Experimental Psychology*, London, Methuen, 1950.

# Index

Abstract intelligence, 3
Abstraction, 20–1, 23–4, 26, 28, 198, 201
Accessory elements, 23, 24
Acquired experience, 197–200
Action and reaction, 195–6
Actually experienced inferences, 36, 38–9
Adaptive behaviour, 202
Affective classifications, 29
*Aha-Erlebnis*, 211
Ajuriaguerra, J. de, 94, 200
Algebra and algebraic structures, 145–6, 236–8
Allers, R., 95
Anagrams, 54
Analysis and problem solving, 65–6, 68
Analytical anticipation, 131–3
Anderson, S. B., 40
Andrew, G., 22
Andrews, T. G., 207, 229
Anglo-Saxon psychologists, 207, 214, 253
Anticipation and anticipatory images, 108, 114, 124–8, 130–5, 140, 186
Apostel, L., 236–7, 267
Apprehension of concepts, 11–18
Apprehension of experience, 150
Apprehension of relations, 10–11, 25
Arc transformed into straight line, 115–19
Archer, E. J., 24
Aristotle, 186, 188, 195
Ascoli, G., 34n.
Aserinsky, E., 97
Ashby, W. R., 202
Assimilation, 149, 200, 226, 266, 268
Association between images, 85
Associationism, 27, 85, 144, 146–7, 151, 212–14, 268
Associative learning, 207, 210, 213, 223

Associativity, 173 and n., 199
Atmosphere-effect, 41–4
Atomic associationism, 151
Attitudes and habits, 46–8, 58–9, 61–3
Auditory images, 98–9
Austin, G. A., 1, 2, 23, 148
Autonomous evolution of images, 91–2
Availability of functions, 56–8

Bang, T., 106, 122
Bartlett, F. C., 1, 8, 235
Behaviour and behaviour theory, 1–2, 147, 199, 202, 207–12, 214–215, 227, 228, 236–8
Behaviourist formulations, 219–22, 249
Berg, E. A., 20
Bergès, J., 140
Bergum, B. O., 18, 25
Berlyne, D., 147, 199, 238–9
*Bewusstheit*, 236
Binet, Alfred, 1, 85, 92, 129, 147, 152, 211, 251
Birch, H. G., 55–6
Blinding phenomenon, 54
Bourne, J. E., jr., 24, 26
Boutan, 211
Brentano, 236
Brouwer, 176
Brown, F. G., 24
Bruner, Jerome, S., 1, 2, 23, 148, 267n.
Bühler, Karl, 152, 208, 211–12
Bulbrook, M. E., 60
Burloud, A., 4, 235
Burt, Cyril, 44, 45, 167
Buss, 25

Cahill, H. E., 24
Chance, 187–90
Chapman, J. P., 42–4, 46–7
Chapman, L. J., 42–4, 46–7
*Child's Conception of Space, The* (Piaget and Inhelder), 250

## Index

Churchill, 177
C.I.E.G. (Centre International d'Epistémologie Génétique), 241, 262
Claparède, E., 148–9, 208, 211
Class inclusion, 168–70, 254–7
Classical problems, 49–50, 60
Classification of images, 91, 107–114, 140
Classifications, 17–19, 29, 33–4, 165–8, 172–4, 200
Cognitive formulations, 219–22
Cognitive functions, 87–90
Cognitive structures, 213–15, 266
Combination and reasoning, 38–9
Combinatorial system, 190–3, 196, 241
Common element, 27
Comparative psychology, 207
Concept apprehension, 11–18
Concept formation, 2, 11–18, 25, 153, 232–4, 268
Concept learning, 25
Conceptualization, 233–4
Connectionism, 214
Consecutive reproduction, 109–10
Conservation, 129, 133–5, 155–65, 199, 235, 241–53
Contiguity theory, 214
Cook, T. W., 53
Copy-responses, 147
Corman, B. R., 68
Cournot, 187
Cowen, E. L., 61n.
Crannell, C. W., 68
Cronbach, 72
Curiosity, 238

Dashiell, J. F., 265
Daltman, P. E., 34
Decision theories, 2
Deduction, 6, 32
Deferred images, 108
Deferred imitation, 90, 100
Dement, W., 97, 139
*Denkpsychologie*, 85, 152–3, 235–6
Dennis, 265
Descartes, 70

Detambel, M. H., 23
*Détour*, 3, 199
Development images, 91–2, 137–9
Dichotomic division, 70
Digital estimations, 105–7
Dilthey, 86
Dimensions and values, 17
*Discours de la Méthode* (Descartes), 70
Discrimination learning, 222–3
Disequilibrium, 201–2
Distinctiveness acquisition, 226
Distributed practice, 25
Dominance of concepts, order of, 33–6
Dove, C. C., 217–19
Drawing and images, 91, 140
Dreams, 94, 139
Duncker, K., 2, 55, 65–6, 151, 235
*Dynamics in Psychology* (Köhler), 223

Education, 6
Eductions, 150, 153, 222
Ehrenfels, von, 213
Ehrenfreund, D., 225
Eidetic images, 85, 93
*Einstellung*, 61n.
Electroencephalograms (E.E.G.s), 95, 97, 197
Electromyograms, 95
Electronic brains, 2
Elkind, D., 157, 160
Ellis, W. D., 10
Empirical learning and laws, 261–4
Empirical reversal, 156
Equilibrium and equilibration, 195–6, 201–2, 212, 267
Equivalences, conservation of, 177
*Ergänzung*, 236
Essential elements, 23–4
Estes, W. K., 207, 228n., 230, 236
Etienne, A., 109
*Etude expérimentale de l'Intelligence* (Binet), 85, 147
Euclidean structures, 182
Euler's rings or circles, 37, 136, 255
Evans, S., 218

*Index*

Everett, I. R., 170
Evocations, mechanism of, 94
Evolution of images, 114–28, 140
Exclusive interpretation, 47–8
Experience, acquired, 197–200
Extinction problems, 62
Eye movements, 96–8, 139

Factor analysis, 145, 149–50
Fields, P. E., 14, 233n.
Figural collections, 166
Figurative aspects of cognitive functions, 87–90, 98
Fixed-ratio schedules of reinforcement, 25
Foerster, O., 93, 95
Form, theory of, 151, 209, 213
Formal operations and reasonings, 37, 190–6, 200
Formation of images, 90–3
Fraisse, P., 20
Frank, Françoise, 106, 116n., 122
Function availability, 56–8
Functional fixedness, 55–6, 58
Functionalists, 207

Galanter, E. H., 2
Gardner, Dr. Riley, 139
Gastaut, H., 95
Gauss, 235
Gelerntner, H., 2
Gellerman, L. W., 7–8, 14, 230
Generality and generalization of responses, 20, 22, 26–8
Generalization of learning, 222–5, 228
*Genèse de l'hypothèse, La* (Claparède), 148
Genetic level of image functions, 90–1, 99–101
Genetic studies, 145, 146, 154–5, 196–7
Genetron, 202
Gengerelli, J. A., 22
Geometrical intuition, 92, 135–9, 141
*Gestalttheoric* and *Gestalt* psychologists, 2, 10, 23, 28, 54, 55, 59, 150–2, 155, 207, 210–13, 215, 222, 230, 235
Global anticipation, 131–2
Goldbeck, R. A., 73
Goldstein, K., 19, 25, 31, 233
Goodnow, J. J., 1, 2, 23, 148
Gottschaldt, K., 50, 51
Gouin-Decarie, T., 199n.
Goustard, M., 265
Grant, D. A., 34
Graphic collections, 166
Graphic estimations, 105–7
Gréco, Pierre, 9, 177 and n., 198, 214n., 230, 231, 237, 258, 260, 262
Green, E. J., 25
Grize, J. B., 202, 267
Groos, K., 100
Groping, 64–5, 148–9, 208–26
Groupings of classes, 165–79
Grouping structures, 172–3, 199
Guillaume, P., 230n., 235
Gulliksen, H. O., 10
Guthrie, 214, 237

Habit-family hierarchy, 238
Habits and attitudes, 46–8, 58–9
Hake, 10
Halt-split method, 70–3
Hall, E. R., 53
Hallucination, 93, 94, 141
Hanfmann, E., 17, 18
Haptic perception, 140
Harlow, H. F., 11, 18, 21–2, 31, 251, 264n.
Harms, E., 1
Harsh, C. M., 218
Haygood, R. C., 26
Heads or tails game, 188–90
Healey, D., 170, 183n.
Hécaen, H., 94
Heidbreder, Edna, 15, 19, 33–4, 36, 229, 231
Hendrickson, 67
Hierarchical classifications, 167
Hilgard, E. R., 207, 214n.
Hobhouse, L. T., 209–10
Homeostats, 202

## Index

Houzik, C. H., 215-18
Hovland, C. J., 17, 24-6, 224
Hull, C. L., 4, 14, 16, 19, 22, 27, 33, 147, 214, 215, 217, 219-22, 225, 228n., 232-3, 235-9, 240n., 249n.
Humphrey, G., 1
Hunter, I. M. L., 7, 8, 44-5
Hunter, W. S., 230
Husserl, 236
Hydrostatic equilibrium, 195-6
Hyperordinal anticipation, 126-7, 186
Hypnagogic reveries, 94
Hypothetico-deductive reasoning, 190, 194

Ideas and learning, 209-10
Identical element, 27
Identity-dissimilarity relation, 10
Ignorance of differences between stimuli, 28-9
Image classification, 91, 107-14, 140
Image development, 91-2
Image evolution, 114-28, 140
Image formation, 90-3
Imaged representation, 86
Imageless thought, 85, 152
Images and drawing, 91, 140
Images and imitation, 91, 101-2, 140
Images and thought, 92, 129-35, 140-1
Images of development, 137-9
Imitation, 90, 91, 100-2, 140
Implication, 148-9
Implicit restrictions of problems, 59-60
Inclusion, quantification of, 168-170, 254-7
Indices or cues, 88
Induction and inductive processes, 5-36
Induction of laws, 7-11, 266
Inference, 6, 36-9
Inferential expectation, 215-17
Information quantity and nature, 25-6

Information theory, 2, 66
Information through complex tests, 31-6
Information through problem solving, 66-9
Infralogical operations, 180
Inhelder, Bärbel, 7, 157-9, 163, 171, 177, 182-4, 187, 189, 191n., 192n., 195n., 197n., 200, 234, 239, 242, 250, 254, 267n.
Innate releasing mechanism, *see* I.R.M.
INRC group (group of the two reversibilities), 190, 194-6
Insight, 208-13, 229
Integrated structures, 164-5
*Intentio*, 236
Interpretation on meaning of words, 42-8
Intuition and groping, 208-26
Intuition of number, 176-8
Intuitionists, 176
Invariants, 156, 164, 241-54
Inversion through rotation of 180°, 257-61
I.R.M. (innate releasing mechanism), 88-9
Irreversible mixing, 187
Isomorphism, 152, 197, 222, 227, 235, 238
Isotropic premises, 44
Israel, H. E., 34

Jackson, 95
Jacobson, E., 95
Jaensch, 93
James, W., 22
Jenkins' three-plate apparatus, 7-8
Jennings, 148
John, E. R., 9
Johnson, D. M., 1, 53
Judd, 67
Juzak, T., 25

Kant, 4
Kardos, 155
Kasanin, J., 17, 18
Katona, G., 67

*Index*

Katz, D., 54, 155, 213
Kendler, H. H. 19, 32, 39
Kendler, T. S., 39
Kennedy, W. A., 25
Kinetic anticipatory images, 124–128
Kinetic reproductive images, 108–110, 114
Kinnaman, A. J., 211
Klein, 195
Kleitmann, N., 97
Klüver, H., 14
Kochen, M., 2
Koffka, K., 213
Köhler, W., 2, 10, 11, 49, 63, 151, 178, 209–13, 222, 223, 226, 232, 235, 238, 240n.
Kohts, 251
Konorski, 224
Koob, H. F., 41
Krechevsky, I., 215, 223
Kubie, L., 94
Külpe, O., 20, 85
Kuo, Z. Y., 218
Kurtz, K. H., 17, 24

Labelling, 233
Ladd, G. Trumball, 97
Lambercier, 109
Language and social transmission, 200–1
Lashley, 23
Laurendeau, M., 157, 160, 161, 177
Lawrence, D. H., 226 and n.
Learning, Chapter 25 *passim*
Learning conditions, 24–5
Learning generalization, 222–5
Learning sets, 31–2, 264n.
Learning situations, 214
Learning transposition, 222–5
Leeds, D. S., 61
Leeper, 23
Lézine, I., 140
Lhermitte, J., 94
Lincoln, R. E., 53
Logic of learning, 205–8
Logical and logico-mathematical structures, 146, 151–2, 154, 198, 240–68
Logicism, 144
Logico-numerical operations, 175–180
Long, L., 14
Long circuits, 3
Lorcnz, K., 88
Lotze, 93
Lovell, K., 157, 160, 170, 183n., 192n., 195n.
Luchins, A. S., 50, 61–3
Luchins, E. H., 61n.
Luquet, G. H., 137

McCulloch, 197
McGeoch, J. A., 67
Maier, N. R. F., 2, 38–9, 50, 55–9, 214, 217, 219–22, 230
Maltzman, I., 4, 61n., 236
Marbe, K., 85, 152, 208, 235
Marks, M. R., 65, 68
Matalon, B., 10, 103, 113, 198, 230, 265
Material reasonings, 37
Matrices, 172–5
Maturation, 197, 241
Mayzner, 54
Meaning and symbolic function, 88–90
Meili, R., 151
Memory-images, 85
Menninger Foundation of Topeka, 139
Mental mazes, 231–2
Messer, 152
Method and problem-solving, 68–73
Methodology, 207, 229
Metzger, 151
Meyerson, I., 86, 129
Mialaret, 22
Michotte, 109
Middleness, 10
Miller, J. G., 9, 224
Mitchell, B., 170
Mixing of series, 187
Mobile equilibrium, 202
Mobility, verbal and practical, 58

## Index

Modalities of learning, 264
Models, 3–6
Monism, 268
Montpellier, G. de, 9, 10
Moore, O. K., 40
Morel, F., 96, 97
Morf, Albert, 198, 254–7
Morgan, A. B., 40
Morgan, C. Lloyd, 209–10
Morgan, W. J., 40
Morrisett, L., 61n.
Motor character of images, 90, 93–9, 139
Multiple classifications, 139
Multiplicative groupings, 173–5
Munn, N. L., 14

Necessary laws, 262–4
Negative stimuli, 26
Nervous system, maturation of, 197
Newell, A., 2
Noegenesis, 149–50
Noelting, G., 158, 191
Non-conservation followed by conservation, 157–64
Non-exclusive interpretation, 47
Non-figural collections, 167
Non-graphical collections, 167
Non-reversal shifts, 32–3
Non-vivid memories, 94
Null transformation, 164
Number, 175–9
Number and intuition, 176–8
Numerical correspondences, 176–8
Numerical invariants, 251–4

Oddity, 10–11
Ogilvie, E., 157, 160
Oléron, Pierre, 7, 8, 10–12, 20, 31, 34 and n., 47, 54, 59, 200, 230
Operational nature of number, 178–9
Operational seriation, 131–3
Operational structures, 146, 148, 149, 155, 197, 200, 202
Operative aspects of cognitive functions, 87–90, 98
Operative intelligence, 128

Order of dominance of concepts, 33–6
Ordinal anticipation, 126–8
Ordinating activity, 199
Oseas, L., 17, 25
Osgood, C. E., 1, 222n., 229, 233, 240n.

Papert, S., 202, 242n., 267
Parasitic elements, 23, 24
Paternotte, F., 110, 114
Pavlovianism, 207, 214, 238, 249n.
Penfield, W., 93, 94, 139
Perceptual constancies, 155
Perceptual strategies, 250, 251
Peterson, 231
*Physica* (Aristotle), 186
Piaget, Jean, 2, 4, 6, 7, 9, 10, 29, 45, 100, 139, 141, 157n., 159, 167, 172, 174, 177 and n., 187, 191n., 192, 194n., 195n., 199n., 207, 227 and n., 234, 236–9, 241n., 242, 247, 249–52, 254, 266, 267
Piéron, Henri, 29, 144, 207
Pinard, A., 157, 160, 161, 177
Pitts, 197
Poincaré, H., 176
Positive stimuli, 26
Principles taught by problem solving, 67–9
Probabilistic analysis and models, 146, 149, 267
Probabilistic laws, 10
Problem solving, 2, 6, 48–73, 147–8, 153, 210–11, 229–32, 268
Progressive matrices, 124
Projective structures, 182
Proportions, 196
Propositional logic, 190–4
Propositional operations, 190–7, 200
Propositions, structure of, 41–6
Pseudo-rotation, 137–8
*Psychology of Reasoning, The* (Binet), 85, 147

Qualitative algebra, 146
Quantification of inclusion, 168–70, 254–7

## Index

Quantity, 242
Quasi-sensory character of images, 93–5
Quastler, H., 10, 73

Rabinowitz, H. S., 55–6
Raven, 173, 174
Razran, 223
Reactions of subject, 28–31
Reasoning, 6, 36–48
Reasoning forms, 36–7
Reductionism, 144, 236–40, 268
Reed, H. B., 15, 24
Reflective abstraction, 201
*Regelbewusstsein* (consciousness of rules), 152
Reid, J. W., 66
Reinforcement, 25
Relations, 10–11, 25, 27–8
Reproductive images, 102–10, 114
Responses, 4–5, 26–31, 238–9, 264
Reversal, 19–20, 164
Reversal shifts, 32–3
Reversibility, 154–6, 158, 164, 172, 190, 194–6, 199, 202
Révesz, G., 7
Rey, André, 50, 52, 65, 95–6, 132–3, 251
Ribot, 95, 251
Richard, J. F., 265
Richardson, J., 15, 18, 25
Rignano, 29–30
Rimold, H. J. A., 69
Rochester, N., 2
Rosenstein, J., 20
Rotation in children's drawings, 137–8
Rowland, A. D., 170, 183n.
Russell, Bertrand, 178

Saugstad, P., 56–8
Scheerer, M., 19, 233
Schema and schemata, 3–6, 36, 149, 166, 196, 198, 225, 238, 264, 266
Scheminsky, F., 95
Schifferli, P., 96–8
Schroeder, 67

Scott, J. P., 29
Sells, S. B., 41–4
Selz, O., 152
Semeiotic function, 89n.
Sensori-motor actions and intelligence, 87, 88, 148, 155, 165, 166, 199, 222, 237, 238, 268
Sensory character of images, 90, 93–9
Serial presentation, 23, 24
Seriation, 44, 130–3, 170–3, 184–5, 199, 200
Set establishment and problems, 61–3
Shaw, J. C., 2
Sigel, I. E., 34
Signs and symbols, 88–9
Simon, H. A., 2
Simultaneous presentation, 23, 24
Simultaneous reproduction, 109–110
Siotis, E., 120, 124
Skinner, 214n., 235
Small, W. S., 211
Smedslund, Jan, 164–5, 198, 242–251, 254 and n.
Smoke, K. L., 16–17, 26, 27
Snyder, F. W., 53
Social transmission and language, 200–1
Solley, C. M., 53
Somersault, images of, 119–22
Spatial images, 92, 135–9
Spatial operations, 179–83
Spatio-temporal laws, 7
Spearman, C. E., 6, 145, 146, 149–150, 153
Speed, 185–6
Specificity of intellectual structures, 234–6
Spence, K. W., 23, 28n., 222–5, 235
Spinoza, 238
Spoken reflection, 148
Spontaneous measurement, 180–181
Square, displacement of, 122–4
Staats, A. W., 58

# Index

Stamping in and stamping out mechanisms, 210, 213
Static reproductive images, 108, 109, 114
Stereognosis, 140
Stern, 208
Stevens, S. S., 23
Stimuli, 4–5, 14, 17, 18, 21–3, 25–9, 34, 36, 222–6, 238–9, 251–3, 266
Stolurow, L. M., 23, 73
Stone, C. P., 11
Strategies, 148
Structural learning, 261–2, 266–267
Structure of problems, 64
Structure of propositions, 41–6
Structurization, 209, 212, 213, 257–68
*Study of Thinking, A* (Bruner, Goodnow and Austin), 148
Subsumption, 5–6
Substance, 247
Suppes, 126
Sweeney, E. J., 60, 61
Syllogisms and syllogistic reasonings, 37, 40–3, 45, 48, 257
Symbolic function, 88–90, 99, 101–102, 165
Symbolic intelligence, 3
Symbolic material, 50
Symbolic significants, 90
Symbolically-based reasonings, 40
Symbols, 88–9
Szekely, L., 68–9
Szeminska, A., 174, 177 and n., 252, 254

Tanner, J. M., 197n.
Temporal laws, 7–9
Temporal maze, 7–9
Temporal operations, 179–80, 183–185
Terrell, G., jr., 25
Thinking, 1, 206–7
Thinking and learning, 227–40
Thompson, M. E., 217–19
Thomson, G., 145, 146

Thorndike, E., 64, 148, 210–11, 214, 232
Thought and images, 92, 129–35, 140–1
Thought psychology, see Denkpsychologie
Three-plate apparatus, 7–8
Tolman, E. C., 215–18, 221, 237
Toulouse, 144
Training and reasoning, 40–1
Transfer of principles, 226
Transfer tests, 251–3
Transformation and transformatory images, 108, 114, 164
Transformation representations, 239
Transformation-responses, 147, 239
Transitivity, 164–5, 241–51
Transposition, 25, 213, 222–5
Tresselt, M. E., 54, 61
Trial and error and learning, 209–210
Trick problems, 60–1

Underwood, B. J., 15, 17, 25
Unification, 236–40
Utilization of information from problem solving, 66–9

Values and dimensions, 17
Van de Geer, J. P., 56
Varied stimuli, 21–3
Varieties of learning, 266–7
Verbal teaching and problem solving, 68–9
*Vierergruppe*, 195
Vinacke, W. E., 1
Vincent, M., 18, 200
Vinh-Bang, 157, 159, 163, 171, 177, 183, 184, 189, 243n.
Visual images, 196–8

Wallon, H., 101n., 202
Walter, Grey, 197
Watson, J. B., 211, 228, 241
Watt, 152
Weight invariants, 242–51

*Index*

Weigl, E., 19
Weiss, W., 26
Wertheimer, M., 2, 50, 150–1, 235, 257
Whitehead, A. N., 178
Whitfield, J. W., 25
Whole number construction, 175–6
Wohlwill, Joachim F., 198, 251–3, 254n.

Wolpert, E. A., 97, 139
Woodworth, R. S., 41–4, 207, 231
Words, interpretation on meaning of, 47–8
Würzburg school, 1, 85, 92, 129, 144, 152, 235
Wyss, Oscar, 94

Young, M. L., 18